Data Warehousing Essentials

Data Warehousing Essentials

Julio Bolton

www.larsen-keller.com

Data Warehousing Essentials
Julio Bolton
ISBN: 978-1-64172-073-1 (Hardback)

Published by Larsen and Keller Education,
5 Penn Plaza,
19th Floor,
New York, NY 10001, USA

Cataloging-in-Publication Data

Data warehousing essentials / Julio Bolton.
p. cm.
Includes bibliographical references and index.
ISBN 978-1-64172-073-1
1. Data warehousing. 2. Database management. 3. Multidimensional databases. I. Bolton, Julio.
QA76.9.D37 D38 2019
005.745--dc23

For more information regarding Larsen and Keller Education and its products, please visit the publisher's website www.larsen-keller.com

Table of Contents

Preface

A data warehouse (DW) is a system used in computing for data analysis and reporting. It is a core component of business intelligence. It stores integrated historical and current data from one or more sources. Data can be characterized according to data integration, time-variance, subject orientation, volatility, granularity, etc. It is then arranged into groups, facts and aggregate facts. The sources of data are cleansed, catalogued, transformed and used for data mining, market research, decision support and online analytical processing. The ways to analyze or retrieve the data, transform, load and extract data and manage the data dictionary are essential components of a data warehousing system. Data warehouses can be designed using the bottom-up, top-down or hybrid design models. This book aims to shed light on some of the unexplored aspects of data warehousing. Most of the topics introduced herein cover new techniques and applications of this field. Those in search of information to further their knowledge will be greatly assisted by this textbook.

A detailed account of the significant topics covered in this book is provided below:

Chapter 1, Data warehouse is a core component of business intelligence. It is used for data reporting and data analysis. This chapter will introduce briefly all the significant aspects of data warehousing such as information processing, data warehouse architecture, data mining, automation, etc. **Chapter 2**, The data in a warehouse is uploaded from various operational sources. It passes through a data store and the cleansed. This is required for ensuring data quality. The diverse operations of data warehousing with respect to database normalization, operational database, data integrity, etc. have been thoroughly discussed in this chapter. **Chapter 3**, Metadata can be described as that data or information which provides information about some other data. Metadata can be of several types, such as descriptive, structural, administrative, statistical and reference metadata. This chapter includes topics like metadata repository, technical and business metadata, metadata management, etc. **Chapter 4**, The process which involves methods of machine learning, database systems and mining to discover different patterns in large data sets is referred to as data mining. All the diverse principles of data mining such as structure mining, data dredging, affinity analysis, etc. have been carefully analyzed in this chapter. **Chapter 5**, Data mining is done with the goal of extracting information from a data set and structuring it comprehensively for future use. It also involves data pre-processing, data management, post-processing of structures, etc. This chapter closely examines the diverse algorithms used in data mining such as GSP algorithm, apriori algorithm, WINEPI, etc.

I would like to make a special mention of my publisher who considered me worthy of this opportunity and also supported me throughout the process. I would also like to thank the editing team at the back-end who extended their help whenever required.

Julio Bolton

1

Introduction to Data Warehousing

Data warehouse is a core component of business intelligence. It is used for data reporting and data analysis. This chapter will introduce briefly all the significant aspects of data warehousing such as information processing, data warehouse architecture, data mining, automation, etc.

A data warehousing is a technique for collecting and managing data from varied sources to provide meaningful business insights. It is a blend of technologies and components which allows the strategic use of data.

It is electronic storage of a large amount of information by a business which is designed for query and analysis instead of transaction processing. It is a process of transforming data into information and making it available to users in a timely manner to make a difference.

The decision support database (Data Warehouse) is maintained separately from the organization's operational database. However, the data warehouse is not a product but an environment. It is an architectural construct of an information system which provides users with current and historical decision support information which is difficult to access or present in the traditional operational data store.

The data warehouse is the core of the BI system which is built for data analysis and reporting.

You many know that a 3NF-designed database for an inventory system many have tables related to each other. For example, a report on current inventory information can include more than 12 joined conditions. This can quickly slow down the response time of the query and report. A data warehouse provides a new design which can help to reduce the response time and helps to enhance the performance of queries for reports and analytics.

Data warehouse system is also known by the following name:

- Decision Support System (DSS).
- Executive Information System.
- Management Information System.
- Business Intelligence Solution.
- Analytic Application.
- Data Warehouse.

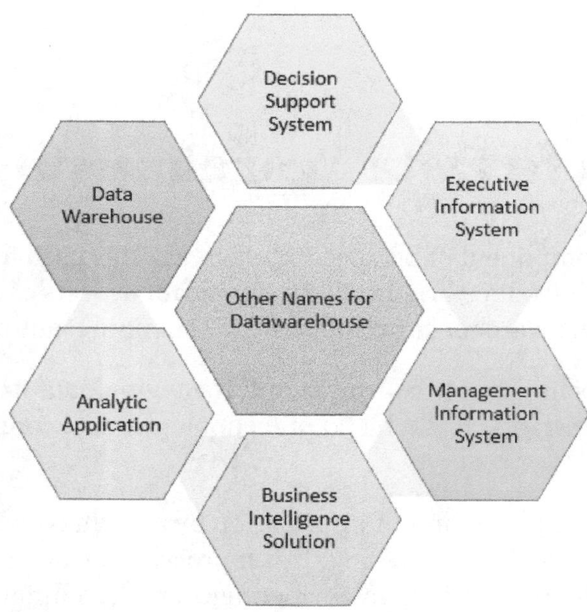

The Data warehouse benefits users to understand and enhance their organization's performance. The need to warehouse data evolved as computer systems became more complex and needed to handle increasing amounts of Information. However, Data Warehousing is a not a new thing.

Here are some key events in evolution of Data Warehouse:

- 1960 - Dartmouth and General Mills in a joint research project, develop the terms dimensions and facts.
- 1970 - A Nielsen and IRI introduces dimensional data marts for retail sales.
- 1983 - Tera Data Corporation introduces a database management system which is specifically designed for decision support.
- Data warehousing started in the late 1980s when IBM worker Paul Murphy and Barry Devlin developed the Business Data Warehouse.
- However, the real concept was given by Inmon Bill. He was considered as a father of data warehouse. He had written about a variety of topics for building, usage, and maintenance of the warehouse & the Corporate Information Factory.

Working of Data Warehouse

A Data Warehouse works as a central repository where information arrives from one or more data sources. Data flows into a data warehouse from the transactional system and other relational databases.

Data may be:

1. Structured
2. Semi-structured

3. Unstructured data

The data is processed, transformed, and ingested so that users can access the processed data in the Data Warehouse through Business Intelligence tools, SQL clients, and spreadsheets. A data warehouse merges information coming from different sources into one comprehensive database.

By merging all of this information in one place, an organization can analyze its customers more holistically. This helps to ensure that it has considered all the information available. Data warehousing makes data mining possible. Data mining is looking for patterns in the data that may lead to higher sales and profits.

Types of Data Warehouse

Three main types of Data Warehouses are:

1. Enterprise Data Warehouse

   Enterprise Data Warehouse is a centralized warehouse. It provides decision support service across the enterprise. It offers a unified approach for organizing and representing data. It also provide the ability to classify data according to the subject and give access according to those divisions.

2. Operational Data Store

   Operational Data Store, which is also called ODS, are nothing but data store required when neither Data warehouse nor OLTP systems support organizations reporting needs. In ODS, Data warehouse is refreshed in real time. Hence, it is widely preferred for routine activities like storing records of the Employees.

3. Data Mart

   A data mart is a subset of the data warehouse. It specially designed for a particular line of business, such as sales, finance, sales or finance. In an independent data mart, data can collect directly from sources.

General Stages of Data Warehouse

Earlier, organizations started relatively simple use of data warehousing. However, over time, more sophisticated use of data warehousing begun.

The following are general stages of use of the data warehouse:

Offline Operational Database

In this stage, data is just copied from an operational system to another server. In this way, loading, processing, and reporting of the copied data do not impact the operational system's performance.

Offline Data Warehouse

Data in the Data warehouse is regularly updated from the Operational Database. The data in Data warehouse is mapped and transformed to meet the Data warehouse objectives.

Real Time Data Warehouse

In this stage, Data warehouses are updated whenever any transaction takes place in operational database. For example, Airline or railway booking system.

Integrated Data Warehouse

In this stage, Data Warehouses are updated continuously when the operational system performs a transaction. The Data warehouse then generates transactions which are passed back to the operational system.

Components of Data Warehouse

Four components of Data Warehouses are:

- Load manager

Load manager is also called the front component. It performs with all the operations associated with the extraction and load of data into the warehouse. These operations include transformations to prepare the data for entering into the Data warehouse.

- Warehouse Manager

Warehouse manager performs operations associated with the management of the data in the warehouse. It performs operations like analysis of data to ensure consistency, creation of indexes and views, generation of denormalization and aggregations, transformation and merging of source data and archiving and baking-up data.

- Query Manager

Query manager is also known as backend component. It performs all the operation operations related to the management of user queries. The operations of this Data warehouse components are direct queries to the appropriate tables for scheduling the execution of queries.

End-user Access Tools

This is categorized into five different groups like:

1. Data Reporting
2. Query Tools
3. Application development tools
4. EIS tools
5. OLAP tools and data mining tools

Who Needs Data Warehouse?

Data warehouse is needed for all types of users like:

- Decision makers who rely on mass amount of data.
- Users who use customized, complex processes to obtain information from multiple data sources.
- It is also used by the people who want simple technology to access the data.
- It also essential for those people who want a systematic approach for making decisions.
- If the user wants fast performance on a huge amount of data which is a necessity for reports, grids or charts, then Data warehouse proves useful.
- Data warehouse is a first step If you want to discover 'hidden patterns' of data-flows and groupings.

Uses of Data Warehouse

Here, are most common sectors where Data warehouse is used:

Airline

In the Airline system, it is used for operation purpose like crew assignment, analyses of route profitability, frequent flyer program promotions, etc.

Banking

It is widely used in the banking sector to manage the resources available on desk effectively. Few banks also used for the market research, performance analysis of the product and operations.

Healthcare

Healthcare sector also used Data warehouse to strategize and predict outcomes, generate patient's treatment reports, share data with tie-in insurance companies, medical aid services, etc.

Public Sector

In the public sector, data warehouse is used for intelligence gathering. It helps government agencies to maintain and analyze tax records, health policy records, for every individual.

Investment and Insurance Sector

In this sector, the warehouses are primarily used to analyze data patterns, customer trends, and to track market movements.

Retain Chain

In retail chains, Data warehouse is widely used for distribution and marketing. It also helps to track items, customer buying pattern, promotions and also used for determining pricing policy.

Telecommunication

A data warehouse is used in this sector for product promotions, sales decisions and to make distribution decisions.

Hospitality Industry

This Industry utilizes warehouse services to design as well as estimate their advertising and promotion campaigns where they want to target clients based on their feedback and travel patterns.

Steps to Implement Data Warehouse

The best way to address the business risk associated with a Data warehouse implementation is to employ a three-prong strategy as below:

1. Enterprise strategy: Here we identify technical including current architecture and tools. We also identify facts, dimensions, and attributes. Data mapping and transformation is also passed.
2. Phased delivery: Data warehouse implementation should be phased based on subject areas. Related business entities like booking and billing should be first implemented and then integrated with each other.
3. Iterative Prototyping: Rather than a big bang approach to implementation, the Data warehouse should be developed and tested iteratively.

Here, are key steps in Data warehouse implementation along with its deliverables.

Step	Tasks	Deliverables
1	Need to define project scope	Scope Definition
2	Need to determine business needs	Logical Data Model
3	Define Operational Data store requirements	Operational Data Store Model
4	Acquire or develop Extraction tools	Extract tools and Software
5	Define Data Warehouse Data requirements	Transition Data Model
6	Document missing data	To Do Project List
7	Maps Operational Data Store to Data Warehouse	D/W Data Integration Map
8	Develop Data Warehouse Database design	D/W Database Design
9	Extract Data from Operational Data Store	Integrated D/W Data Extracts
10	Load Data Warehouse	Initial Data Load
11	Maintain Data Warehouse	On-going Data Access and Subsequent Loads

Best practices to implement a Data Warehouse

- Decide a plan to test the consistency, accuracy, and integrity of the data.
- The data warehouse must be well integrated, well defined and time stamped.
- While designing Data warehouse make sure you use right tool, stick to life cycle, take care about data conflicts and ready to learn you're your mistakes.
- Never replace operational systems and reports.
- Don't spend too much time on extracting, cleaning and loading data.
- Ensure to involve all stakeholders including business personnel in Data warehouse implementation process. Establish that Data warehousing is a joint/ team project. You don't want to create Data warehouse that is not useful to the end users.
- Prepare a training plan for the end users.

Advantages of Data Warehouse

- Data warehouse allows business users to quickly access critical data from some sources all in one place.
- Data warehouse provides consistent information on various cross-functional activities. It is also supporting ad-hoc reporting and query.
- Data Warehouse helps to integrate many sources of data to reduce stress on the production system.
- Data warehouse helps to reduce total turnaround time for analysis and reporting.
- Restructuring and Integration make it easier for the user to use for reporting and analysis.
- Data warehouse allows users to access critical data from the number of sources in a single place. Therefore, it saves user's time of retrieving data from multiple sources.
- Data warehouse stores a large amount of historical data. This helps users to analyze different time periods and trends to make future predictions.

Disadvantages of Data Warehouse

- Not an ideal option for unstructured data.
- Creation and Implementation of Data Warehouse is surely time confusing affair.
- Data Warehouse can be outdated relatively quickly.
- Difficult to make changes in data types and ranges, data source schema, indexes, and queries.
- The data warehouse may seem easy, but actually, it is too complex for the average users.
- Despite best efforts at project management, data warehousing project scope will always increase.

- Sometime warehouse users will develop different business rules.
- Organizations need to spend lots of their resources for training and Implementation purpose.

The Future of Data Warehousing

- Change in Regulatory constrains may limit the ability to combine source of disparate data. These disparate sources may include unstructured data which is difficult to store.
- As the size of the databases grows, the estimates of what constitutes a very large database continue to grow. It is complex to build and run data warehouse systems which are always increasing in size. The hardware and software resources are available today do not allow to keep a large amount of data online.
- Multimedia data cannot be easily manipulated as text data, whereas textual information can be retrieved by the relational software available today. This could be a research subject.

Data Warehouse Tools

There are many Data Warehousing tools are available in the market. Here, are some most prominent one:

1. MarkLogic

MarkLogic is useful data warehousing solution that makes data integration easier and faster using an array of enterprise features. This tool helps to perform very complex search operations. It can query different types of data like documents, relationships, and metadata.

2. Oracle

Oracle is the industry-leading database. It offers a wide range of choice of data warehouse solutions for both on-premises and in the cloud. It helps to optimize customer experiences by increasing operational efficiency.

3. Amazon RedShift

Amazon Redshift is Data warehouse tool. It is a simple and cost-effective tool to analyze all types of data using standard SQL and existing BI tools. It also allows running complex queries against petabytes of structured data, using the technique of query optimization.

Characteristics of Data Warehouse

Subject Oriented

Data warehouses are designed to help you analyze data. For example, to learn more about your company's sales data, you can build a data warehouse that concentrates on sales. Using this data warehouse, you can answer questions such as "Who was our best customer for this item last year?" or "Who is likely to be our best customer next year?" This ability to define a data warehouse by subject matter, sales in this case, makes the data warehouse subject oriented.

Integrated

Integration is closely related to subject orientation. Data warehouses must put data from disparate sources into a consistent format. They must resolve such problems as naming conflicts and inconsistencies among units of measure. When they achieve this, they are said to be integrated.

Nonvolatile

Nonvolatile means that, once entered into the data warehouse, data should not change. This is logical because the purpose of a data warehouse is to enable you to analyze what has occurred.

Time Variant

A data warehouse's focus on change over time is what is meant by the term time variant. In order to discover trends and identify hidden patterns and relationships in business, analysts need large amounts of data. This is very much in contrast to online transaction processing (OLTP) systems, where performance requirements demand that historical data be moved to an archive.

Contrasting OLTP and Data Warehousing Environments

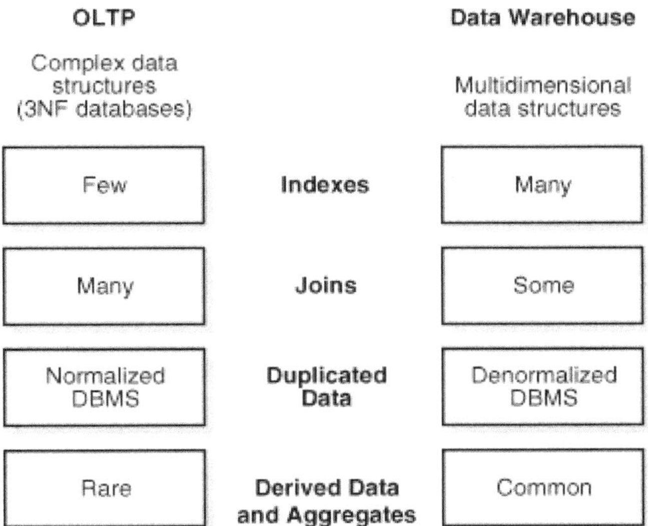

Figure: Contrasting OLTP and data warehousing environments

One major difference between the types of system is that data warehouses are not usually in third normal form (3NF), a type of data normalization common in OLTP environments.

Data warehouses and OLTP systems have very different requirements. Here are some examples of differences between typical data warehouses and OLTP systems:

- Workload

Data warehouses are designed to accommodate *ad hoc* queries and data analysis. You might not know the workload of your data warehouse in advance, so a data warehouse should be optimized to perform well for a wide variety of possible query and analytical operations.

OLTP systems support only predefined operations. Your applications might be specifically tuned or designed to support only these operations.

- Data modifications

A data warehouse is updated on a regular basis by the ETL process (run nightly or weekly) using bulk data modification techniques. The end users of a data warehouse do not directly update the data warehouse except when using analytical tools, such as data mining, to make predictions with associated probabilities, assign customers to market segments, and develop customer profiles.

In OLTP systems, end users routinely issue individual data modification statements to the database. The OLTP database is always up to date, and reflects the current state of each business transaction.

- Schema design

Data warehouses often use denormalized or partially denormalized schemas (such as a star schema) to optimize query and analytical performance.

OLTP systems often use fully normalized schemas to optimize update/insert/delete performance, and to guarantee data consistency.

- Typical operations

A typical data warehouse query scans thousands or millions of rows. For example, "Find the total sales for all customers last month."

A typical OLTP operation accesses only a handful of records. For example, "Retrieve the current order for this customer."

- Historical data

Data warehouses usually store many months or years of data. This is to support historical analysis and reporting.

OLTP systems usually store data from only a few weeks or months. The OLTP system stores only historical data as needed to successfully meet the requirements of the current transaction.

Data Warehouse Components

Sourcing, Acquisition, Cleanup and Transformation Tools

A significant portion of the implementation effort is spent extracting data from operational systems and putting it in a format suitable for informational applications that run off the data warehouse.

The data sourcing, cleanup, transformation and migration tools perform all of the conversions, summarizations, key changes, structural changes and condensations needed to transform disparate data into information that can be used by the decision support tool. They produce the programs and control statements, including the COBOL programs, MVS job-control language (JCL), UNIX scripts, and SQL data definition language (DDL) needed to move data into the data warehouse for multiple operational systems. These tools also maintain the meta data. The functionality includes:

- Removing unwanted data from operational databases.
- Converting to common data names and definitions.
- Establishing defaults for missing data.
- Accommodating source data definition changes.

The data sourcing, cleanup, extract, transformation and migration tools have to deal with some significant issues including:

- Database heterogeneity. DBMSs are very different in data models, data access language, data navigation, operations, concurrency, integrity, recovery etc.
- Data heterogeneity. This is the difference in the way data is defined and used in different models – homonyms, synonyms, unit compatibility (U.S. vs. metric), different attributes for the same entity and different ways of modeling the same fact.

These tools can save a considerable amount of time and effort. However, significant shortcomings do exist. For example, many available tools are generally useful for simpler data extracts.

Frequently, customized extract routines need to be developed for the more complicated data extraction procedures.

Meta Data

Meta data is data about data that describes the data warehouse. It is used for building, maintaining, managing and using the data warehouse. Meta data can be classified into:

- Technical meta data, which contains information about warehouse data for use by warehouse designers and administrators when carrying out warehouse development and management tasks.
- Business meta data, which contains information that gives users an easy-to-understand perspective of the information stored in the data warehouse.

Equally important, meta data provides interactive access to users to help understand content and find data. One of the issues dealing with meta data relates to the fact that many data extraction tool capabilities to gather meta data remain fairly immature. Therefore, there is often the need to create a meta data interface for users, which may involve some duplication of effort.

Meta data management is provided via a meta data repository and accompanying software. Meta data repository management software, which typically runs on a workstation, can be used to map the source data to the target database; generate code for data transformations; integrate and transform the data; and control moving data to the warehouse.

As user's interactions with the data warehouse increase, their approaches to reviewing the results of their requests for information can be expected to evolve from relatively simple manual analysis for trends and exceptions to agent-driven initiation of the analysis based on user-defined thresholds. The definition of these thresholds, configuration parameters for the software agents using them, and the information directory indicating where the appropriate sources for the information can be found are all stored in the meta data repository as well.

Access Tools

The principal purpose of data warehousing is to provide information to business users for strategic decision-making. These users interact with the data warehouse using front-end tools. Many of these tools require an information specialist, although many end users develop expertise in the tools. Tools fall into four main categories: query and reporting tools, application development tools, online analytical processing tools, and data mining tools.

Query and Reporting tools can be divided into two groups: reporting tools and managed query tools. Reporting tools can be further divided into production reporting tools and report writers.

Production reporting tools let companies generate regular operational reports or support high-volume batch jobs such as calculating and printing paychecks. Report writers, on the other hand, are inexpensive desktop tools designed for end-users.

Managed query tools shield end users from the complexities of SQL and database structures by inserting a meta layer between users and the database. These tools are designed for easy-to-use, point-and-click operations that either accept SQL or generate SQL database queries.

Often, the analytical needs of the data warehouse user community exceed the built-in capabilities of query and reporting tools. In these cases, organizations will often rely on the tried-and-true approach of in-house application development using graphical development environments such as PowerBuilder, Visual Basic and Forte. These application development platforms integrate well with popular OLAP tools and access all major database systems including Oracle, Sybase, and Informix.

OLAP tools are based on the concepts of dimensional data models and corresponding databases, and allow users to analyze the data using elaborate, multidimensional views. Typical business applications include product performance and profitability, effectiveness of a sales program or marketing campaign, sales forecasting and capacity planning. These tools assume that the data is organized in a multidimensional model.

A critical success factor for any business today is the ability to use information effectively. Data mining is the process of discovering meaningful new correlations, patterns and trends by digging into large amounts of data stored in the warehouse using artificial intelligence, statistical and mathematical techniques.

Data Marts

The concept of a data mart is causing a lot of excitement and attracts much attention in the data warehouse industry. Mostly, data marts are presented as an alternative to a data warehouse that takes significantly less time and money to build. However, the term data mart means different things to different people. A rigorous definition of this term is a data store that is subsidiary to a data warehouse of integrated data. The data mart is directed at a partition of data (often called a subject area) that is created for the use of a dedicated group of users. A data mart might, in fact, be a set of denormalized, summarized, or aggregated data. Sometimes, such a set could be placed on the data warehouse rather than a physically separate store of data. In most instances, however, the data mart is a physically separate store of data and is resident on separate database server, often a local area network serving a dedicated user group. Sometimes the data mart simply comprises relational OLAP technology which creates highly denormalized dimensional model (e.g., star schema) implemented on a relational database. The resulting hypercubes of data are used for analysis by groups of users with a common interest in a limited portion of the database.

These types of data marts, called dependent data marts because their data is sourced from the data warehouse, have a high value because no matter how they are deployed and how many different enabling technologies are used, different users are all accessing the information views derived from the single integrated version of the data.

Unfortunately, the misleading statements about the simplicity and low cost of data marts sometimes result in organizations or vendors incorrectly positioning them as an alternative to the data warehouse. This viewpoint defines independent data marts that in fact, represent fragmented point solutions to a range of business problems in the enterprise. This type of implementation should be rarely deployed in the context of an overall technology or applications architecture. Indeed, it is missing the ingredient that is at the heart of the data warehousing concept — that of data integration. Each independent data mart makes its own assumptions about how to consolidate the data, and the data across several data marts may not be consistent.

Moreover, the concept of an independent data mart is dangerous — as soon as the first data mart is created, other organizations, groups, and subject areas within the enterprise embark on the task of building their own data marts. As a result, you create an environment where multiple operational systems feed multiple non-integrated data marts that are often overlapping in data content, job scheduling, connectivity and management. In other words, you have transformed a complex many-to-one problem of building a data warehouse from operational and external data sources to a many-to-many sourcing and management nightmare.

Data Warehouse Administration and Management

Data warehouses tend to be as much as 4 times as large as related operational databases, reaching terabytes in size depending on how much history needs to be saved. They are not synchronized in real time to the associated operational data but are updated as often as once a day if the application requires it.

In addition, almost all data warehouse products include gateways to transparently access multiple enterprise data sources without having to rewrite applications to interpret and utilize the data.

Furthermore, in a heterogeneous data warehouse environment, the various databases reside on disparate systems, thus requiring inter-networking tools. The need to manage this environment is obvious.

Managing data warehouses includes security and priority management; monitoring updates from the multiple sources; data quality checks; managing and updating meta data; auditing and reporting data warehouse usage and status; purging data; replicating, subsetting and distributing data; backup and recovery and data warehouse storage management.

Information Delivery System

The information delivery component is used to enable the process of subscribing for data warehouse information and having it delivered to one or more destinations according to some user-specified scheduling algorithm. In other words, the information delivery system distributes warehouse-stored data and other information objects to other data warehouses and end-user products such as spreadsheets and local databases. Delivery of information may be based on time of day or on the completion of an external event. The rationale for the delivery systems component is based on the fact that once the data warehouse is installed and operational, its users don't have to be aware of its location and maintenance. All they need is the report or an analytical view of data at a specific point in time. With the proliferation of the Internet and the World Wide Web such a delivery system may leverage the convenience of the Internet by delivering warehouse-enabled information to thousands of end-users via the ubiquitous worldwide network.

In fact, the Web is changing the data warehousing landscape since at the very high level the goals of both the Web and data warehousing are the same: easy access to information. The value of data warehousing is maximized when the right information gets into the hands of those individuals who need it, where they need it and they need it most. However, many corporations have struggled with complex client/server systems to give end users the access they need. The issues become even more difficult to resolve when the users are physically remote from the data warehouse location. The Web removes a lot of these issues by giving users universal and relatively inexpensive access to data. Couple this access with the ability to deliver required information on demand and the result is a web-enabled information delivery system that allows users dispersed across continents to perform a sophisticated business-critical analysis and to engage in collective decision-making.

Information Processing

Information processing refers to the manipulation of digitized information by computers and other digital electronic equipment, known collectively as information technology (IT).

Information processing systems include business software, operating systems, computers, networks and mainframes. Whenever data needs to be transferred or operated upon in some way, this is referred to as information processing.

A computer information processor processes information to produce understandable results. The processing may include the acquisition, recording, assembly, retrieval or dissemination of information. For example, in printing a text file, an information processor works to translate and format the digital information for printed form.

Information processing began decades ago as businesses and governments sought to be able to process large amounts of data, often statistical or calculated from gathered data. The desire to travel into space further fueled the need to process large amounts of data and the information processing revolution gained more momentum. The 21st century has seen an explosion of data and the amount of information processed very day has reached gigantic proportions. Information is processed by billions of devices, hundreds of satellites and millions of software applications. Trillions of bytes are processed every minute.

Information processing is still in a growth phase; larger systems and more prolific ownership has created a steady increase in the amount of information processed globally.

Online Analytical Processing Server

Online Analytical Processing Server (OLAP) is based on the multidimensional data model. It allows managers, and analysts to get an insight of the information through fast, consistent, and interactive access to information. This topic cover the types of OLAP, operations on OLAP, difference between OLAP, and statistical databases and OLTP.

Types of OLAP Servers

We have four types of OLAP servers:

- Relational OLAP (ROLAP).
- Multidimensional OLAP (MOLAP).
- Hybrid OLAP (HOLAP).
- Specialized SQL Servers.

Relational OLAP

ROLAP servers are placed between relational back-end server and client front-end tools. To store and manage warehouse data, ROLAP uses relational or extended-relational DBMS.

ROLAP includes the following:

- Implementation of aggregation navigation logic.
- Optimization for each DBMS back end.
- Additional tools and services.

Multidimensional OLAP

MOLAP uses array-based multidimensional storage engines for multidimensional views of data. With multidimensional data stores, the storage utilization may be low if the data set is sparse. Therefore, many MOLAP server use two levels of data storage representation to handle dense and sparse data sets.

Hybrid OLAP

Hybrid OLAP is a combination of both ROLAP and MOLAP. It offers higher scalability of ROLAP and faster computation of MOLAP. HOLAP servers allow to store the large data volumes of detailed information. The aggregations are stored separately in MOLAP store.

SQL Servers Specialized

Specialized SQL servers provide advanced query language and query processing support for SQL queries over star and snowflake schemas in a read-only environment.

OLAP Operations

Since OLAP servers are based on multidimensional view of data, we will discuss OLAP operations in multidimensional data.

Here is the list of OLAP operations:

- Roll-up
- Drill-down
- Slice and dice
- Pivot (rotate)

Roll-up

Roll-up performs aggregation on a data cube in any of the following ways:

- By climbing up a concept hierarchy for a dimension.
- By dimension reduction.

The following diagram illustrates how roll-up works:

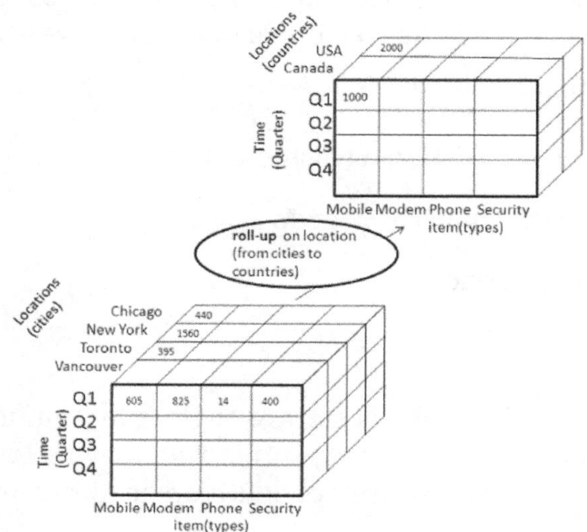

- Roll-up is performed by climbing up a concept hierarchy for the dimension location.
- Initially the concept hierarchy was "street < city < province < country".
- On rolling up, the data is aggregated by ascending the location hierarchy from the level of city to the level of country.
- The data is grouped into cities rather than countries.
- When roll-up is performed, one or more dimensions from the data cube are removed.

Drill-down

Drill-down is the reverse operation of roll-up. It is performed by either of the following ways:

- By stepping down a concept hierarchy for a dimension.
- By introducing a new dimension.

The following diagram illustrates how drill-down works:

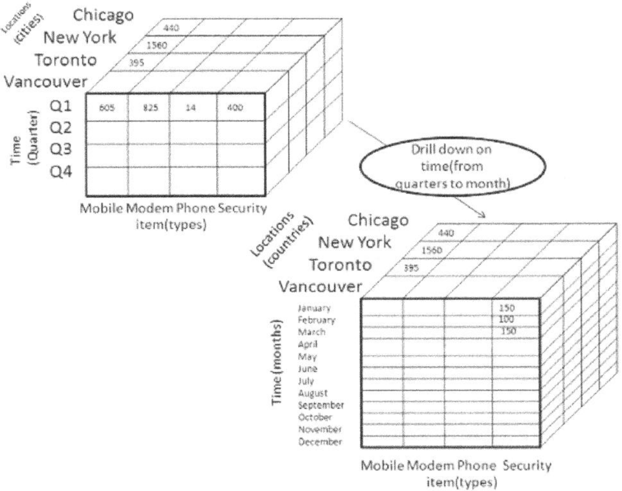

- Drill-down is performed by stepping down a concept hierarchy for the dimension time.
- Initially the concept hierarchy was "day < month < quarter < year."
- On drilling down, the time dimension is descended from the level of quarter to the level of month.
- When drill-down is performed, one or more dimensions from the data cube are added.
- It navigates the data from less detailed data to highly detailed data.

Slice

The slice operation selects one particular dimension from a given cube and provides a new sub-cube. Consider the following diagram that shows how slice works.

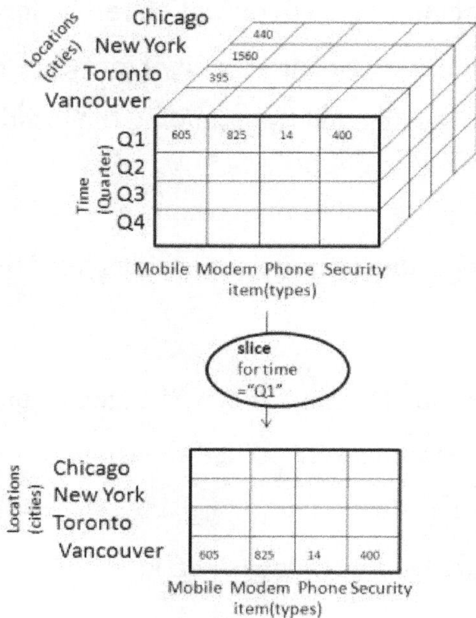

- Here Slice is performed for the dimension "time" using the criterion time = "Q1".
- It will form a new sub-cube by selecting one or more dimensions.

Dice

Dice selects two or more dimensions from a given cube and provides a new sub-cube. Consider the following diagram that shows the dice operation.

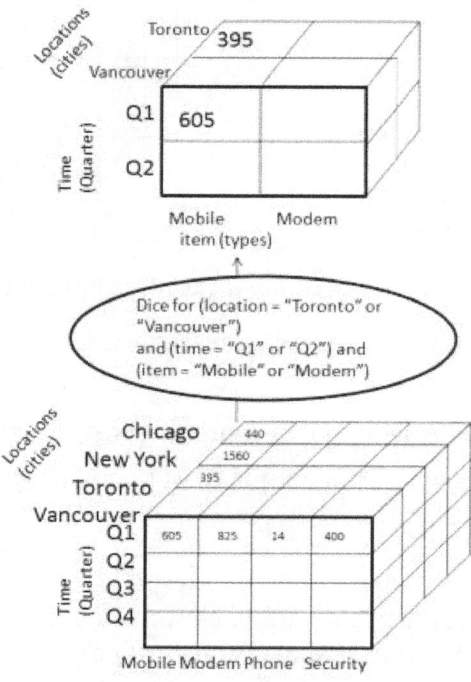

The dice operation on the cube based on the following selection criteria involves three dimensions.

- (location = "Toronto" or "Vancouver").
- (time = "Q1" or "Q2").
- (item =" Mobile" or "Modem").

Pivot

The pivot operation is also known as rotation. It rotates the data axes in view in order to provide an alternative presentation of data. Consider the following diagram that shows the pivot operation.

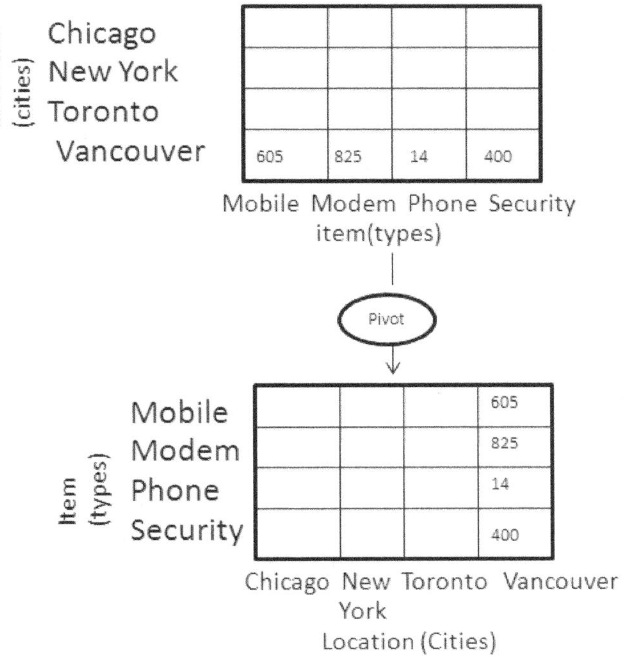

OLAP vs. OLTP

Sr. No.	Data Warehouse (OLAP)	Operational Database (OLTP)
1	Involves historical processing of information.	Involves day-to-day processing.
2	OLAP systems are used by knowledge workers such as executives, managers and analysts.	OLTP systems are used by clerks, DBAs, or database professionals.
3	Useful in analyzing the business.	Useful in running the business.
4	It focuses on Information out.	It focuses on Data in.
5	Based on Star Schema, Snowflake, Schema and Fact Constellation Schema.	Based on Entity Relationship Model.
6	Contains historical data.	Contains current data.

7	Provides summarized and consolidated data.	Provides primitive and highly detailed data.
8	Provides summarized and multidimensional view of data.	Provides detailed and flat relational view of data.
9	Number or users is in hundreds.	Number of users is in thousands.
10	Number of records accessed is in millions.	Number of records accessed is in tens.
11	Database size is from 100 GB to 1 TB	Database size is from 100 MB to 1 GB.
12	Highly flexible.	Provides high performance.

Data Mining

Data mining is the process of sorting through large data sets to identify patterns and establish relationships to solve problems through data analysis. Data mining tools allow enterprises to predict future trends.

Data Mining Parameters

In data mining, association rules are created by analyzing data for frequent if/then patterns, then using the support and confidence criteria to locate the most important relationships within the data. Support is how frequently the items appear in the database, while confidence is the number of times if/then statements are accurate.

Other data mining parameters include Sequence or Path Analysis, Classification, Clustering and Forecasting. Sequence or Path Analysis parameters look for patterns where one event leads to another later event. A Sequence is an ordered list of sets of items, and it is a common type of data structure found in many databases. A Classification parameter looks for new patterns, and might result in a change in the way the data is organized. Classification algorithms predict variables based on other factors within the database.

Four stages of data mining

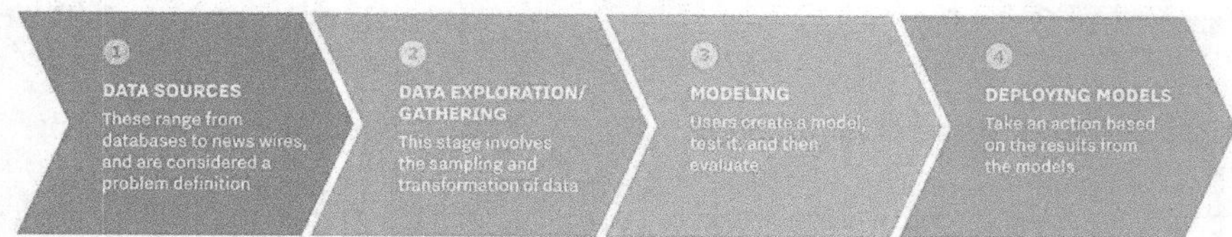

Clustering parameters find and visually document groups of facts that were previously unknown. Clustering groups a set of objects and aggregates them based on how similar they are to each other.

There are different ways a user can implement the cluster, which differentiate between each clustering model. Fostering parameters within data mining can discover patterns in data that can lead to reasonable predictions about the future, also known as predictive analysis.

Data Mining Tools and Techniques

Data mining techniques are used in many research areas, including mathematics, cybernetics, genetics and marketing. While data mining techniques are a means to drive efficiencies and predict customer behavior, if used correctly, a business can set itself apart from its competition through the use of predictive analysis.

Web mining, a type of data mining used in customer relationship management, integrates information gathered by traditional data mining methods and techniques over the web. Web mining aims to understand customer behavior and to evaluate how effective a particular website is.

Other data mining techniques include network approaches based on multitask learning for classifying patterns, ensuring parallel and scalable execution of data mining algorithms, the mining of large databases, the handling of relational and complex data types, and machine learning. Machine learning is a type of data mining tool that designs specific algorithms from which to learn and predict.

Benefits of Data Mining

In general, the benefits of data mining come from the ability to uncover hidden patterns and relationships in data that can be used to make predictions that impact businesses.

Specific data mining benefits vary depending on the goal and the industry. Sales and marketing departments can mine customer data to improve lead conversion rates or to create one-to-one marketing campaigns. Data mining information on historical sales patterns and customer behaviors can be used to build prediction models for future sales, new products and services.

Companies in the financial industry use data mining tools to build risk models and detect fraud. The manufacturing industry uses data mining tools to improve product safety, identify quality issues, manage the supply chain and improve operations.

Key Features of Data Mining

- Automatic pattern predictions based on trend and behavior analysis.
- Prediction based on likely outcomes.
- Creation of decision-oriented information.
- Focus on large data sets and databases for analysis.
- Clustering based on finding and visually documented groups of facts not previously known.

The Data Mining Process: Technological Infrastructure Required:

1. Database Size: For creating a more powerful system more data is required to processed and maintained.
2. Query complexity: For querying or processing more complex queries and the greater the number of queries, the more powerful system is required.

Uses

1. Data mining techniques are useful in many research projects, including mathematics, cybernetics, genetics and marketing.
2. With data mining, a retailer could manage and use point-of-sale records of customer purchases to send targeted promotions based on an individual's purchase history.

The retailer could also develop products and promotions to appeal to specific customer segments based on mining demographic data from comment or warranty cards.

Data Warehouse Architectures

Data Warehouse Architecture: Basic

Figure shows a simple architecture for a data warehouse. End users directly access data derived from several source systems through the data warehouse.

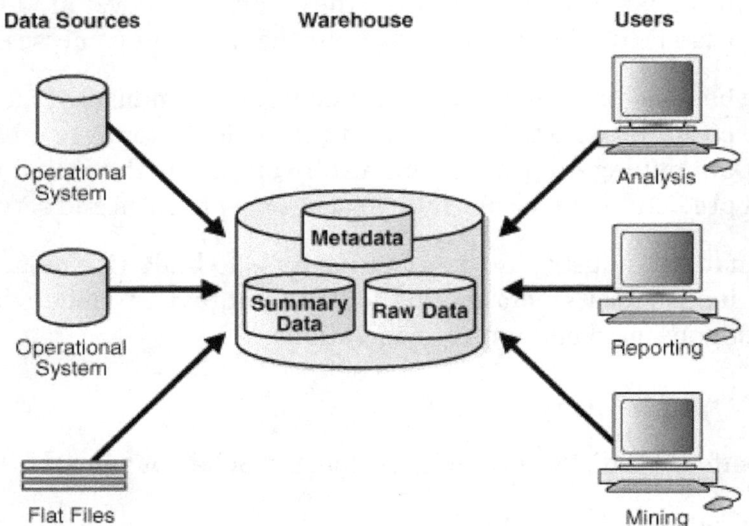

Figure: Architecture of a data warehouse

In figure, the metadata and raw data of a traditional OLTP system is present, as is an additional type of data, summary data. Summaries are very valuable in data warehouses because they pre-compute long operations in advance. For example, a typical data warehouse query is to retrieve something such as August sales.

Data Warehouse Architecture: With a Staging Area

You must clean and process your operational data before putting it into the warehouse, as shown in figure. You can do this programmatically, although most data warehouses use a **staging area** instead. A staging area simplifies building summaries and general warehouse management. Figure illustrates this typical architecture.

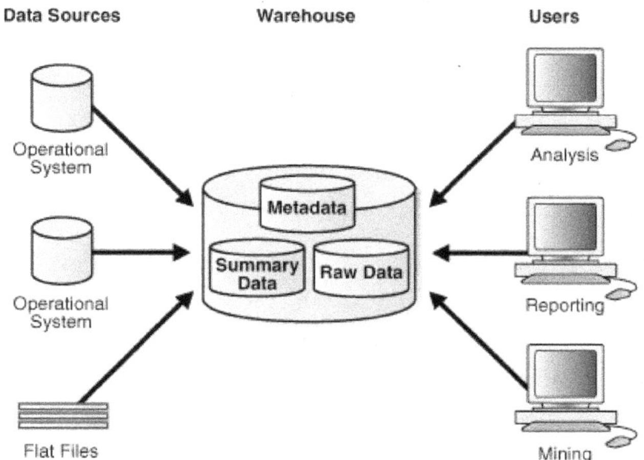

Figure: Architecture of a data warehouse with a staging area

Data Warehouse Architecture: with a Staging Area and Data Marts

Although the architecture in figure is quite common, you may want to customize your warehouse's architecture for different groups within your organization. You can do this by adding data marts, which are systems designed for a particular line of business. Figure illustrates an example where purchasing, sales, and inventories are separated. In this example, a financial analyst might want to analyze historical data for purchases and sales or mine historical data to make predictions about customer behavior.

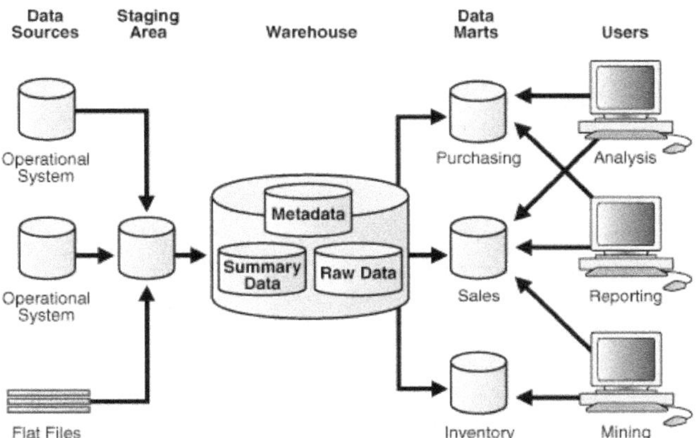

Figure: Architecture of a data warehouse with a staging area and data marts

Single-Tier Architecture

The objective of a single layer is to minimize the amount of data stored. This goal is to remove data redundancy. This architecture is not frequently used in practice.

Two-Tier Architecture

Two-layer architecture separates physically available sources and data warehouse. This architecture is not expandable and also not supporting a large number of end-users. It also has connectivity problems because of network limitations.

Three-Tier Architecture

Traditional data warehouse architecture employs a three-tier structure composed of the following tiers:

- Bottom tier: This tier contains the database server used to extract data from many different sources, such as from transactional databases used for front-end applications.
- Middle tier: The middle tier houses an OLAP server, which transforms the data into a structure better suited for analysis and complex querying. The OLAP server can work in two ways: either as an extended relational database management system that maps the operations on multidimensional data to standard relational operations (Relational OLAP), or using a multidimensional OLAP model that directly implements the multidimensional data and operations.
- Top tier: The top tier is the client layer. This tier holds the tools used for high-level data analysis, querying reporting, and data mining.

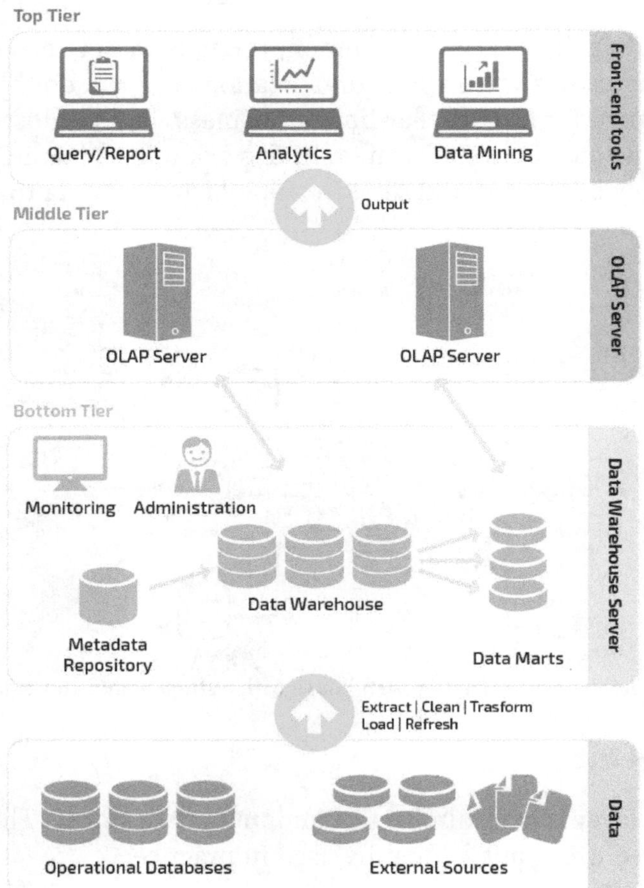

Kimball vs. Inmon

Two pioneers of data warehousing named Bill Inmon and Ralph Kimball had different approaches to data warehouse design.

Ralph Kimball's approach stressed the importance of data marts, which are repositories of data belonging to particular lines of business. The data warehouse is simply a combination of different data marts that facilitates reporting and analysis. The Kimball data warehouse design uses a "bottom-up" approach.

Bill Inmon regarded the data warehouse as the centralized repository for all enterprise data. In this approach, an organization first creates a normalized data warehouse model. Dimensional data marts are then created based on the warehouse model. This is known as a top-down approach to data warehousing.

Data Warehouse Bus Architecture

Data warehouse Bus determines the flow of data in your warehouse. The data flow in a data warehouse can be categorized as Inflow, Upflow, Downflow, Outflow and Meta flow.

While designing a Data Bus, one needs to consider the shared dimensions, facts across data marts.

Data Marts

A data mart is an access layer which is used to get data out to the users. It is presented as an option for large size data warehouse as it takes less time and money to build. However, there is no standard definition of a data mart is differing from person to person.

In a simple word Data mart is a subsidiary of a data warehouse. The data mart is used for partition of data which is created for the specific group of users.

Data marts could be created in the same database as the Data warehouse or a physically separate Database.

Data Warehouse Models

In a traditional architecture there are three common data warehouse models: virtual warehouse, data mart, and enterprise data warehouse:

- A virtual data warehouse is a set of separate databases, which can be queried together, so a user can effectively access all the data as if it was stored in one data warehouse.
- A data mart model is used for business-line specific reporting and analysis. In this data warehouse model, data is aggregated from a range of source systems relevant to a specific business area, such as sales or finance.
- An enterprise data warehouse model prescribes that the data warehouse contain aggregated data that spans the entire organization. This model sees the data warehouse as the heart of the enterprise's information system, with integrated data from all business units.

Star Schema vs. Snowflake Schema

The star schema and snowflake schema are two ways to structure a data warehouse.

The star schema has a centralized data repository, stored in a fact table. The schema splits the fact table into a series of denormalized dimension tables. The fact table contains aggregated data to be used for reporting purposes while the dimension table describes the stored data.

Denormalized designs are less complex because the data is grouped. The fact table uses only one link to join to each dimension table. The star schema's simpler design makes it much easier to write complex queries.

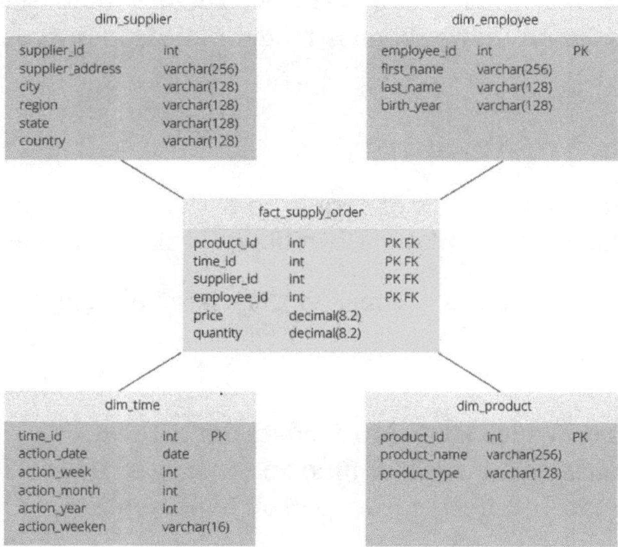

The snowflake schema is different because it normalizes the data. Normalization means efficiently organizing the data so that all data dependencies are defined, and each table contains minimal redundancies. Single dimension tables thus branch out into separate dimension tables.

The snowflake schema uses less disk space and better preserves data integrity. The main disadvantage is the complexity of queries required to access data—each query must dig deep to get to the relevant data because there are multiple joins.

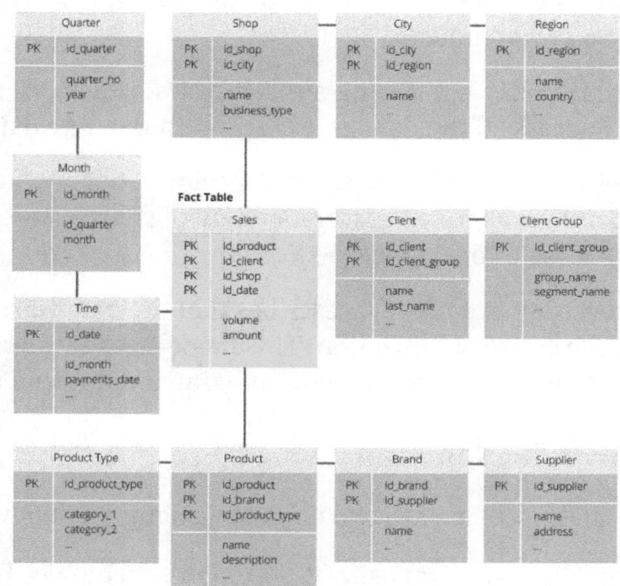

ETL vs. ELT

ETL and ELT are two different methods of loading data into a warehouse.

Extract, Transform, Load (ETL) first extracts the data from a pool of data sources, which are typically transactional databases. The data is held in a temporary staging database. Transformation operations are then performed, to structure and convert the data into a suitable form for the target data warehouse system. The structured data is then loaded into the warehouse, ready for analysis.

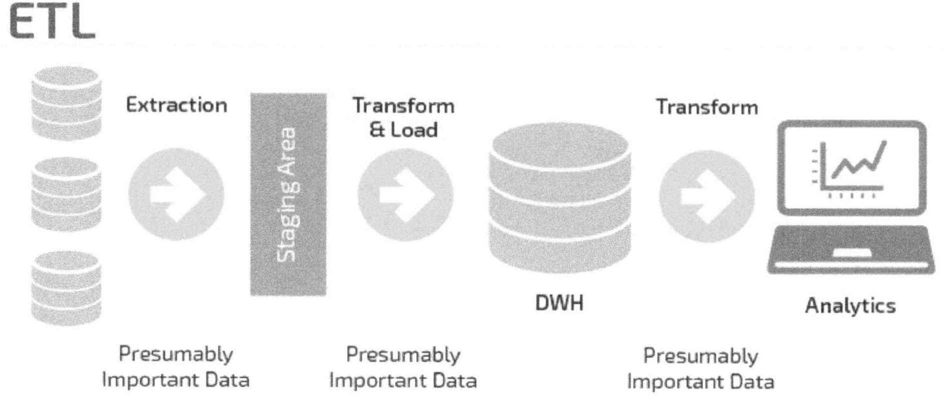

With Extract Load Transform (ELT), data is immediately loaded after being extracted from the source data pools. There is no staging database, meaning the data is immediately loaded into the single, centralized repository. The data is transformed inside the data warehouse system for use with business intelligence tools and analytics.

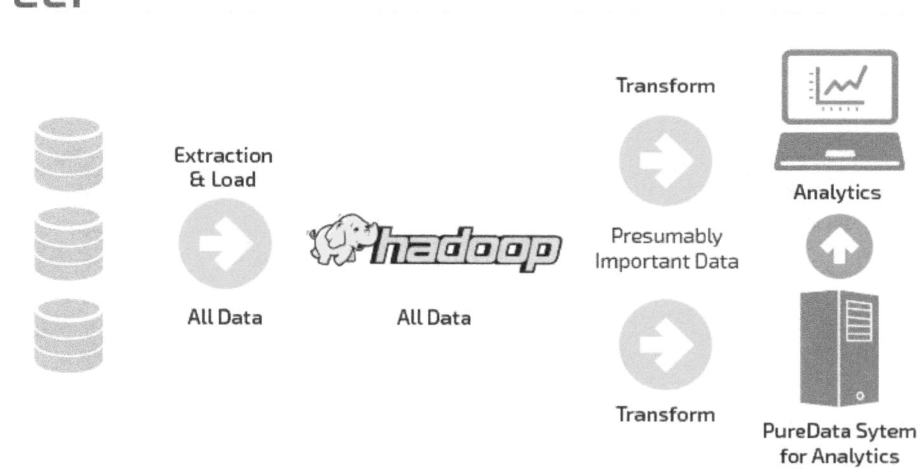

Organizational Maturity

The structure of an organization's data warehouse also depends on its current situation and needs.

The basic structure lets end users of the warehouse directly access summary data derived from source systems and perform analysis, reporting, and mining on that data. This structure is useful for when data sources derive from the same types of database systems.

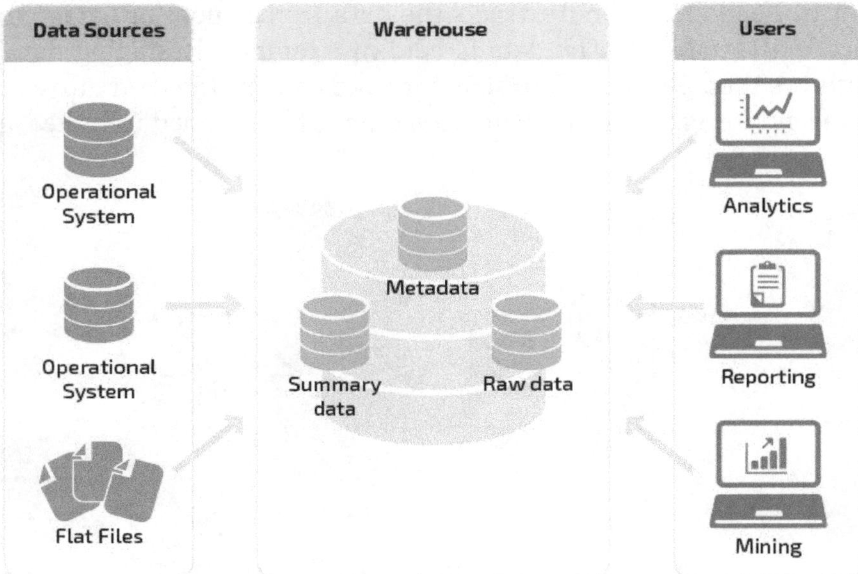

A warehouse with a staging area is the next logical step in an organization with disparate data sources with many different types and formats of data. The staging area converts the data into a summarized structured format that is easier to query with analysis and reporting tools.

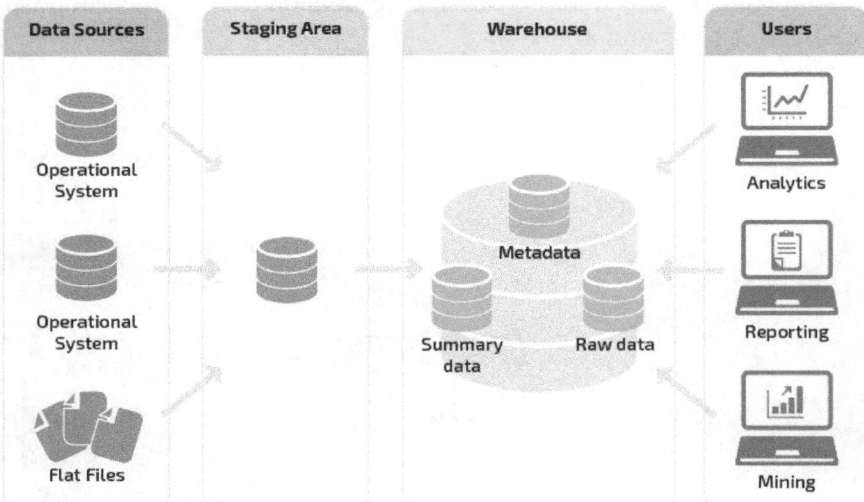

A variation on the staging structure is the addition of data marts to the data warehouse. The data marts store summarized data for a particular line of business, making that data easily accessible for specific forms of analysis. For example, adding data marts can allow a financial analyst to more easily perform detailed queries on sales data, to make predictions about customer behavior. Data marts make analysis easier by tailoring data specifically to meet the needs of the end user.

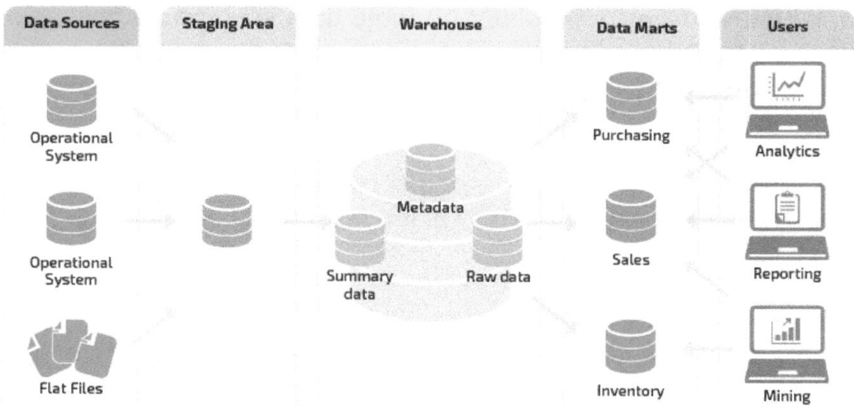

New Data Warehouse Architectures

In recent years, data warehouses are moving to the cloud. The new cloud-based data warehouses do not adhere to the traditional architecture; each data warehouse offering has a unique architecture.

This section summarizes the architectures used by two of the most popular cloud-based warehouses: Amazon Redshift and Google BigQuery.

Amazon Redshift

Amazon Redshift is a cloud-based representation of a traditional data warehouse.

Redshift requires computing resources to be provisioned and set up in the form of clusters, which contain a collection of one or more nodes. Each node has its own CPU, storage, and RAM. A leader node compiles queries and transfers them to compute nodes, which execute the queries.

On each node, data is stored in chunks, called slices. Redshift uses a columnar storage, meaning each block of data contains values from a single column across a number of rows, instead of a single row with values from multiple columns.

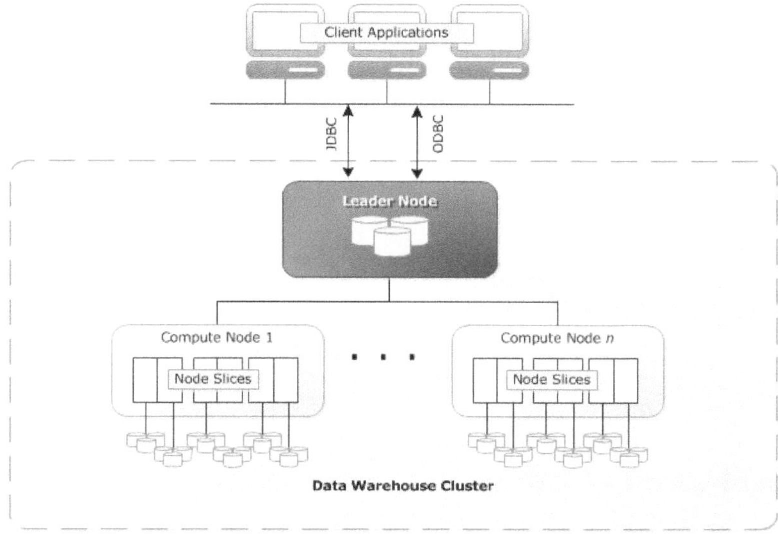

Redshift uses an MPP architecture, breaking up large data sets into chunks which are assigned to slices within each node. Queries perform faster because the compute nodes process queries in each slice simultaneously. The Leader Node aggregates the results and returns them to the client application.

Client applications, such as BI and analytics tools, can directly connect to Redshift using open source PostgreSQL, JDBC and ODBC drivers. Analysts can thus perform their tasks directly on the Redshift data.

Redshift can load only structured data. It is possible to load data to Redshift using pre-integrated systems including Amazon S3 and DynamoDB, by pushing data from any on-premise host with SSH connectivity, or by integrating other data sources using the Redshift API.

Google BigQuery

BigQuery's architecture is serverless, meaning Google dynamically manages the allocation of machine resources. All resource management decisions are, therefore, hidden from the user.

BigQuery lets clients load data from Google Cloud Storage and other readable data sources. The alternative option is to stream data, which allows developers to add data to the data warehouse in real-time, row-by-row, as it becomes available.

BigQuery uses a query execution engine named Dremel, which can scan billions of rows of data in just a few seconds. Dremel uses massively parallel querying to scan data in the underlying Colossus file management system. Colossus distributes files into chunks of 64 megabytes among many computing resources named nodes, which are grouped into clusters.

Dremel uses a columnar data structure, similar to Redshift. A tree architecture dispatches queries among thousands of machines in seconds.

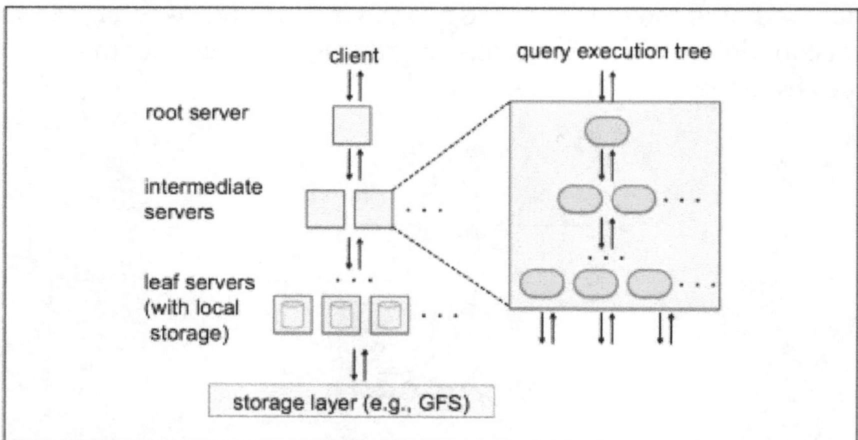

Figure: Tree architecture of Dremel

Panoply

Panoply provides end-to-end data management-as-a-service. Its unique self-optimizing architecture utilizes machine learning and natural language processing (NLP) to model and streamline the data journey from source to analysis, reducing the time from data to value as close as possible to none.

Panoply's smart data infrastructure includes the following features:

- Analyzing of queries and data: Identifying the best configuration for each use case, adjusting it over time, and building indexes, sortkeys, diskeys, data types, vacuuming, and partitioning.
- Identifying queries that do not follow best practices: Such as those that include nested loops or implicit casting – and rewrites them to an equivalent query requiring a fraction of the runtime or resources.
- Optimizing server configurations over time based on query patterns and by learning which server setup works best. The platform switches server types seamlessly and measures the resulting performance.

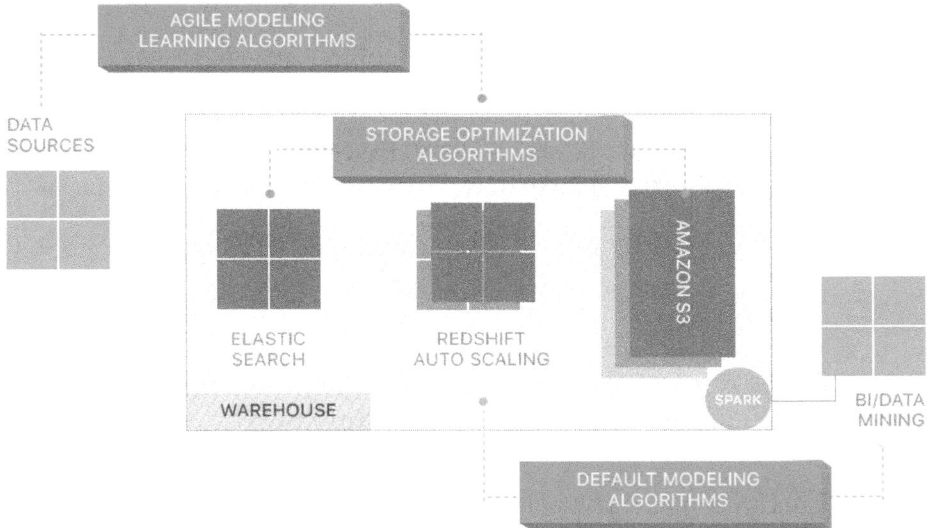

Beyond Cloud Data Warehouses

Cloud-based data warehouses are a big step forward from traditional architectures. However, users still face several challenges when setting them up:

- Loading data to cloud data warehouses is non-trivial, and for large-scale data pipelines, it requires setting up, testing, and maintaining an ETL process. This part of the process is typically done with third-party tools.
- Updates, upserts and deletions can be tricky and must be done carefully to prevent degradation in query performance.
- Semi-structured data is difficult to deal with - needs to be normalized into a relational database format, which requires automation for large data streams.
- Nested structures are typically not supported in cloud data warehouses. You will need to flatten nested tables into a format the data warehouse can understand.

- Optimizing your cluster: There are different options for setting up a Redshift cluster to run your workloads. Different workloads, data sets, or even different types of queries might require a different setup. To stay optimal you'll need to continually revisit and tweak your setup.
- Query optimization: User queries may not follow best practices, and consequently will take much longer to run. You may find yourselves working with users or automated client applications to optimize queries so that the data warehouse can perform as expected.
- Backup and recovery: While the data warehouse vendors provide numerous options for backing up your data, they are not trivial to set up and require monitoring and close attention.

Panoply is a Smart Data Warehouse that adds a layer of automation that takes care of all of the complex tasks above, saving valuable time and helping you get from data to insight in minutes.

Data warehouse Architecture Best Practices

To design Data Warehouse Architecture, you need to follow below given best practices:

- Use a data model which is optimized for information retrieval which can be the dimensional mode, denormalized or hybrid approach.
- Need to assure that Data is processed quickly and accurately. At the same time, you should take an approach which consolidates data into a single version of the truth.
- Carefully design the data acquisition and cleansing process for Data warehouse.
- Design a metadata architecture which allows sharing of metadata between components of Data Warehouse.
- Consider implementing an ODS model when information retrieval need is near the bottom of the data abstraction pyramid or when there are multiple operational sources required to be accessed.
- One should make sure that the data model is integrated and not just consolidated. In that case, you should consider 3NF data model. It is also ideal for acquiring ETL and Data cleansing tools.

Data Warehouse Design Approaches

It has been said there are as many ways to build data warehouses as there are companies to build them. Each data warehouse is unique because it must adapt to the needs of business users in different functional areas, whose companies face different business conditions and competitive pressures.

Nonetheless, four major approaches to building a data warehousing environment exist. These architectures are generally referred to as:

1) Top-down
2) Bottom-up

3) Hybrid
4) Federated

Most organizations—wittingly or not—follow one or another of these approaches as a blueprint for development.

Although we have been building data warehouses since the early 1990s, there is still a great deal of confusion about the similarities and differences among these architectures. This is especially true of the "top-down" and "bottom-up" approaches, which have existed the longest and occupy the polar ends of the development spectrum.

As a result, some companies fail to adopt a clear vision for the way the data warehousing environment can and should evolve. Others, paralyzed by confusion or fear of deviating from prescribed tenets for success, cling too rigidly to one approach or another, undermining their ability to respond flexibly to new or unexpected situations. Ideally, organizations need to borrow concepts and tactics from each approach to create environments that uniquely meets their needs.

Semantic and Substantive Differences The two most influential approaches are championed by industry heavyweights Bill Inmon and Ralph Kimball, both prolific authors and consultants in the data warehousing field. Inmon, who is credited with coining the term "data warehousing" in the early 1990s, advocates a top-down approach, in which companies first build a data warehouse followed by data marts. Kimball's approach, on the other hand, is often called bottom-up because it starts and ends with data marts, negating the need for a physical data warehouse altogether.

On the surface, there is considerable friction between top-down and bottom-up approaches. But in reality, the differences are not as stark as they may appear. Both approaches advocate building a robust enterprise architecture that adapts easily to changing business needs and delivers a single version of the truth. In some cases, the differences are more semantic than substantive in nature. For example, both approaches collect data from source systems into a single data store, from which data marts are populated. But while "top-down" subscribers call this a data warehouse, "bottom-up" adherents often call this a "staging area."

Nonetheless, significant differences exist between the two approaches Data warehousing professionals need to understand the substantial, subtle, and semantic differences among the approaches and which industry "gurus" or consultants advocate each approach. This will provide a clearer understanding of the different routes to achieve data warehousing success and how to translate between the advice and rhetoric of the different approaches.

Top-down Approach

The top-down approach views the data warehouse as the linchpin of the entire analytic environment. The data warehouse holds atomic or transaction data that is extracted from one or more source systems and integrated within a normalized, enterprise data model. From there, the data is summarized, dimensionalized, and distributed to one or more "dependent" data marts. These data marts are "dependent" because they derive all their data from a centralized data warehouse.

Sometimes, organizations supplement the data warehouse with a staging area to collect and store source system data before it can be moved and integrated within the data warehouse. A separate staging area is particularly useful if there are numerous source systems, large volumes of data, or small batch windows with which to extract data from source systems.

The major benefit of a "top-down" approach is that it provides an integrated, flexible architecture to support downstream analytic data structures. First, this means the data warehouse provides a departure point for all data marts, enforcing consistency and standardization so that organizations can achieve a single version of the truth. Second, the atomic data in the warehouse lets organizations re-purpose that data in any number of ways to meet new and unexpected business needs. For example, a data warehouse can be used to create rich data sets for statisticians, deliver operational reports, or support operational data stores (ODS) and analytic applications. Moreover, users can query the data warehouse if they need cross-functional or enterprise views of the data.

On the downside, a top-down approach may take longer and cost more to deploy than other approaches, especially in the initial increments. This is because organizations must create a reasonably detailed enterprise data model as well as the physical infrastructure to house the staging area, data warehouse, and the marts before deploying their applications or reports. (Of course, depending on the size of an implementation, organizations can deploy all three "tiers" within a single database.) This initial delay may cause some groups with their own IT budgets to build their own analytic applications. Also, it may not be intuitive or seamless for end users to drill through from a data mart to a data warehouse to find the details behind the summary data in their reports.

Bottom-up Approach

In a bottom-up approach, the goal is to deliver business value by deploying dimensional data marts as quickly as possible. Unlike the top-down approach, these data marts contain all the data—both atomic and summary—that users may want or need, now or in the future. Data is modeled in a star schema design to optimize usability and query performance. Each data mart builds on the next, reusing dimensions and facts so users can query across data marts, if desired, to obtain a single version of the truth as well as both summary and atomic data.

The "bottom-up" approach consciously tries to minimize back-office operations, preferring to focus an organization's effort on developing dimensional designs that meet end-user requirements. The "bottom-up" staging area is non-persistent, and may simply stream flat files from source systems to data marts using the file transfer protocol. In most cases, dimensional data marts are logically stored within a single database. This approach minimizes data redundancy and makes it easier to extend existing dimensional models to accommodate new subject areas.

Pros/Cons

The major benefit of a bottom-up approach is that it focuses on creating user-friendly, flexible data structures using dimensional, star schema models. It also delivers value rapidly because it doesn't lay down a heavy infrastructure up front.

Without an integration infrastructure, the bottom-up approach relies on a "dimensional bus" to ensure that data marts are logically integrated and stovepipe applications are avoided. To integrate data marts logically, organizations use "conformed" dimensions and facts when building new data marts. Thus, each new data mart is integrated with others within a logical enterprise dimensional model.

Another advantage of the bottom-up approach is that since the data marts contain both summary and atomic data, users do not have to "drill through" from a data mart to another structure to obtain detailed or transaction data. The use of a staging area also eliminates redundant extracts and overhead required to move source data into the dimensional data marts.

One problem with a bottom-up approach is that it requires organizations to enforce the use of standard dimensions and facts to ensure integration and deliver a single version of the truth. When data marts are logically arrayed within a single physical database, this integration is easily done. But in a distributed, decentralized organization, it may be too much to ask departments and business units to adhere and reuse references and rules for calculating facts. There can be a tendency for organizations to create "independent" or non-integrated data marts.

In addition, dimensional marts are designed to optimize queries, not support batch or transaction processing. Thus, organizations that use a bottom-up approach need to create additional data structures outside of the bottom-up architecture to accommodate data mining, ODSs, and operational reporting requirements. However, this may be achieved simply by pulling a subset of data from a data mart at night when users are not active on the system.

Hybrid Approach

The hybrid approach tries to blend the best of both "top-down" and "bottom-up" approaches. It attempts to capitalize on the speed and user-orientation of the "bottom-up" approach without sacrificing the integration enforced by a data warehouse in a "top down" approach. Pieter Mimno, an independent consultant who teaches at TDWI conferences, is currently the most vocal proponent of this approach.

The hybrid approach recommends spending about two weeks developing an enterprise model in third normal form before developing the first data mart. The first several data marts are also designed in third normal form but deployed using star schema physical models. This dual modeling approach fleshes out the enterprise model without sacrificing the usability and query performance of a star schema.

The hybrid approach relies on an extraction, transformation, and load (ETL) tool to store and manage the enterprise and local models in the data marts as well as synchronize the differences between them. This lets local groups, for example, develop their own definitions or rules for data elements that are derived from the enterprise model without sacrificing long-term integration. Organizations also use the ETL tool to extract and load data from source systems into the dimensional data marts at both the atomic and summary levels. Most ETL tools today can create summary tables on the fly.

After deploying the first few "dependent" data marts, an organization then backfills a data warehouse behind the data marts, instantiating the "fleshed out" version of the enterprise data model. The organization then transfers atomic data from the data marts to the data warehouse and consolidates redundant data feeds, saving the organization time, money, and processing resources.

Organizations typically backfill a data warehouse once business users request views of atomic data across multiple data marts.

The major benefit of a hybrid approach is that it combines rapid development techniques within an enterprise architecture framework. It develops an enterprise data model iteratively and only develops a heavyweight infrastructure once it's really needed (e.g. when executives start asking for reports that cross data mart boundaries.)

However, backfilling a data warehouse can be a highly disruptive process that delivers no ostensible value and therefore may never be funded. In addition, few query tools can dynamically and intelligently query atomic data in one database (i.e. the data warehouse) and summary data in another database (i.e. the data marts.) Users may be confused when to query which database.

This approach also relies heavily on an ETL tool to synchronize meta data between enterprise and local versions, develop aggregates, load detail data, and orchestrate the transition to a data warehousing infrastructure. Although ETL tools have matured considerably, they can never enforce adherence to architecture. The hybrid approach may make it too easy for local groups to stray irrevocably from the enterprise data model.

Federated Approach

The federated approach is sometimes confused with the hybrid approach above or "hub-and-spoke" data warehousing architectures that are a reflection of a top-down approach.

However, the federated approach—as defined by its most vocal proponent, Doug Hackney—is not a methodology or architecture per se, but a concession to the natural forces that undermine the best laid plans for deploying a perfect system. A federated approach rationalizes the use of whatever means possible to integrate analytical resources to meet changing needs or business conditions. In short, it's a salve for the soul of the stressed out data warehousing project manager who must sacrifice architectural purity to meet the immediate (and ever-changing) needs of his business users.

Hackney says the federated approach is "an architecture of architectures." It recommends how to integrate a multiplicity of heterogeneous data warehouses, data marts, and packaged applications that companies have already deployed and will continue to implement in spite of the IT group's best effort to enforce standards and adhere to a specific architecture.

Hackney concedes that a federated architecture will never win awards for elegance or be drawn up on clean white boards as an "optimal solution." He says it provides the "maximum amount of architecture possible in a given political and implementation reality." The approach merely encourages organizations to share the "highest value" metrics, dimensions, and measures wherever possible, however possible. This may mean, for example, creating a common staging area to eliminate redundant data feeds or building a data warehouse that sources data from multiple data marts, data warehouses, or analytic applications.

The major problem with the federated approach is that it is not well documented. There are only a few columns written on the subject. But perhaps this is enough, as it doesn't prescribe a specific end-state or approach. Another potential problem is that without a specific architecture in mind, a federated approach can perpetuate the continued decentralization and fragmentation of analytical resources, making it harder to deliver an enterprise view in the end. Also, integrating meta data is a pernicious problem in a heterogeneous, ever-changing environment.

In conclusion, the four approaches described here represent the dominant strains of data warehousing methodologies. Data warehousing managers need to be aware of these methodologies but not wedded to them. These methodologies have shaped the debate about data warehousing best practices, and comprise the building blocks for methodologies developed by practicing consultants.

Ultimately, organizations need to understand the strengths and limitations of each methodology and then pursue their own way through the data warehousing thicket. Since each organization must respond to unique needs and business conditions, having a foundation of best practice models to start with augurs a successful outcome.

Data Warehouse Automation

Data warehouse automation describe the automation of the following:

1. Simplified capture of the data warehouse design.
2. Automated build (i.e. Generate Code).
3. Automated deployment of code to the Server.
4. Automated batch execution of the ETL code on the Server.
5. Automated monitoring and reporting of the batch execution.

Generally this is achieved through a data warehouse automation tool. You could also manually create scripts to generate code and automate the Build, Deploy Run processes.

Reasons why we Need it

In the past, data warehousing has taken too long and the result have been too inflexible. This led to much frustration in the business community. As a result businesses have turned to other solutions like big data and self-service BI. However a Data Warehouse provides additional benefits over other solutions (i.e. Self Service BI). For example:

- The ability to keep history,
- A single source of the truth,
- End user productivity,
- Reduced risk of reliance on key individuals,
- Data augmentation, and
- Query performance etc.

The problem isn't the Data Warehouse concept, it's still an extremely useful method of managing information. The problem has been our execution of Data Warehouse development as an industry.

This is where Data Warehouse Automation comes in. It doesn't throw out the idea of a Data Warehouse in search of a better way; instead it directly addresses the real problem, being the execution of Data Warehouse development.

Let's face it, Data is Dirty. There is no quick and easy way to solve that, no matter what tool you use. It takes skill and experience to derive usable information from dirty data. If you are going to invest that time, why not invest it in a data warehouse. A Data Warehouse is:

- A long term asset,
- Fit for multiple purposes,
- Supports multiple reports, dashboards and analysis.

Benefits of Data Warehouse Automation

- It's fast: Dramatically reduce your development time.
- It's flexible: Respond to changing business requirements quickly and easily.
- Stay focused: On what really matters. Concentrate on reporting and analytics instead of stuck in ETL code.
- Quality: Data Warehouse Automation tools produce tested, high performance, complete and readable code. At least Dimodelo Architect does!
- Consistency and Continuity: It produces consistent code, naming standards etc. Developers come and go, but as long as they keep using the same tool, it's easy for one developer to understand the work of another.

Who

Data Warehouse Automation tools are used by professional Data Warehouse developers to enhance their productivity. It's even possible for a technical data analyst with some training and support to maintain their own Data Warehouses.

When

The need for data warehouse automation is right now. Certainly that is what the business has been telling IT for years. Seriously there are mature data warehouse automation tools on the market right now.

Where

You need the flexibility to deliver a Data Warehouse, on your desktop (development environment), on-premise or in the Cloud. Your solution should be able to deploy to multiple environments and support all three scenario simultaneously.

Dimension

Dimensions are a common way of analyzing data. The dimensional model is laid out for ease of use and to be logical and understandable to business users. Dimensions define the dimensional model and spell out the who, what, where, when, why, and how of the situation. They add context and meaning to the measures contained in the associated fact table.

In a dimension table, there is one row per product, one row per customer, one row per facility, one row per time unit, or one row per geographic region, and the granularity or level of detail of these rows depends on how finely detailed the business user wants the data. For instance, is it enough to know the average dollar value of each sale? Or do you need to know the average dollar value of a sale for each day of the year? Do you need to know how much of the sale value was for perishable items versus nonperishable items? Do you need to know purchases down to the line item level? It's very important to understand what the business reporting needs are before you start designing a data warehouse. You simply cannot be a cowboy and start slinging data around with data warehousing and dimensional design - there's too much at stake: Too much data is involved in a data warehouse, the project visibility is too high, and it's too costly to undo careless mistakes. You must plan. You must know how granular the level of detail needs to be.

Structuring Dimensions

At this point, if you're thinking "cube," think about the flat surfaces of the cube - those are the dimensions. Dimensions control query filtering - for example, "...where region like West" in T-SQL or "WHERE (Region. West)" in MDX - and supply almost all labeling in the output result sets that are turned into reports. Dimensions provide the "by" words for a report - "sales by month by product," "inventory by category by region." When you think about it, dimensions are the natural way a business user would talk about business. Each dimension contains data from a single domain, such as the time, product, or geographic area domain. Dimensions act like decoders when you "flatten" the lookup table hierarchy. If the three tables on the left were part of an entity relationship diagram (ERD) for an online transaction processing (OLTP) database, Product_Category and Product_Subcategory would be lookup tables in a hierarchy, with Product_Category higher in the hierarchy than Product_Subcategory. The purpose of a lookup table is twofold: to enforce domain integrity by limiting the list of codes that can be used in the modified table, and to help reduce data redundancy by adhering to a production level of third normal form.

In a dimensional model, you'd consider flattening the hierarchy of products, categories, and subcategories, as you can see in the Product_ With_Category table. Each row in the Product_With_ Category dimension contains all the category content that's relevant for that row, in addition to all the product information. You don't need the one-to-many relationships of an ERD because you shouldn't have to worry about domain integrity. The data has already gone through the extraction, transformation, and loading (ETL) process and has (presumably) been scrubbed and validated before loading into the data warehouse. But what about redundancy? With a data warehouse, the goal is not to reduce redundancy - data warehousing involves a different mindset from the transactional, operational database. If you're going to be building multidimensional cubes, you're better off flattening the hierarchies than not.

Flattening hierarchies also makes the join paths between the dimensions and their associated fact tables much simpler, resulting in better performance and faster query results (we hope). The one-to-many relationships between the dimension and its associated fact table, aren't meant to protect data integrity. These relationships are meant to associate keys in the fact table with the expanded definitions, which are found in the dimensions.

In any database there are hierarchies. Geographic hierarchies occur where zip codes aggregate into countries, countries into states, states into countries. With temporal hierarchies, hours aggregate into days, days into weeks and months, months into quarters, and quarters into years. In spatial hierarchies, rooms aggregate into buildings, and buildings into campuses or city blocks, and so on.

Hierarchies such as these and the product category-subcategory hierarchy in figures are used in reporting and summarizing results. Depending on what information users require, they might use the hierarchies differently from other users. One of the most common scenarios is the dichotomy between marketing and manufacturing: What manufacturing considers one product might be many products to marketing, as when hospital scrubs were co-opted by young adults as the latest fashion statement. When generating reports, manufacturing might not want to use product subcategories, whereas marketing would.

The flattening example is the type of denormalization you'll often see in a dimensional model. We denormalize to avoid an excessive number of join operations. In future columns I'll examine dimensional denormalization more closely, but for now, just remember to denormalize in such a way that you lose nothing except the OLTP structural complexity.

Dimensional Granularity

Dimensions also have grain, and the granularity of a dimension depends on the reporting requirements - just like the fact table's granularity. Unlike any other database modeling scheme, dimensional modeling is truly customer-driven.

How fine-grained do you want your dimensions to be? Obviously, the level of detail of the dimension table has to be consistent with the level of detail of the fact table that it modifies. If you have a fact table that tells you that customer A bought product B at store C in region F on date D and paid for the purchase using E, and that the sale was credited to sales associate G, then all those dimensions, A through G, had better be able to define and describe the A through G identifiers in the fact table.

One school of thought holds that a data warehouse should contain only summary data and that all available detail data should be stored in the associated OLTP source databases. That approach might work in some cases. However, we believe that fact tables and dimensions are an archive of historical activity and should contain the finest level of detail that you'll ever need for a report. One of the largest data warehouses in the world belongs to Wal-Mart - it's measured in petabytes (thousands of terabytes) and holds one and a half years of data at the individual sale level. If you need to be able to analyze individual sales in your organization, you'll need the finest level of granularity. It's better to create a data warehouse that stores data with a fine level of detail and not need that detail, than to start with summarized data and then realize you need more detail.

Understandability and Performance

The twin properties of a data warehouse are understandability and performance. By flattening hierarchies and not losing any data in the process, you make the dimension more understandable to the people who use the data. What can you do to enhance performance? You guessed it - flatten the hierarchies! One of the most common user activities in a dimensional model is drilling down to get more details. Drilling down means adding more row headers to the result set. Drilling up simply takes away those row headers. You could drill down through the product category into a specific product subcategory until you found all the products in that subcategory, and never leave the Product_With_Category dimension.

The Sales_Territory dimension is an excellent example of a dimension suited for drilldown. You can start with the Americas (zone), move on to the United States, Western region, Colorado, Denver County, 80208, and do all that with a single table, meaning no joins (at least not until you want some sales facts that relate to zip code 80208). Sales_Territory is a richly defined geographic dimension with a flattened hierarchy.

Flattening hierarchies is the same as eliminating snowflaking in the star schema. Hierarchies expressed as separate tables create snowflakes, which complicate the user presentation and often intimidate users, causing them to shy away from your data warehouse. Snowflaking (normalizing the hierarchy) causes most data warehouse applications to run relatively slowly because of all the joins in the background, lowering the quality of the user experience. The savings on disk space that you achieve with snowflaking isn't worth it. And finally, snowflaking defeats the purpose of bitmap indexing, which SQL Server Analysis Services uses internally to optimize query response.

Aggregate

Aggregates are the summarization of fact related data for the purpose of improved performance. There are many occasions when the customer wants to be able to quickly answer a question where the data is at a higher grain than we collect. To avoid slow responses due to system summing data up to higher levels we can pre-calculate these requests, storing the summarized data in a separate star. Aggregates can be considered to be conformed fact tables since they must provide the same query results as the detailed fact table.

Imagine that you have a fact table like this in which the granularity is date, product and customer:

Customer ID	Item No	Order Date	Unit Sales	Profit
1	143	04/05/2012	1	1.52
1	150	04/05/2012	3	3.9
1	8	10/06/2012	1	2.48
1	77	10/06/2012	1	1.37
1	92	10/06/2012	1	1.33

1	95	10/06/2012	1	2.87
1	18	28/07/2012	1	2.3
1	37	28/07/2012	1	1.03
1	61	28/07/2012	1	2.01
1	83	28/07/2012	1	2.37
1	120	28/07/2012	1	2.24
1	8	13/08/2012	1	2.48
1	58	13/08/2012	1	2.79
1	100	16/12/2012	1	2.18
1	122	16/12/2012	1	2.47
1	83	12/05/2013	1	2.37
1	148	12/05/2013	1	2.17
1	37	29/11/2013	1	1.03
1	116	29/11/2013	1	2.03
2	46	07/04/2012	1	2.24
2	110	07/04/2012	1	2.84
2	49	06/05/2012	1	2.2
2	60	06/05/2012	1	1.91
2	26	22/05/2012	1	1.69

Every value that you see for "unit sales" is the number of units of a particular product that were sold to a particular customer on a particular day. (Here, to help make the point of aggregation slightly clearer, we've shown the day of sale as an actual date rather than as a pointer. And yes, we realize that these European-style dates are still in the future – but we'll treat them as the past for purposes of this demonstration.)

We could run queries against this fact table, and it would return data. For example, we could ask for the total unit sales of Item No. 150 to Customer 1 on May 4, 2012, and the answer we'd get is three.

We could also run a query that returns the total sales of Item No. 150 to the same customer not just for the 4th of May but for that entire month. In order to do this, the system would scan the fact table looking for 31 separate date entries listing sales of that product to Customer 1 and then aggregate the unit-sale values from the returned rows. That would be a relatively slow process.

An alternative is to create a fact table that already contains one or more levels of aggregation. For example, we could aggregate this fact table by month. That would involve finding all the sales of Item No. 150 to Customer 1 in, say, January 2012, aggregating the data, and putting the results in a single row. We then, of course, would have to do the same for the other months, the other products and the other customers.

The new table would look like this:

Customer ID	Item No	Order date	Unit Sales	Profit
1	150	Jan 2012	11	11.52
1	150	Feb 2012	3	3.9
1	150	March 2012	2	2.48
1	150	April 2012	1	1.37
1	150	May 2012	1	1.33
1	150	June 2012	2	2.87

Now when we had a query that looked for a monthly sales total, we could run it against the aggregate fact table and find the answer much more rapidly. And of course, this isn't the only aggregate fact table that we could generate. For example, if we knew the counties that different customers were located in, we could aggregate their data on that basis.

We could also aggregate by both date and customer up to the level of the month and county, as in this table excerpt (with Herefordshire being a county in England, for the uninitiated):

Customer ID	Item No	Order date	Unit Sales	Profit
Herefordshire	150	Jan 2012	111	121.52
Herefordshire	150	Feb 2010	63	73.9

In other words, we could create a series of aggregate fact tables, and when a query comes in, we could run it against the appropriate aggregated table.

An aggregate fact table is simply one that combines multiple rows of data, loses some detail and aggregates numerical values.

Aggregation Versus Pre-aggregation

Whenever the display level of data on a report must differ from the level at which the data is initially captured, aggregation, that is, the rolling up of data, must occur. By default, aggregation occurs dynamically with a SQL statement at report run-time.

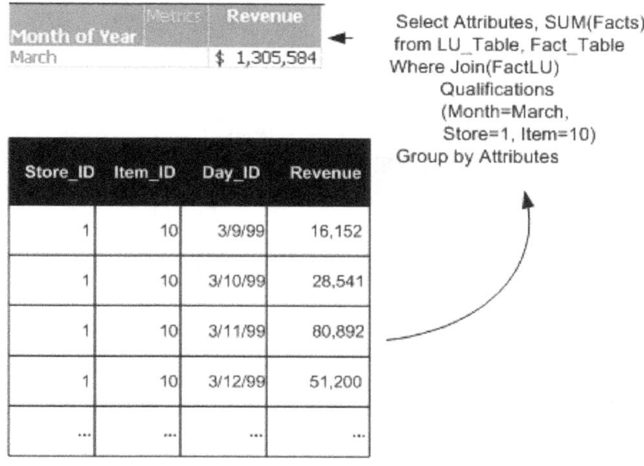

For example, sales data is stored by day in a fact table. A report requesting month-level data is executed. The daily values from the fact table are selected, sorted, and added to produce the monthly totals, as shown below.

Aggregation can also be completed before reports are executed; the results of the aggregation are stored in an aggregate table. This process is called pre-aggregation. You can build these pre-aggregated—or aggregate—tables as part of the ETL process. If sales data is frequently requested at the month level, as in the previous example, an aggregate table with the sales data rolled up to the month level is useful.

Pre-aggregation eliminates the reading, sorting, and calculation of data from many database rows in a large, lower-level fact table at run time, as shown in the following example.

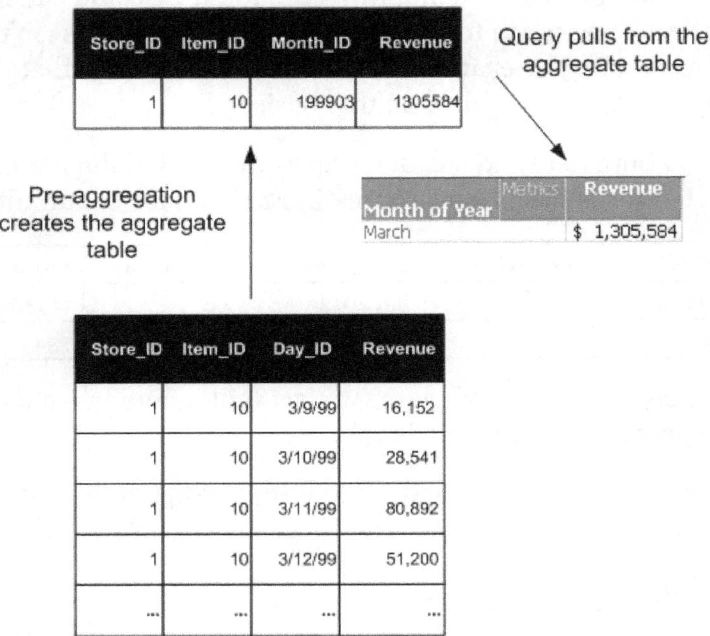

If the daily sales fact table is the lowest-level fact table and contains atomic-level data, it is referred to as a base table. In these terms, an aggregate table is any fact table whose data is derived by aggregating data from an existing base table.

Degree of Aggregation

While MOLAP can provide fast performance when it answers a question, it requires a completely aggregated schema to answer most questions. That is, every possible combination of aggregate associations must be generated when the multidimensional cube is built. This ensures that all possible questions can be answered. This scenario becomes very difficult to maintain as the number of attributes and the amount of data increase, and therefore is not very scalable.

In a ROLAP environment, the degree of aggregation can be as dense or as sparse as is appropriate for your users. A densely aggregated warehouse has a large number of aggregate tables while a sparsely aggregated warehouse has fewer. Sparse aggregation refers to the fact that a given project only requires as many aggregate fact tables as is useful to its users.

ROLAP, therefore, provides much greater flexibility than MOLAP. Only the aggregate combinations that you determine are beneficial must be created. That is, if the aggregate table is useful in answering frequently-asked queries, its presence provides a response as fast as a MOLAP system can provide. However, if a certain aggregate combination is rarely or never used, the space in the RDBMS does not need to be consumed and the resources to build that table during the batch process do not need to be used.

Not every attribute level or hierarchy intersection is suitable for pre-aggregation. Build aggregate tables only if they can benefit users, since the creation and maintenance of aggregate tables requires additional work by the database administrator. Also, do not waste database space for tables that will not be used.

Consider the following factors when deciding whether to create aggregate tables:

- The frequency of queries at that level: Determining the frequency of queries at a specific level.
- The relationship between the parent and child: Considering any related parent-child relationships.
- The compression ratio: Compression ratio.

References

- Components-of-a-data-warehouse-4213: tdan.com, Retrieved 16 April 2018
- Information-processing-25605: techopedia.com, Retrieved 28 June 2018
- Data-mining: searchsqlserver.techtarget.com, Retrieved 09 July 2018
- Data-warehouse-architecture-traditional-vs-cloud, data-warehouse-guide: panoply.io, Retrieved 07 May 2018
- Business-intelligence/data-warehousing-dimension-basics: itprotoday.com, Retrieved 17 April 2018
- What-are-aggregate-tables-and-aggregate-fact-tables: searchdatamanagement.techtarget.com, Retrieved 10 June 2018

2

Data Warehousing Operations

The data in a warehouse is uploaded from various operational sources. It passes through a data store and the cleansed. This is required for ensuring data quality. The diverse operations of data warehousing with respect to database normalization, operational database, data integrity, etc. have been thoroughly discussed in this chapter.

Data Integrity

It is important that data adhere to a predefined set of rules, as determined by the database administrator or application developer. As an example of data integrity, consider the tables employees and departments and the business rules for the information in each of the tables, as illustrated in figure.

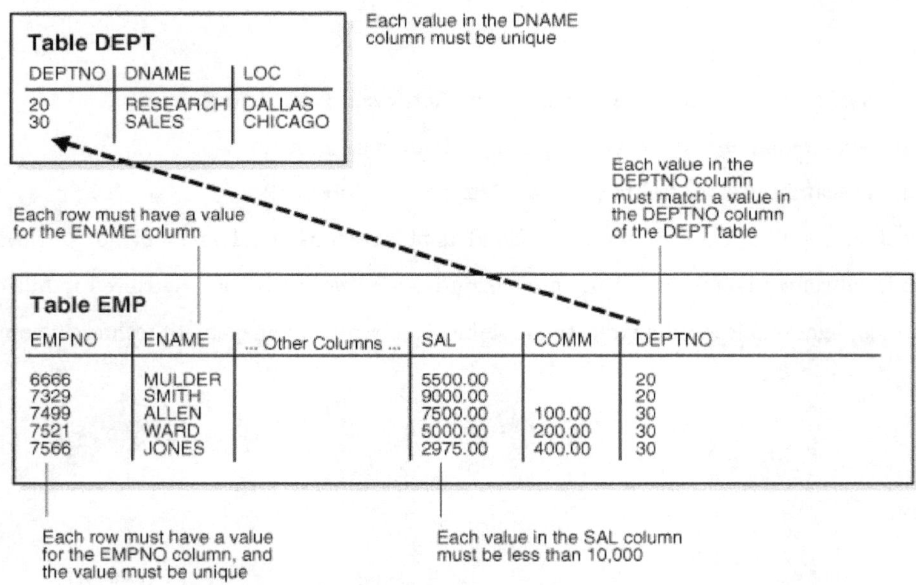

Figure: Examples of Data Integrity

Note that some columns in each table have specific rules that constrain the data contained within them.

Types of Data Integrity

- Null Rule

A null rule is a rule defined on a single column that allows or disallows inserts or updates of rows containing a null (the absence of a value) in that column.

- Unique Column Values

A unique value rule defined on a column (or set of columns) allows the insert or update of a row only if it contains a unique value in that column (or set of columns).

- Primary Key Values

A primary key value rule defined on a key (a column or set of columns) specifies that each row in the table can be uniquely identified by the values in the key.

- Referential Integrity Rules

A referential integrity rule is a rule defined on a key (a column or set of columns) in one table that guarantees that the values in that key match the values in a key in a related table (the referenced value).

Referential integrity also includes the rules that dictate what types of data manipulation are allowed on referenced values and how these actions affect dependent values. The rules associated with referential integrity are:

- Restrict: Disallows the update or deletion of referenced data.
- Set to Null: When referenced data is updated or deleted, all associated dependent data is set to NULL.
- Set to Default: When referenced data is updated or deleted, all associated dependent data is set to a default value.
- Cascade: When referenced data is updated, all associated dependent data is correspondingly updated. When a referenced row is deleted, all associated dependent rows are deleted.
- No Action: Disallows the update or deletion of referenced data. This differs from RESTRICT in that it is checked at the end of the statement, or at the end of the transaction if the constraint is deferred. (Oracle uses No Action as its default action.)

Complex Integrity Checking

Complex integrity checking is a user-defined rule for a column (or set of columns) that allows or disallows inserts, updates, or deletes of a row based on the value it contains for the column (or set of columns).

Integrity Constraints Description

An integrity constraint is a declarative method of defining a rule for a column of a table. Oracle supports the following integrity constraints:

- NOT NULL constraints for the rules associated with nulls in a column.
- UNIQUE key constraints for the rule associated with unique column values.
- PRIMARY KEY constraints for the rule associated with primary identification values.

- FOREIGN KEY constraints for the rules associated with referential integrity. Oracle supports the use of FOREIGN KEY integrity constraints to define the referential integrity actions, including:
  - Update and delete No Action.
  - Delete CASCADE.
  - Delete SET NULL.
- CHECK constraints for complex integrity rules.

Advantages of Integrity Constraints

Here we describe some of the advantages that integrity constraints have over other alternatives, which include:

- Enforcing business rules in the code of a database application.
- Using stored procedures to completely control access to data.
- Enforcing business rules with triggered stored database procedures.

Declarative Ease

Define integrity constraints using SQL statements. When you define or alter a table, no additional programming is required. The SQL statements are easy to write and eliminate programming errors. Oracle controls their functionality. For these reasons, declarative integrity constraints are preferable to application code and database triggers. The declarative approach is also better than using stored procedures, because the stored procedure solution to data integrity controls data access, but integrity constraints do not eliminate the flexibility of ad hoc data access.

Centralized Rules

Integrity constraints are defined for tables (not an application) and are stored in the data dictionary. Any data entered by any application must adhere to the same integrity constraints associated with the table. By moving business rules from application code to centralized integrity constraints, the tables of a database are guaranteed to contain valid data, no matter which database application manipulates the information. Stored procedures cannot provide the same advantage of centralized rules stored with a table. Database triggers can provide this benefit, but the complexity of implementation is far greater than the declarative approach used for integrity constraints.

Maximum Application Development Productivity

If a business rule enforced by an integrity constraint changes, then the administrator need only change that integrity constraint and all applications automatically adhere to the modified constraint. In contrast, if the business rule was enforced by the code of each database application, developers would have to modify all application source code and recompile, debug, and test the modified applications.

Immediate User Feedback

Oracle stores specific information about each integrity constraint in the data dictionary. You can design database applications to use this information to provide immediate user feedback about integrity constraint violations, even before Oracle runs and checks the SQL statement. For example, an Oracle Forms application can use integrity constraint definitions stored in the data dictionary to check for violations as values are entered into the fields of a form, even before the application issues a statement.

Superior Performance

The semantics of integrity constraint declarations are clearly defined, and performance optimizations are implemented for each specific declarative rule. The Oracle optimizer can use declarations to learn more about data to improve overall query performance. (Also, taking integrity rules out of application code and database triggers guarantees that checks are only made when necessary.)

Flexibility for Data Loads and Identification of Integrity Violations

You can disable integrity constraints temporarily so that large amounts of data can be loaded without the overhead of constraint checking. When the data load is complete, you can easily enable the integrity constraints, and you can automatically report any new rows that violate integrity constraints to a separate exceptions table.

The Performance Cost of Integrity Constraints

The advantages of enforcing data integrity rules come with some loss in performance. In general, the cost of including an integrity constraint is, at most, the same as executing a SQL statement that evaluates the constraint.

Types of Integrity Constraints

You can use the following integrity constraints to impose restrictions on the input of column values:

- NOT NULL Integrity Constraints.
- UNIQUE Key Integrity Constraints.
- PRIMARY KEY Integrity Constraints.
- Referential Integrity Constraints.
- CHECK Integrity Constraints.

NOT NULL Integrity Constraints

By default, all columns in a table allow nulls. Null means the absence of a value. A NOT NULL constraint requires a column of a table contain no null values. For example, you can define a NOT NULL constraint to require that a value be input in the last_name column for every row of the employees table.

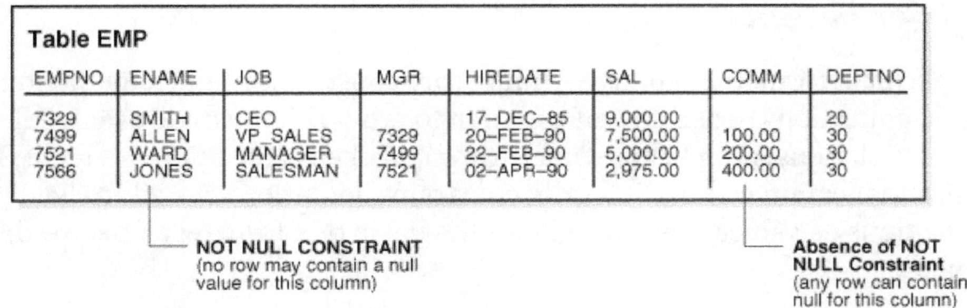

Figure: NOT NULL Integrity Constraints

UNIQUE Key Integrity Constraints

A UNIQUE key integrity constraint requires that every value in a column or set of columns (key) be unique—that is, no two rows of a table have duplicate values in a specified column or set of columns.

For example, in figure a UNIQUE key constraint is defined on the DNAME column of the dept table to disallow rows with duplicate department names.

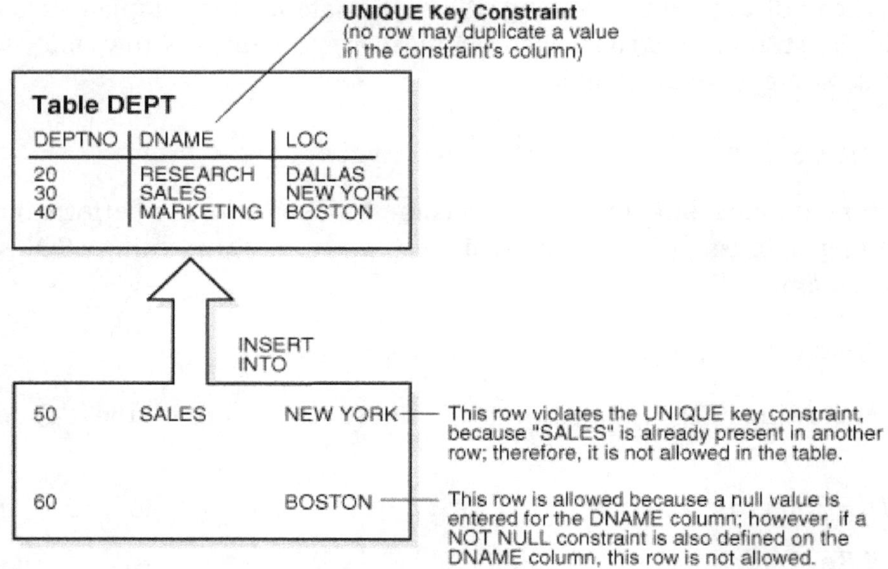

Figure: A UNIQUE Key Constraint

Unique Keys

The columns included in the definition of the UNIQUE key constraint are called the unique key. Unique key is often incorrectly used as a synonym for the terms UNIQUE key constraint or UNIQUE index. However, note that key refers only to the column or set of columns used in the definition of the integrity constraint.

If the UNIQUE key consists of more than one column, then that group of columns is said to be a composite unique key. For example, in figure the customer table has a UNIQUE key constraint defined on the composite unique key: the area and phone columns.

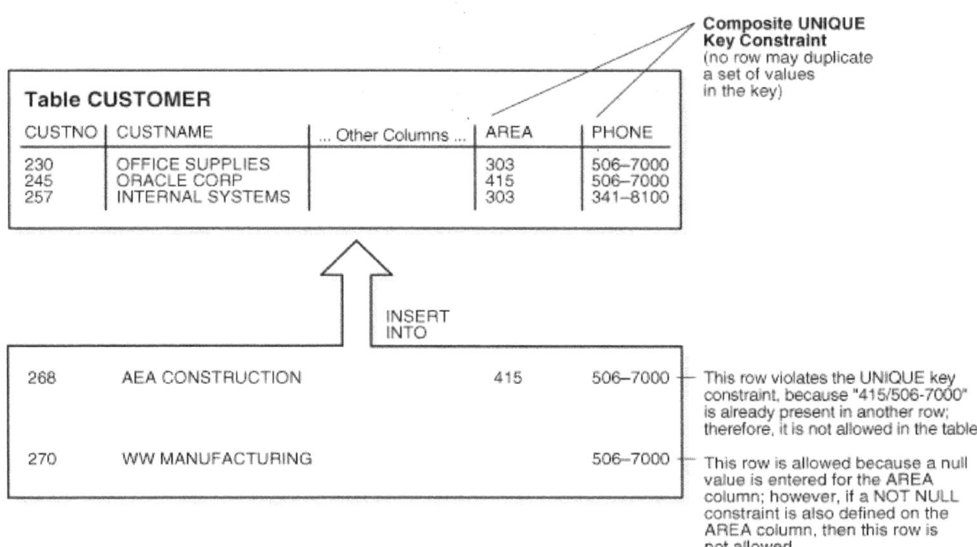

Figure: A Composite UNIQUE Key Constraint

This UNIQUE key constraint lets you enter an area code and telephone number any number of times, but the combination of a given area code and given telephone number cannot be duplicated in the table. This eliminates unintentional duplication of a telephone number.

UNIQUE Key Constraints and Indexes

Oracle enforces unique integrity constraints with indexes. For example, in figure Oracle enforces the UNIQUE key constraint by implicitly creating a unique index on the composite unique key. Therefore, composite UNIQUE key constraints have the same limitations imposed on composite indexes: up to 32 columns can constitute a composite unique key.

If a usable index exists when a unique key constraint is created, the constraint uses that index rather than implicitly creating a new one.

Combine UNIQUE Key and NOT NULL Integrity Constraints

In figures UNIQUE key constraints allow the input of nulls unless you also define NOT NULL constraints for the same columns. In fact, any number of rows can include nulls for columns without NOT NULL constraints because nulls are not considered equal to anything. A null in a column (or in all columns of a composite UNIQUE key) always satisfies a UNIQUE key constraint.

Columns with both unique keys and NOT NULL integrity constraints are common. This combination forces the user to enter values in the unique key and also eliminates the possibility that any new row's data will ever conflict with an existing row's data.

PRIMARY KEY Integrity Constraints

Each table in the database can have at most one PRIMARY KEY constraint. The values in the group of one or more columns subject to this constraint constitute the unique identifier of the row. In effect, each row is named by its primary key values.

The Oracle implementation of the PRIMARY KEY integrity constraint guarantees that both of the following are true:

- No two rows of a table have duplicate values in the specified column or set of columns.
- The primary key columns do not allow nulls. That is, a value must exist for the primary key columns in each row.

Primary Keys

The columns included in the definition of a table's PRIMARY KEY integrity constraint are called the primary key. Although it is not required, every table should have a primary key so that:

- Each row in the table can be uniquely identified.
- No duplicate rows exist in the table.

Figure illustrates a PRIMARY KEY constraint in the dept table and examples of rows that violate the constraint.

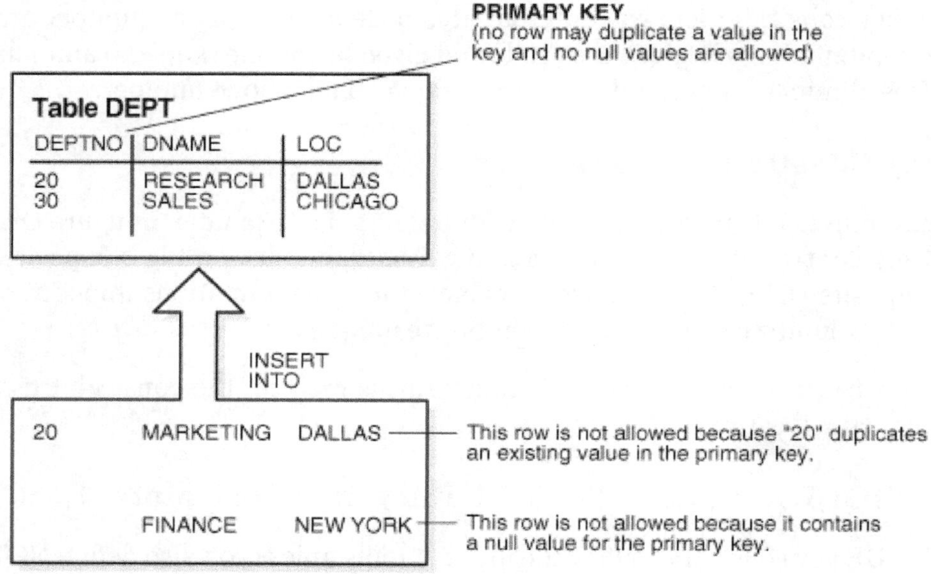

Figure: A Primary Key Constraint

Primary Key Constraints and Indexes

Oracle enforces all PRIMARY KEY constraints using indexes. In Figure the primary key constraint created for the deptno column is enforced by the implicit creation of:

- A unique index on that column.
- A NOT NULL constraint for that column.

Composite primary key constraints are limited to 32 columns, which is the same limitation imposed on composite indexes. The name of the index is the same as the name of the constraint. Also, you can specify the storage options for the index by including the ENABLE clause in the CREATE

TABLE or ALTER TABLE statement used to create the constraint. If a usable index exists when a primary key constraint is created, then the primary key constraint uses that index rather than implicitly creating a new one.

Referential Integrity Constraints

Different tables in a relational database can be related by common columns, and the rules that govern the relationship of the columns must be maintained. Referential integrity rules guarantee that these relationships are preserved.

The following terms are associated with referential integrity constraints.

Term	Definition
Foreign key	The column or set of columns included in the definition of the referential integrity constraint that reference a referenced key.
Referenced key	The unique key or primary key of the same or different table that is referenced by a foreign key.
Dependent or child table	The table that includes the foreign key. Therefore, it is the table that is dependent on the values present in the referenced unique or primary key.
Referenced or parent table	The table that is referenced by the child table's foreign key. It is this table's referenced key that determines whether specific inserts or updates are allowed in the child table.

A referential integrity constraint requires that for each row of a table, the value in the foreign key matches a value in a parent key.

Figure shows a foreign key defined on the deptno column of the emp table. It guarantees that every value in this column must match a value in the primary key of the dept table (also the deptno column). Therefore, no erroneous department numbers can exist in the deptno column of the emp table.

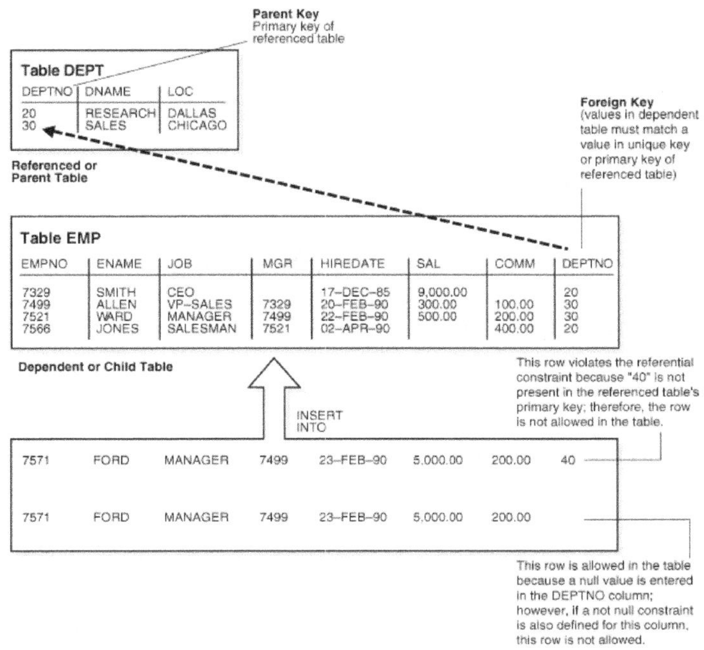

Figure: Referential Integrity Constraints

Foreign keys can be defined as multiple columns. However, a composite foreign key must reference a composite primary or unique key with the same number of columns and the same data types. Because composite primary and unique keys are limited to 32 columns, a composite foreign key is also limited to 32 columns.

Self-Referential Integrity Constraints

Another type of referential integrity constraint, shown in figure is called a self-referential integrity constraint. This type of foreign key references a parent key in the same table.

In figure the referential integrity constraint ensures that every value in the mgr column of the emp table corresponds to a value that currently exists in the empno column of the same table, but not necessarily in the same row, because every manager must also be an employee. This integrity constraint eliminates the possibility of erroneous employee numbers in the mgr column.

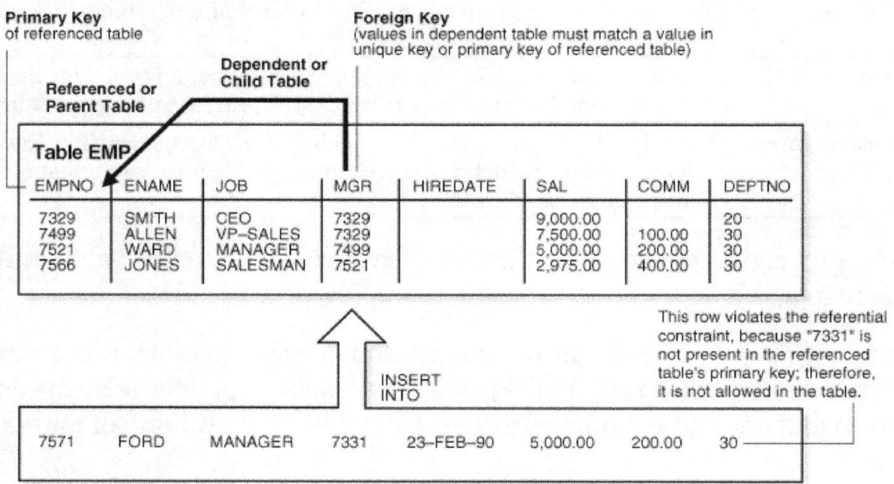

Figure: Single Table Referential Constraints

Nulls and Foreign Keys

The relational model permits the value of foreign keys either to match the referenced primary or unique key value, or be null. If any column of a composite foreign key is null, then the non-null portions of the key do not have to match any corresponding portion of a parent key.

Actions Defined by Referential Integrity Constraints

Referential integrity constraints can specify particular actions to be performed on the dependent rows in a child table if a referenced parent key value is modified. The referential actions supported by the FOREIGN KEY integrity constraints of Oracle are UPDATE and DELETE NO ACTION, and DELETE CASCADE.

Delete No Action

The No Action (default) option specifies that referenced key values cannot be updated or deleted if the resulting data would violate a referential integrity constraint. For example, if a primary key value is referenced by a value in the foreign key, then the referenced primary key value cannot be deleted because of the dependent data.

Delete Cascade

A delete cascades when rows containing referenced key values are deleted, causing all rows in child tables with dependent foreign key values to also be deleted. For example, if a row in a parent table is deleted, and this row's primary key value is referenced by one or more foreign key values in a child table, then the rows in the child table that reference the primary key value are also deleted from the child table.

Delete Set Null

A delete sets null when rows containing referenced key values are deleted, causing all rows in child tables with dependent foreign key values to set those values to null. For example, if employee_id references manager_id in the TMP table, then deleting a manager causes the rows for all employees working for that manager to have their manager_id value set to null.

DML Restrictions with Respect to Referential Actions

Table outlines the DML statements allowed by the different referential actions on the primary/unique key values in the parent table, and the foreign key values in the child table.

Table: DML Statements Allowed by Update and Delete No Action

DML Statement	Issued Against Parent Table	Issued Against Child Table
INSERT	Always OK if the parent key value is unique.	OK only if the foreign key value exists in the parent key or is partially or all null.
UPDATE No Action	Allowed if the statement does not leave any rows in the child table without a referenced parent key value.	Allowed if the new foreign key value still references a referenced key value.
DELETE No Action	Allowed if no rows in the child table reference the parent key value.	Always OK.
DELETE Cascade	Always OK.	Always OK.
DELETE Set Null	Always OK.	Always OK.

Concurrency Control, Indexes and Foreign Keys

You almost always index foreign keys. The only exception is when the matching unique or primary key is never updated or deleted.

Oracle maximizes the concurrency control of parent keys in relation to dependent foreign key values. You can control what concurrency mechanisms are used to maintain these relationships, and, depending on the situation, this can be highly beneficial.

No Index on the Foreign Key

Figure illustrates the locking mechanisms used by Oracle when no index is defined on the foreign key and when rows are being updated or deleted in the parent table. Inserts into the parent table do not require any locks on the child table.

Unindexed foreign keys cause DML on the primary key to get a share row exclusive table lock (also sometimes called a share-subexclusive table lock, SSX) on the foreign key table. This prevents DML on the table by other transactions. The SSX lock is released immediately after it is obtained. If multiple primary keys are updated or deleted, the lock is obtained and released once for each row.

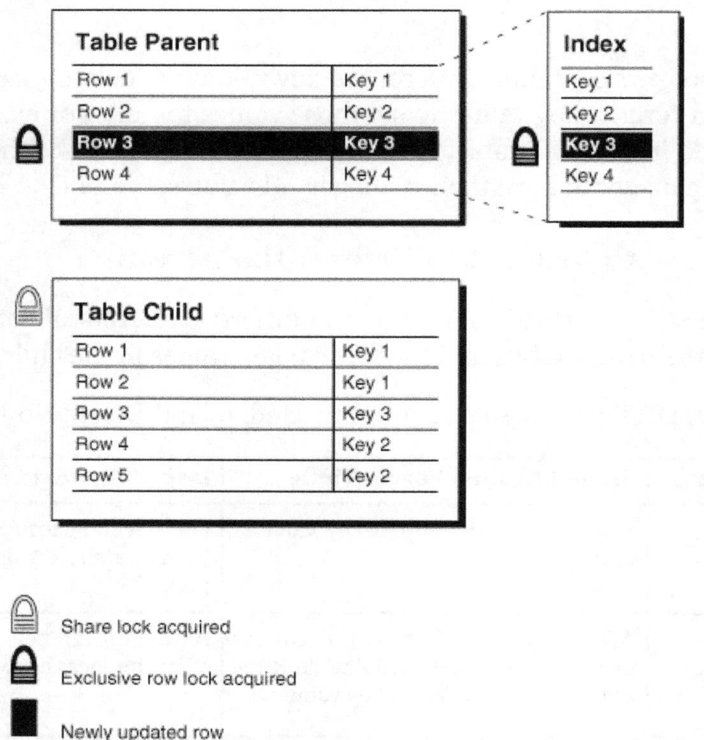

Figure: Locking Mechanisms When No Index Is Defined on the Foreign Key

Index on the Foreign Key

Figure illustrates the locking mechanisms used when an index is defined on the foreign key, and new rows are inserted, updated, or deleted in the child table.

Indexed foreign keys cause a row share table lock (also sometimes called a subshare table lock, SS). This prevents other transactions from exclusive locking the whole table, but it does not block DML on the parent or the child table.

This situation is preferable if there is any update or delete activity on the parent table while update activity is taking place on the child table. Inserts, updates, and deletes on the parent table do not require any locks on the child table, although updates and deletes will wait for row-level locks on the indexes of the child table to clear.

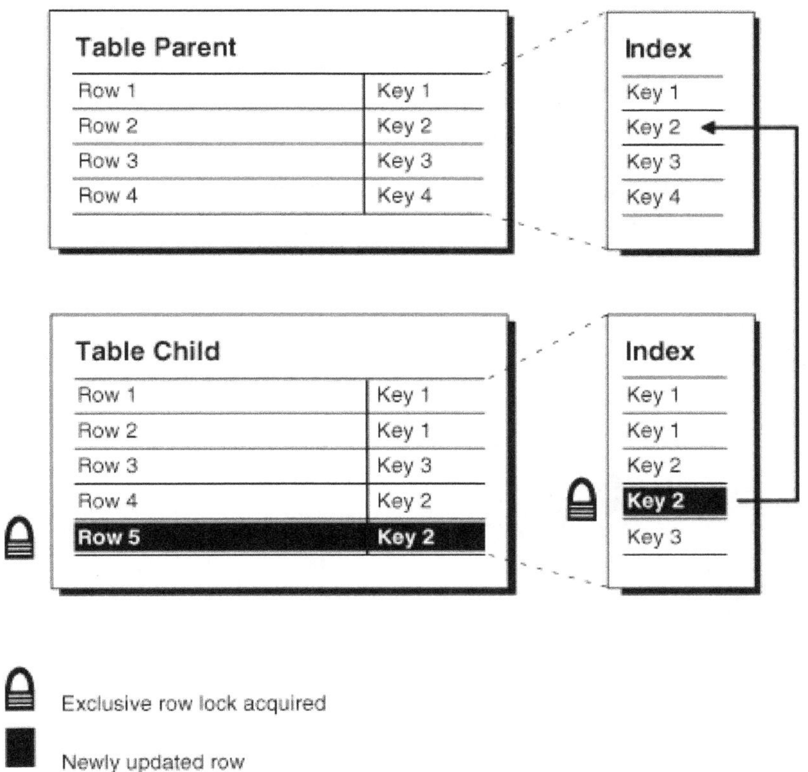

Figure: Locking Mechanisms When Index Is Defined on the Foreign Key

If the child table specifies ON DELETE CASCADE, then deletes from the parent table can result in deletes from the child table. In this case, waiting and locking rules are the same as if you deleted yourself from the child table after performing the delete from the parent table.

CHECK Integrity Constraints

A CHECK integrity constraint on a column or set of columns requires that a specified condition be true or unknown for every row of the table. If a DML statement results in the condition of the CHECK constraint evaluating to false, then the statement is rolled back.

The Check Condition

CHECK constraints let you enforce very specific integrity rules by specifying a check condition. The condition of a CHECK constraint has some limitations:

- It must be a Boolean expression evaluated using the values in the row being inserted or updated, and
- It cannot contain subqueries; sequences; the SQL functions SYSDATE, UID, USER, or USERENV; or the pseudocolumns LEVEL or ROWNUM.

In evaluating CHECK constraints that contain string literals or SQL functions with globalization support parameters as arguments (such as TO_CHAR, TO_DATE, and TO_NUMBER), Oracle uses the database globalization support settings by default. You can override the defaults by specifying globalization support parameters explicitly in such functions within the CHECK constraint definition.

Multiple CHECK Constraints

A single column can have multiple CHECK constraints that reference the column in its definition. There is no limit to the number of CHECK constraints that you can define on a column.

If you create multiple CHECK constraints for a column, design them carefully so their purposes do not conflict. Do not assume any particular order of evaluation of the conditions. Oracle does not verify that CHECK conditions are not mutually exclusive.

Database Normalization

Database normalization is process used to organize a database into tables and columns. The idea is that a table should be about a *specific* topic and that only those columns which support that topic are included. For example, a spreadsheet containing information about sales people and customers serves several purposes:

- Identify sales people in your organization.
- List all customers your company calls upon to sell product.
- Identify which sales people call on specific customers.

By limiting a table to one purpose you reduce the number of duplicate data that is contained within your database, which helps eliminate some issues stemming from database modifications. To assist in achieving these objectives, some rules for database table organization have been developed. The stages of organization are called normal forms; there are three normal forms most databases adhere to using. As tables satisfy each successive normalization form, they become less prone to database modification anomalies and more focused toward a sole purpose or topic.

Reasons for Normalization

There are three main reasons to normalize a database. The first is to minimize duplicate data, the second is to minimize or avoid data modification issues, and the third is to simplify queries. As we go through the various states of normalization we'll discuss how each form addresses these issues, but to start, let's look at some data which hasn't been normalized and discuss some potential pitfalls. Consider the following table:

SalesStaff						
EmployeeID	SalesPerson	SalesOffice	OfficeNumber	Customer1	Customer2	Customer3
1003	Mary Smith	Chicago	312-555-1212	Ford	GM	
1004	John Hunt	New York	212-555-1212	Dell	HP	Apple
1005	Martin Hap	Chicago	312-555-1212	Boeing		

The first thing to notice is this table serves many purposes including:

1. Identifying the organization's salespeople.
2. Listing the sales offices and phone numbers.
3. Associating a salesperson with a sales office.
4. Showing each salesperson's customers.

As a DBA this raises a red flag. Having the table serve many purposes introduces many of the challenges; namely, data duplication, data update issues, and increased effort to query data.

Data Duplication and Modification Anomalies

Notice that for each SalesPerson we have listed both the SalesOffice and OfficeNumber. This information is duplicated for each SalesPerson. Duplicated information presents two problems:

1. It increases storage and decrease performance.
2. It becomes more difficult to maintain data changes.

For example

- Consider if we move the Chicago office to Evanston, IL. To properly reflect this in our table, we need to update the entries for all the SalesPersons currently in Chicago. Our table is a small example, but you can see if it were larger, that potentially this could involve hundreds of updates.
- Also consider what would happen if John Hunt quits. If we remove his entry, then we lose the information for New York.

These situations are modification anomalies. There are three modification anomalies that can occur:

Insert Anomaly

There are facts we cannot record until we know information for the entire row. In our example we cannot record a new sales office until we also know the sales person. Why? Because in order to create the record, we need provide a primary key. In our case this is the EmployeeID.

EmployeeID	SalesPerson	SalesOffice	OfficeNumber	Customer1	Customer2	Customer3
1003	Mary Smith	Chicago	312-555-1212	Ford	GM	
1004	John Hunt	New York	212-555-1212	Dell	HP	Apple
1005	Martin Hap	Chicago	312-555-1212	Boeing		
???	???	Atlanta	312-555-1212			

Update Anomaly

The same information is recorded in multiple rows. For instance if the office number changes, then there are multiple updates that need to be made. If these updates are not successfully completed across all rows, then an inconsistency occurs.

EmployeeID	SalesPerson	SalesOffice	OfficeNumber	Customer1	Customer2	Customer3
1003	Mary Smith	Chicago	312-555-1212	Ford	GM	
1004	John Hunt	New York	212-555-1212	Dell	HP	Apple
1005	Martin Hap	Chicago	312-555-1212	Boeing		

Deletion Anomaly

Deletion of a row can cause more than one set of facts to be removed. For instance, if John Hunt retires, then deleting that row cause use to lose information about the New York office.

EmployeeID	SalesPerson	SalesOffice	OfficeNumber	Customer1	Customer2	Customer3
1003	Mary Smith	Chicago	312-555-1212	Ford	GM	
1004	John Hunt	New York	212-555-1212	Dell	HP	Apple
1005	Martin Hap	Chicago	312-555-1212	Boeing		

Search and Sort Issues

The last reason we'll consider is making it easier to search and sort your data. In the SalesStaff table if you want to search for a specific customer such as Ford, you would have to write a query like

```
SELECT SalesOffice
FROM SalesStaff
WHERE Customer1 = 'Ford' OR
   Customer2 = 'Ford' OR
   Customer3 = 'Ford'
```

Clearly if the customer were somehow in one column our query would be simpler. Also, consider if you want to run a query and sort by customer. The way the table is currently defined, this isn't possible, unless you use three separate queries with a UNION. These anomalies can be eliminated or reduced by properly separating the data into different tables, to house the data in tables which serve a single purpose. The process to do this is called normalization, and the various stages you can achieve are called the normal forms.

Normalization

Here are the most commonly used normal forms:

- First normal form(1NF).
- Second normal form(2NF).
- Third normal form(3NF).
- Boyce & Codd normal form (BCNF).

First Normal Form (1NF)

As per the rule of first normal form, an attribute (column) of a table cannot hold multiple values. It should hold only atomic values.

Example: Suppose a company wants to store the names and contact details of its employees. It creates a table that looks like this:

emp_id	emp_name	emp_address	emp_mobile
101	Herschel	New Delhi	8912312390
102	Jon	Kanpur	8812121212 9900012222
103	Ron	Chennai	7778881212
104	Lester	Bangalore	9990000123 8123450987

Two employees (Jon & Lester) are having two mobile numbers so the company stored them in the same field as you can see in the table above.

This table is not in 1NF as the rule says "each attribute of a table must have atomic (single) values", the emp_mobile values for employees Jon & Lester violates that rule.

To make the table complies with 1NF we should have the data like this:

emp_id	emp_name	emp_address	emp_mobile
101	Herschel	New Delhi	8912312390
102	Jon	Kanpur	8812121212
102	Jon	Kanpur	9900012222
103	Ron	Chennai	7778881212
104	Lester	Bangalore	9990000123
104	Lester	Bangalore	8123450987

Second Normal Form (2NF)

A table is said to be in 2NF if both the following conditions hold:

- Table is in 1NF (First normal form).
- No non-prime attribute is dependent on the proper subset of any candidate key of table.

An attribute that is not part of any candidate key is known as non-prime attribute.

Example: Suppose a school wants to store the data of teachers and the subjects they teach. They create a table that looks like this: Since a teacher can teach more than one subjects, the table can have multiple rows for a same teacher.

teacher_id	subject	teacher_age
111	Maths	38
111	Physics	38
222	Biology	38
333	Physics	40
333	Chemistry	40

Candidate Keys: {teacher_id, subject}
Non-prime attribute: teacher_age

The table is in 1 NF because each attribute has atomic values. However, it is not in 2NF because non-prime attribute teacher_age is dependent on teacher_id alone which is a proper subset of candidate key. This violates the rule for 2NF as the rule says "**no** non-prime attribute is dependent on the proper subset of any candidate key of the table".

To make the table complies with 2NF we can break it in two tables like this:

teacher_details table:

teacher_id	teacher_age
111	38
222	38
333	40

teacher_subject table:

teacher_id	subject
111	Maths
111	Physics
222	Biology
333	Physics
333	Chemistry

Now the tables comply with Second normal form (2NF).

Third Normal form (3NF)

A table design is said to be in 3NF if both the following conditions hold:

- Table must be in 2NF.
- Transitive functional dependency of non-prime attribute on any super key should be removed.

An attribute that is not part of any candidate key is known as non-prime attribute.

In other words 3NF can be explained like this: A table is in 3NF if it is in 2NF and for each functional dependency X-> Y at least one of the following conditions hold:

- X is a super key of table.
- Y is a prime attribute of table.

An attribute that is a part of one of the candidate keys is known as prime attribute.

Example: Suppose a company wants to store the complete address of each employee, they create a table named employee_details that looks like this:

emp_id	emp_name	emp_zip	emp_state	emp_city	emp_district
1001	John	282005	UP	Agra	Dayal Bagh
1002	Ajeet	222008	TN	Chennai	M-City
1006	Lora	282007	TN	Chennai	Urrapakkam
1101	Lilly	292008	UK	Pauri	Bhagwan
1201	Steve	222999	MP	Gwalior	Ratan

Super keys: {emp_id}, {emp_id, emp_name}, {emp_id, emp_name, emp_zip}... so on Candidate Keys: {emp_id}

Non-prime attributes: all attributes except emp_id are non-prime as they are not part of any candidate keys.

Here, emp_state, emp_city & emp_district dependent on emp_zip. And, emp_zip is dependent on emp_id that makes non-prime attributes (emp_state, emp_city & emp_district) transitively dependent on super key (emp_id). This violates the rule of 3NF.

To make this table complies with 3NF we have to break the table into two tables to remove the transitive dependency:

employee table:

emp_id	emp_name	emp_zip
1001	John	282005
1002	Ajeet	222008
1006	Lora	282007
1101	Lilly	292008
1201	Steve	222999

employee_zip table:

emp_zip	emp_state	emp_city	emp_district
282005	UP	Agra	Dayal Bagh
222008	TN	Chennai	M-City
282007	TN	Chennai	Urrapakkam
292008	UK	Pauri	Bhagwan
222999	MP	Gwalior	Ratan

Boyce Codd Normal Form (BCNF)

It is an advance version of 3NF that's why it is also referred as 3.5NF. BCNF is stricter than 3NF. A table complies with BCNF if it is in 3NF and for every functional dependency X->Y, X should be the super key of the table.

Example: Suppose there is a company wherein employees work in more than one department. They store the data like this:

emp_id	emp_nationality	emp_dept	dept_type	dept_no_of_emp
1001	Austrian	Production and planning	D001	200
1001	Austrian	stores	D001	250
1002	American	design and technical support	D134	100
1002	American	Purchasing department	D134	600

Functional dependencies in the table above:
emp_id -> emp_nationality
emp_dept -> {dept_type, dept_no_of_emp}

Candidate key: {emp_id, emp_dept}

The table is not in BCNF as neither emp_id nor emp_dept alone are keys.

To make the table comply with BCNF we can break the table in three tables like this: emp_nationality table:

emp_id	emp_nationality
1001	Austrian
1002	American

emp_dept table:

emp_dept	dept_type	dept_no_of_emp
Production and planning	D001	200
stores	D001	250
design and technical support	D134	100
Purchasing department	D134	600

emp_dept_mapping table:

emp_id	emp_dept
1001	Production and planning
1001	stores

1002	design and technical support
1002	Purchasing department

Functional dependencies:
emp_id -> emp_nationality
emp_dept -> {dept_type, dept_no_of_emp}

Candidate keys:
For first table: emp_id
For second table: emp_dept
For third table: {emp_id, emp_dept}

This is now in BCNF as in both the functional dependencies left side part is a key.

Extract, Transform and Load

ETL is an abbreviation of Extract, Transform and Load. In this process, an ETL tool extracts the data from different RDBMS source systems then transforms the data like applying calculations, concatenations, etc. and then load the data into the Data Warehouse system.

It's tempting to think a creating a Data warehouse is simply extracting data from multiple sources and loading into database of a Data warehouse. This is far from the truth and requires a complex ETL process. The ETL process requires active inputs from various stakeholders including developers, analysts, testers, top executives and is technically challenging.

In order to maintain its value as a tool for decision-makers, Data warehouse system needs to change with business changes. ETL is a recurring activity (daily, weekly, monthly) of a Data warehouse system and needs to be agile, automated, and well documented.

Importance of ETL

- It helps companies to analyze their business data for taking critical business decisions.
- Transactional databases cannot answer complex business questions that can be answered by ETL.
- A Data Warehouse provides a common data repository
- ETL provides a method of moving the data from various sources into a data warehouse.
- As data sources change, the Data Warehouse will automatically update.
- Well-designed and documented ETL system is almost essential to the success of a Data Warehouse project.
- Allow verification of data transformation, aggregation and calculations rules.
- ETL process allows sample data comparison between the source and the target system.

- ETL process can perform complex transformations and requires the extra area to store the data.
- ETL helps to Migrate data into a Data Warehouse. Convert to the various formats and types to adhere to one consistent system.
- ETL is a predefined process for accessing and manipulating source data into the target database.
- ETL offers deep historical context for the business.
- It helps to improve productivity because it codifies and reuses without a need for technical skills.

ETL Process in Data Warehouses

ETL is a 3-step process:

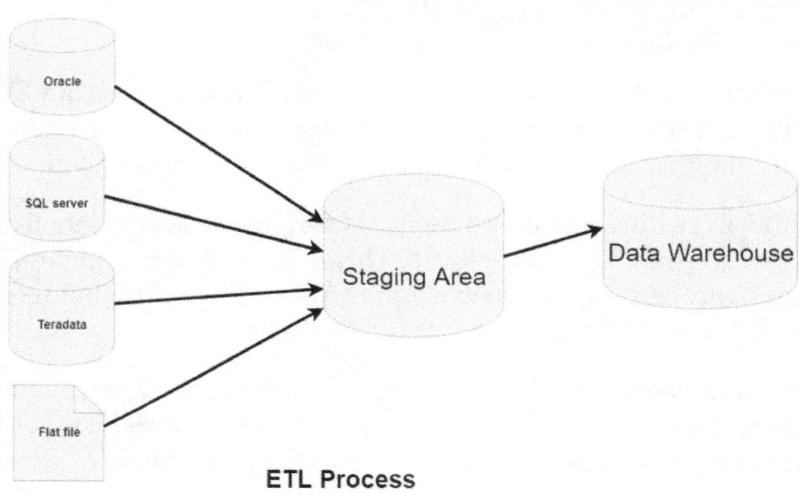

ETL Process

Step 1: Extraction

In this step, data is extracted from the source system into the staging area. Transformations if any are done in staging area so that performance of source system in not degraded. Also, if corrupted data is copied directly from the source into Data warehouse database, rollback will be a challenge. Staging area gives an opportunity to validate extracted data before it moves into the Data warehouse.

Data warehouse needs to integrate systems that have different DBMS, Hardware, Operating Systems and Communication Protocols. Sources could include legacy applications like Mainframes, customized applications, Point of contact devices like ATM, Call switches, text files, spreadsheets, ERP, data from vendors, partners amongst others.

Hence one need a logical data map before data is extracted and loaded physically. This data map describes the relationship between sources and target data.

Three data extraction methods:

- Full Extraction.
- Partial Extraction- without update notification.
- Partial Extraction- with update notification.

Irrespective of the method used, extraction should not affect performance and response time of the source systems. These source systems are live production databases. Any slow down or locking could affect company's bottom line.

Some validations are done during extraction:

- Reconcile records with the source data.
- Make sure that no spam/unwanted data loaded.
- Data type check.
- Remove all types of duplicate/fragmented data.
- Check whether all the keys are in place or not.

Step 2: Transformation

Data extracted from source server is raw and not usable in its original form. Therefore it needs to be cleansed, mapped and transformed. In fact, this is the key step where ETL process adds value and changes data such that insightful BI reports can be generated.

In this step, you apply a set of functions on extracted data. Data that does not require any transformation is called as direct move or pass through data.

In transformation step, you can perform customized operations on data. For instance, if the user wants sum-of-sales revenue which is not in the database. Or if the first name and the last name in a table is in different columns. It is possible to concatenate them before loading.

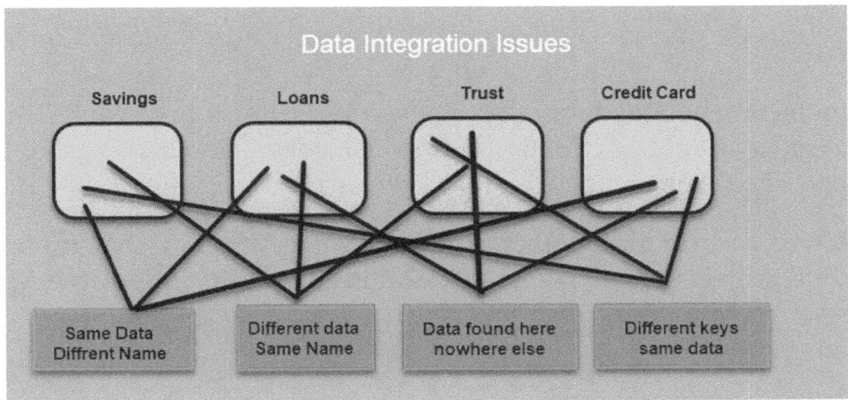

Following are data integrity problems:

1. Different spelling of the same person like Jon, John, etc.

2. There are multiple ways to denote company name like Google, Google Inc.
3. Use of different names like Cleaveland, Cleveland.
4. There may be a case that different account numbers are generated by various applications for the same customer.
5. In some data required files remains blank.
6. Invalid product collected at POS as manual entry can lead to mistakes.

Validations are done during this stage

- Filtering: Select only certain columns to load.
- Using rules and lookup tables for Data standardization.
- Character Set Conversion and encoding handling.
- Conversion of Units of Measurements like Date Time Conversion, currency conversions, numerical conversions, etc.
- Data threshold validation check. For example, age cannot be more than two digits.
- Data flow validation from the staging area to the intermediate tables.
- Required fields should not be left blank.
- Cleaning (for example, mapping NULL to 0 or Gender Male to "M" and Female to "F" etc.)
- Split a column into multiples and merging multiple columns into a single column.
- Transposing rows and columns,
- Use lookups to merge data
- Using any complex data validation (e.g., if the first two columns in a row are empty then it automatically reject the row from processing)

Step 3: Loading

Loading data into the target data warehouse database is the last step of the ETL process. In a typical Data warehouse, huge volume of data needs to be loaded in a relatively short period (nights). Hence, load process should be optimized for performance.

In case of load failure, recover mechanisms should be configured to restart from the point of failure without data integrity loss. Data Warehouse admins need to monitor, resume, cancel loads as per prevailing server performance.

Types of Loading

- Initial Load: Populating all the Data Warehouse tables.
- Incremental Load: Applying ongoing changes as when needed periodically.

- Full Refresh: Erasing the contents of one or more tables and reloading with fresh data.

Load Verification

- Ensure that the key field data is neither missing nor null.
- Test modeling views based on the target tables.
- Check that combined values and calculated measures.
- Data checks in dimension table as well as history table.
- Check the BI reports on the loaded fact and dimension table.

ETL Tools

There are many Data Warehousing tools are available in the market. Here, are some most prominent one:

1. MarkLogic

MarkLogic is a data warehousing solution which makes data integration easier and faster using an array of enterprise features. It can query different types of data like documents, relationships, and metadata.

2. Oracle

Oracle is the industry-leading database. It offers a wide range of choice of Data Warehouse solutions for both on-premises and in the cloud. It helps to optimize customer experiences by increasing operational efficiency.

3. Amazon RedShift

Amazon Redshift is Data warehouse tool. It is a simple and cost-effective tool to analyze all types of data using standard SQL and existing BI tools. It also allows running complex queries against petabytes of structured data.

Best Practices ETL Process

- Never try to cleanse all the data

Every organization would like to have all the data clean, but most of them are not ready to pay to wait or not ready to wait. To clean it all would simply take too long, so it is better not to try to cleanse all the data.

- Never cleanse Anything

Always plan to clean something because the biggest reason for building the Data Warehouse is to offer cleaner and more reliable data.

- Determine the cost of cleansing the data

Before cleansing all the dirty data, it is important for you to determine the cleansing cost for every dirty data element.

- To speed up query processing, have auxiliary views and indexes

To reduce storage costs, store summarized data into disk tapes. Also, the trade-off between the volume of data to be stored and its detailed usage is required. Trade-off at the level of granularity of data to decrease the storage costs.

Operational Database

An operational database is a database that is used to manage and store data in real time. An operational database is the source for a data warehouse. Elements in an operational database can be added and removed on the fly. These databases can be either SQL or NoSQL-based, where the latter is geared toward real-time operations.

An operational database is a database that stores data inside of an enterprise. They can contain things like payroll records, customer information and employee data. They are critical to data warehousing and business analytics operations.

The key characteristic of operational databases is their orientation toward real-time operations, compared with conventional databases that rely on batch processing. With operational databases, records can be added, removed and modified in real time. Operational database management systems can be based on SQL but a growing number are using NoSQL and non-structured data.

Examples of an Operational Database

Sensors

A city continuously collects sensor data from a network of air quality stations distributed throughout the city. The operational database creates the data. Separate analytical databases use the data to generate air quality warnings or to report sustainability metrics.

Machine Data

An energy company continuously records data from solar panel systems distributed throughout its grid. This is integrated with systems in areas such as maintenance and grid operations.

Science

A national weather service continuously collects data from automated weather stations that is used generate timely weather forecasts and as a historical record for researchers.

Internet of Things

A medical device manufacturer provides a service to remotely monitor medical devices in the field and send alerts when a device isn't performing to specifications.

Communications

A message app receives and delivers millions of messages per hour.

Media

A blogging service writes millions of blog posts and comments to its database each day.

Applications

A sales platform allows salespeople in the field to update sales data such as contacts, leads, opportunities and quotes using a mobile app.

User Interfaces

An ecommerce company records user clicks on their website. This information is then used to generate product recommendations and marketing offers by the operational database in real time. The clicks are also used by a variety of systems as a source of customer analytics data.

Transactions

A bank records transactions such as transfers, interest payments and withdrawals using an operational database. This data is used by a variety of batch processes that perform functions such as updating accounts.

Operational Database Management Systems

As organizations embrace digital transformation with mobile and cloud-capable applications, they encounter different types of data requirements that aren't optimally supported by the leading relational products. This has enabled NoSQL and in-memory database management systems (DBMSes) to gain market share. Additionally, it has caused the market leaders to enhance their offerings to support additional data models and engines.

Given the dizzying number of competing operational DBMS products, it can be confusing to match application requirements to an ideal operational DBMS, especially with so many choices. Here's an overview of the leading operational database management systems in the market to help enterprises get started.

Aerospike

Aerospike is an open source, in-memory NoSQL DBMS. It's a key-value data store designed to deliver high performance and rapid data access for real-time big data applications.

This NoSQL DBMS provides a simplified environment and setup for developers building and operating modern applications at scale, with minimal upfront administrative work. It can make sense to use Aerospike for caching data, storing session information or when personalizing user experiences on web portals and mobile applications.

Aerospike can be licensed as open source or commercially. The commercial edition adds more features, which are unavailable in the open source edition, as well as technical support. Aerospike runs on Linux.

Support is available for many different Linux distributions, including prebuilt binaries for Red Hat, Ubuntu, CentOS and Debian.

Amazon DynamoDB

The DynamoDB NoSQL cloud database as a service supports both document and key-value store models, providing flexibility for development of web, gaming, internet of things and many other types of applications. Amazon DynamoDB is designed to provide high performance at a large scale with low latency.

Amazon DynamoDB eliminates the need to handle tasks such as hardware and software provisioning, setup and configuration, software patches, upgrades, operating a distributed database cluster or partitioning data over multiple instances as it scales.

DynamoDB is a service; there's no notion of a database server or schema. Its core components are tables, items and attributes. The highest-level object in DynamoDB is a table, but not a traditional relational table; rather, it's a table that's composed of as many items as you want.

All the data is stored on solid-state drives and is replicated three ways across different availability zones, thereby delivering redundancy and fault tolerance.

Apache Cassandra/DataStax

Apache Cassandra is an open source, distributed key-value NoSQL DBMS. It was originally developed at Facebook, and was later released as an open source project. Additionally, a free packaged distribution of Apache Cassandra -- DataStax Community Edition -- and a commercial edition are available from DataStax.

Apache Cassandra was created for online applications that require fast performance and no downtime. It works best when most, if not all, access is to look up data based on a primary key value. It was built to handle very large amounts of data spread out across commodity servers and to deliver high availability without a single point of failure.

Available for Linux, Windows and Mac OS X operating systems, Apache Cassandra is open source and free to download.

EnterpriseDB/PostgreSQL

PostgreSQL, an open source RDBMS, serves as the foundation for the EnterpriseDB (EDB) Postgres Platform. PostgreSQL is made available under the terms of the PostgreSQL License. The EDB

Postgres Platform from EnterpriseDB is offered as a subscription service for production and non-production systems.

The platform is open source-based and brings together multiple components for managing structured and unstructured data in a federated model. It comprises a DBMS, three fully integrated tool suites, a range of deployment options, and support and services.

Oracle users looking for a less costly option can take advantage of the EDM Postgres platform's Database Compatibility Technology for Oracle, which allows users to switch existing applications from Oracle to run on EDB Postgres, with minimal to no changes required.

EDB Postgres software can be deployed on bare metal or virtually, including in container environments or in public, private and/or hybrid cloud environments.

IBM DB2

IBM DB2 is a relational DBMS with strong availability and performance capabilities. Along with its relational/SQL core, DB2 also boasts integrated support for a number of NoSQL capabilities, including XML, graph store and Java Script Object Notation, or JSON.

Used by organizations of all sizes, DB2 provides a data platform for both transactional and analytical operations, as well as continuous availability of data to keep transactional workflows and analytics operating efficiently.

DB2 is available for Linux, Unix and Windows (LUW) workstations, on IBM iSeries midrange computers and on IBM mainframes running z/OS. It's the only leading operational DBMS with native mainframe support.

DB2 boasts strong hybrid transaction/analytical processing capabilities with BLU acceleration column store support on LUW platforms, as well as tight integration with the IBM DB2 Analytics Accelerator on the mainframe. As such, it is well-suited for organizations that need to use a single DBMS to run mixed transactional and analytical workloads.

Pricing for DB2 LUW is based on the processor value unit (PVU), which is the unit of measure that IBM uses to license its software. IBM applies a PVU count to each core of a processor, and the pricing is based on the total number of PVUs made available to DB2. DB2 for z/OS is licensed using the IBM Monthly License Charge model.

MarkLogic Server

The MarkLogic Server NoSQL DBMS is designed to make heterogeneous data integration easier and faster using a combination of enterprise features.

MarkLogic Server is a document-based DBMS that can perform a complex search and query across multiple types of data, including documents, relationships and metadata. It can handle data such as JSON, XML and Resource Description Framework natively, and offers enterprise features such as ACID (atomicity, consistency, isolation and durability) transactions, automated failover and security.

MarkLogic Server's Search & Query capability lets users search through billions of text documents with subsecond response times. Search indexes scan metadata and relationship data inside the document and set up automatic alerting.

There are multiple editions of MarkLogic Server for varying levels of enterprise functionality and support, as well as a free edition for developers.

Microsoft SQL Server

Microsoft SQL Server 2016 is a relational DBMS for Windows platforms that can be used for building, deploying and managing applications located on premises or in the cloud.

Microsoft SQL Server 2016 provides strong analytics, in-memory processing and security capabilities.

Organizations looking to extend their relational databases to the cloud can benefit from the Stretch Database feature of SQL Server, which can be used to store some data on premises and to send infrequently used data to Microsoft's Azure Cloud. Applications using the database can access all of the data regardless of where it's stored.

Although Microsoft SQL Server 2016 is well-known for its strong support and integration with the Microsoft Windows operating system, Microsoft began offering SQL Server on Linux in 2016, enabling the DBMS to compete on non-Windows platforms.

SQL Server 2016 can be licensed based on the number of users and devices that access SQL Server, or per core, which offers a more precise and consistent measure of computing power, regardless of whether SQL Server is deployed on physical servers, on premises, virtually or in the cloud.

MongoDB

MongoDB is an open source document store, NoSQL DBMS designed for running modern applications that rely on structured and unstructured data with a flexible schema and rapidly changing data requirements. MongoDB is designed to make it easier for organizations to develop and run applications that address performance, availability and scalability, and to support a variety of data types.

MongoDB's document data model lets developers easily store and combine data of any structure, without sacrificing data access or indexing functionality. This enables database administrators to dynamically modify the schema with no downtime.

MongoDB is licensed both as open source, under the GNU Affero General Public License, and as a commercial offering. The commercial edition, MongoDB Enterprise Server, is available as part of the MongoDB Enterprise Advanced subscription, which adds advanced security, administrative features, support and on-demand training not available in the open source edition.

MySQL

MySQL is a popular open source RDBMS known for its ability to support web-based and online publishing applications, in addition to a wide range of applications.

Although MySQL doesn't have the same range and span of features and functionality as the big three RDBMS offerings (Oracle Database, Microsoft SQL Server and IBM DB2), it generally costs less and is easier to deploy.

MySQL runs on most Linux, Unix and Windows platforms. Although it can be used in a wide range of applications, MySQL is most often associated with web-based applications and online publishing. MySQL is the M in the open source enterprise LAMP stack.

MySQL is owned by Oracle. Developers can use MySQL under the GNU General Public License, but commercial organizations must buy a commercial license from Oracle to deploy MySQL.

Neo4j

Neo4j is a native graph database system that provides valuable insight based on data relationships built into the fabric of the product, including the data model, query language and storage engine. Much like how RDBMSes are founded on a mathematical basis (set theory), graph database systems are built on the mathematical foundation of graph theory.

The Neo4j graph DBMS delivers high performance and availability, with its native graph capabilities for data storage and access.

It's well-suited for applications and data where the relationship between the data elements is as important as the data itself. Example use cases include social media connections, delivery routing and dispatching, public transportation links, curriculum prerequisites, network topologies and recommendation engines, such as those used by online retail sites.

Neo4j data and its connections are physically stored as relationships. The database engine relates data by following pointers from data point to related data point, providing faster processing than relational joins or writing joins in other NoSQL databases.

Data relationships are stored and processed as they occur, providing quick responsiveness and flexibility when making database changes and creating Agile development.

Oracle Database 12c

The overall market leader, Oracle Database 12c, is an RDBMS designed for both on-premises and cloud uses. It can be deployed on a choice of clustered or single servers. A comprehensive feature set enables Oracle Database 12c to be used to support multiple types of applications, including transaction processing, business intelligence and content management applications.

Oracle's multi-tenant architecture simplifies the process of consolidating databases in the cloud, enabling customers to manage many databases as one, without changing their applications. A single multi-tenant container can host and manage hundreds of pluggable databases to dramatically reduce costs and to simplify administration.

Oracle Database 12c provides a Database In-Memory Column Store, which can be used to boost the performance of database queries. Existing applications can automatically and transparently take advantage of in-memory processing without needing any changes or losing any existing Oracle Database capabilities.

Oracle Database 12c is available primarily in three editions. Perpetual and term licenses are based on the number of named users and devices that will have access to the software, or the number of processors on which the database will run.

Redis

Redis is a lightweight, flexible, key-value store, open source DBMS. It provides a highly scalable data store that can be shared by multiple processes, applications or servers.

A key-value database is ideal when almost all of the access to data is requested using a key, such as when looking up product details by a product number. The details can be any type of information -- and can even vary from product to product.

Redis is frequently used for applications with high-availability and low-latency requirements, such as gaming, retail and mobile. The schema flexibility of key-value databases such as Redis helps users to excel at session management, serving ad content and managing user or product profiles.

Redis is available as open source via a BSD license or as an enterprise edition available both as Redis Labs Enterprise Cluster and Redis Cloud.

Riak

Riak from Basho Technologies is a fault-tolerant, highly available, scalable, distributed multimodel, NoSQL DBMS. It enables application developers to store, manage and secure unstructured data. The DBMS is designed to enable storage of and access to various types of unstructured data that requires continuous availability.

Riak is a good choice for supporting highly scalable applications that access large amounts of unstructured data, and that require around-the-clock availability. It's designed to support fast development and ease of operations. The key-value store enables storage and access of various types of unstructured data at a massive scale with high availability.

However, Riak is more accurately referred to as a multimodel platform, supporting key-value, object store and search, all from the same platform.

The Riak DBMS can be deployed to multiple servers, and it provides continuous functionality in the presence of hardware and network failures. Riak is available in three versions: open source, supported enterprise and cloud storage.

SAP HANA

SAP HANA is a column-oriented, in-memory RDBMS. HANA is architected to enable applications to support both transactional and analytical processing on a single system with one copy of the data. It's designed to handle high transaction rates and complex queries.

Running on SUSE Linux and Red Hat Enterprise Linux, SAP HANA enables real-time analytics on transactional systems at a large scale and on a variety of data, including structured, unstructured, spatial, time series and streaming data.

It provides features that support development for SAP and custom-built applications. SAP HANA combines database, advanced analytics, enterprise information management and application server capabilities, all running in-memory, on one data copy and on a single platform.

SAP HANA supports multi-tenancy and data tiering, which enables petabyte-scale deployments for warm data (data that's less frequently accessed) to be stored on the disk, and offers a choice of deployment models and partners.

The DBMS can be deployed on-premises, in the cloud or as a hybrid of both.

Which Operational DBMS is Right for you?

The products covered in this article all provide core operational DBMS capabilities. Varying application and enterprise requirements will make certain categories of DBMSes and individual products stronger or weaker.

Be sure to consider and understand the storage and access mechanisms, the data consistency capabilities (ACID vs. BASE) and the total cost of ownership of the DBMS over its usage lifetime as you evaluate your operational DBMS choices.

Also, be aware that many organizations use multiple operational database management systems, not just one, to fit disparate application requirements (also known as polyglot persistence).

In the end, it's up to each organization to review the products closely and determine which best meets its needs. These overviews provide a good starting point for determining, which of the operational database management systems are the best fit for your company's project requirements.

References

- Get-ready-to-learn-sql-database-normalization-explained-in-simple-english: essentialsql.com, Retrieved 16 April 2018
- Normalization-in-dbms: beginnersbook.com, Retrieved 12 June 2018
- Etl-extract-load-process: guru99.com, Retrieved 20 April 2018
- Operational-database-odb-5711: techopedia.com, Retrieved 28 May 2018
- A-look-at-the-leading-operational-database-management-systems: searchdatamanagement.techtarget.com, Retrieved 18 March 2018

3

Metadata

Metadata can be described as that data or information which provides information about some other data. Metadata can be of several types, such as descriptive, structural, administrative, statistical and reference metadata. This chapter includes topics like metadata repository, technical and business metadata, metadata management, etc.

Metadata is data about data. In other words, it's information that's used to describe the data that's contained in something like a web page, document, or file. Another way to think of metadata is as a short explanation or summary of what the data is.

A simple example of metadata for a document might include a collection of information like the author, file size, date the document was created, and keywords to describe the document. Metadata for a music file might include the artist's name, the album, and the year it was released.

For computer files, metadata can be stored within the file itself or elsewhere, like is the case with some EPUB book files that keep metadata in an associated ANNOT file.

Metadata represents behind-the-scenes information that's used everywhere, by every industry, in multiple ways. It's ubiquitous in information systems, social media, websites, software, music services, and online retailing. Metadata can be created manually to pick and choose what's included, but it can also be generated automatically based on the data.

Types of Metadata

Metadata comes in several types and is used for a variety of broad purposes that can be roughly categorized as business, technical, or operational.

- Descriptive metadata properties include title, subject, genre, author, and creation date, for example.
- Rights metadata might include copyright status, rights holder, or license terms.
- Technical metadata properties include file types, size, creation date and time, and type of compression. Technical metadata is often used for digital object management and interoperability.
- Preservation metadata is used in navigation. Example preservation metadata properties include an item's place in a hierarchy or sequence.
- Markup languages include metadata used for navigation and interoperability. Properties might include heading, name, date, list, and paragraph.

Metadata in Database

Database objects have various attributes that describe them; you can obtain information about a particular schema object by performing a DESCRIBE operation. The result can be accessed as an object of the Metadata class by passing object attributes as arguments to the various methods of the Metadata class.

You can perform an explicit DESCRIBE operation on the database as a whole, on the types and properties of the columns contained in a *ResultSet* class, or on any of the following schema and subschema objects, such as tables, types, sequences, views, type attributes, columns, procedures, type methods, arguments, functions, collections, results, packages, synonyms, and lists

You must specify the type of the attribute you are looking for. By using the *getAttributeCount()*, *getAttributeId()*, and *getAttributeType()* methods of the *MetaData* class, you can scan through each available attribute.

All DESCRIBE information is cached until the last reference to it is deleted. Users are in this way prevented from accidentally trying to access DESCRIBE information that is already freed.

You obtain metadata by calling the *getMetaData()* method on the Connection class in case of an explicit describe, or by calling the *getColumnListMetaData()* method on the *ResultSet* class to get the metadata of the result set columns. Both methods return a *MetaData* object with the describing information. The *MetaData* class provides the *getxxx()* methods to access this information.

Types and Attributes

When performing *DESCRIBE* operations, be aware of the following issues:

- The *ATTR_TYPECODE* returns typecodes that represent the type supplied when you created a new type by using the *CREATE TYPE* statement. These typecodes are of the enumerated type *TypeCode*, which are represented by *OCCI_TYPECODE* constants.
- The *ATTR_DATA_TYPE* returns types that represent the datatypes of the database columns. These values are of enumerated type *Type*. For example, *LONG* types return *OCCI_SQLT_LNG* types.

Describing Database Metadata

Describing database metadata is equivalent to an explicit DESCRIBE operation. The object to describe must be an object in the schema. In describing a type, you call the *getMetaData()* method from the connection, passing the name of the object or a *RefAny* object. To do this, you must initialize the environment in the OBJECT mode. The *getMetaData()* method returns an object of type *MetaData*. Each type of *MetaData* object has a list of attributes that are part of the describe tree. The describe tree can then be traversed recursively to point to subtrees containing more information. More information about an object can be obtained by calling the *getxxx()* methods.

If you need to construct a browser that describes the database and its objects recursively, then you can access information regarding the number of attributes for each object in the database (including the database), the attribute ID listing, and the attribute types listing. By using this information, you can recursively traverse the describe tree from the top node (the database) to the columns in the tables, the attributes of a type, the parameters of a procedure or function, and so on.

For example, consider the typical case of describing a table and its contents. You call the *getMetaData()* method from the connection, passing the name of the table to be described. The *MetaData* object returned contains the table information. Since you are aware of the type of the object that you want to describe (table, column, type, collection, function, procedure, and so on), you can obtain the attribute list. You can retrieve the value into a variable of the type specified in the table by calling the corresponding *getxxx()* method.

Example: How to obtain metadata about attributes of a simple database table

This example demonstrates how to obtain metadata about attributes of a simple database table:

```
/* Create an environment and a connection to the HR database */

.

.

/* Call the getMetaData method on the Connection object obtainedv*/

MetaData emptab_metaData = connection->getMetaData(

"EMPLOYEES", MetaData::PTYPE_TABLE);

/* Now that you have the metadata information on the EMPLOYEES table,

  call the getxxx methods using the appropriate attributes */


/* Call getString */

cout<<"Schema:"<<

        (emptab_metaData.getString(MetaData::ATTR_OBJ_SCHEMA))<<endl;


if(emptab_metaData.getInt(

        emptab_metaData::ATTR_PTYPE)==MetaData::PTYPE_TABLE)

  cout<<"EMPLOYEES is a table"<<endl;

else

  cout<<"EMPLOYEES is not a table"<<endl;


/* Call getInt to get the number of columns in the table */

int columnCount=emptab_metaData.getInt(MetaData::ATTR_NUM_COLS);

cout<<"Number of Columns:"<<columnCount<<endl;
```

```
/* Call getTimestamp to get the timestamp of the table object */
Timestamp tstamp = emptab_metaData.getTimestamp(MetaData::ATTR_TIMESTAMP);
/* Now that you have the value of the attribute as a Timestamp object,
  you can call methods to obtain the components of the timestamp */
int year;
unsigned int month, day;
tstamp.getData(year, month, day);

/* Call getVector for attributes of list type, e.g. ATTR_LIST_COLUMNS */
vector<MetaData>listOfColumns;
listOfColumns=emptab_metaData.getVector(MetaData::ATTR_LIST_COLUMNS);

/* Each of the list elements represents a column metadata,
  so now you can access the column attributes*/
for (int i=0;i<listOfColumns.size();i++
{
  MetaData columnObj=listOfColumns[i];
  cout<<"Column Name:"<<(columnObj.getString(MetaData::ATTR_NAME))<<endl;
  cout<<"Data Type:"<<(columnObj.getInt(MetaData::ATTR_DATA_TYPE))<<endl;
  .
  .
  /* and so on to obtain metadata on other column specific attributes */
}
```

Example: How to obtain metadata from a column containing user-defined types.

This example demonstrates how to obtain metadata from a column that contains user-defined types database table:

```
/* Create an environment and a connection to the HR database */
...
/* Call the getMetaData method on the Connection object obtained */
MetaData custtab_metaData = connection->getMetaData(
   "CUSTOMERS", MetaData::PTYPE_TABLE);
```

```
/* Have metadata information on CUSTOMERS table; call the getxxx methods */
/* Call getString */
cout<<"Schema:"<<(custtab_metaData.getString(MetaData::ATTR_OBJ_SCHEMA))
   <<endl;
if(custtab_metaData.getInt(custtab_metaData::ATTR_PTYPE)==MetaData::PTYPE_
TABLE)
  cout<<"CUSTOMERS is a table"<<endl;
else
  cout<<"CUSTOMERS is not a table"<<endl;

/* Call getVector to obtain list of columns in the CUSTOMERS table */
vector<MetaData>listOfColumns;
listOfColumns=custtab_metaData.getVector(MetaData::ATTR_LIST_COLUMNS);

/* Assuming metadata for column cust_address_typ is fourth element in list*/
MetaData customer_address=listOfColumns[3];

/* Obtain the metadata for the customer_address attribute */
int typcode = customer_address.getInt(MetaData::ATTR_TYPECODE);
if(typcode==OCCI_TYPECODE_OBJECT)
  cout<<"customer_address is an object type"<<endl;
else
  cout<<"customer_address is not an object type"<<endl;

string objectName=customer_address.getString(MetaData::ATTR_OBJ_NAME);

/* Now that you have the name of the address object,
  the metadata of the attributes of the type can be obtained by using
  getMetaData on the connection by passing the object name
*/
MetaData address = connection->getMetaData(objectName);
```

```
/* Call getVector to obtain the list of the address object attributes */
vector<MetaData> attributeList =
   address.getVector(MetaData::ATT_LIST_TYPE_ATTRS);

/* and so on to obtain metadata on other address object specific attributes */
```

Example: How to obtain object oetadata from a reference

This example demonstrates how to obtain metadata about an object when using a reference to it:

```
Type ADDRESS(street VARCHAR2(50), city VARCHAR2(20));
Table Person(id NUMBER, addr REF ADDRESS);

/* Create an environment and a connection to the HR database */
.
.
/* Call the getMetaData method on the Connection object obtained */
MetaData perstab_metaData = connection->getMetaData(
   "Person", MetaData::PTYPE_TABLE);

/* Now that you have the metadata information on the Person table,
  call the getxxx methods using the appropriate attributes */
/* Call getString */
cout<<"Schema:"<<(perstab_metaData.getString(MetaData::ATTR_OBJ_SCHE-
MA))<<endl;

if(perstab_metaData.getInt(perstab_metaData::ATTR_PTYPE)==MetaData::PTYPE_
TABLE)
  cout<<"Person is a table"<<endl;
else
  cout<<"Person is not a table"<<endl;

/* Call getVector to obtain the list of columns in the Person table*/
vector<MetaData>listOfColumns;
```

```
listOfColumns=perstab_metaData.getVector(MetaData::ATTR_LIST_COLUMNS);

/* Each of the list elements represents a column metadata,
  so now get the datatype of the column by passing ATTR_DATA_TYPE
  to getInt */
for(int i=0;i<numCols;i++)
{
  int dataType=colList[i].getInt(MetaData::ATTR_DATA_TYPE);
  /* If the datatype is a reference, get the Ref and obtain the metadata
   about the object by passing the Ref to getMetaData */
  if(dataType==SQLT_REF)
   RefAny refTdo=colList[i].getRef(MetaData::ATTR_REF_TDO);

  /* Now you can obtain the metadata about the object as shown
  MetaData tdo_metaData=connection->getMetaData(refTdo);

  /* Now that you have the metadata about the TDO, you can obtain the metadata
   about the object */
}
```

Example: How to obtain metadata about a select list from a *ResultSet* object.

This example demonstrates how to obtain metadata about a select list from a *ResultSet*:

```
/* Create an environment and a connection to the database */
...
/* Create a statement and associate it with a select clause */
string sqlStmt="SELECT * FROM EMPLOYEES";
Statement *stmt=conn->createStatement(sqlStmt);

/* Execute the statement to obtain a ResultSet */
```

```
ResultSet *rset=stmt->executeQuery();

/* Obtain the metadata about the select list */
vector<MetaData>cmd=rset->getColumnListMetaData();

/* The metadata is a column list and each element is a column metaData */
int dataType=cmd[i].getInt(MetaData::ATTR_DATA_TYPE);
...
```

The *getMetaData* method is called for the *ATTR_COLLECTION_ELEMENT* attribute only.

Business Metadata

In IT, Business Metadata is adding additional text or statement around a particular word that adds value to data. Business Metadata is about creating definitions, business rules. For example, when tables and columns are created the following business metadata would be more useful for generating reports to functional and technical team. The advantage is of this business metadata is whether they are technical or non-technical, everybody would understand what is going on within the organization.

Typically, the following information needs to be provided to describe business metadata:

- DW Table Name.
- DW Column Name.
- Business Name: Short and descriptive header information.
- Definition: Extended description with brief overview of the business rules for the field.
- Field Type: A flag may indicate whether a given field stores the key or a discrete value, whether is active or not, or what data type is it. The content of that field (or fields) may vary upon business needs.

Table's Metadata: While creating a table, metadata for definition of a table, source system name, source entity names, business rules to transform the source table, and the usage of the table in reports should be added in order to make them available for taking metadata reports. Column's Metadata: Similarly for columns, source column name (mapping), business rules to transform the source column name, and the usage of the column in reports should be added for taking metadata reports.

Column's Metadata: Similarly for columns, source column name (mapping), business rules to transform the source column name, and the usage of the column in reports should be added for taking metadata reports

Business Metadata Example

Entity (Table) Name	Attribute (Column)	Attribute Definition
TARGET AUTO LOAN BY WEB	Auto Loan Identifier	The number that uniquely identifies an AUTO LOAN
	Auto Loan Amount	The amount of auto loan that has been approved. Mapping: SOURCE_AUTO_LOAN_BY_WEB.AUTO_LOAN_AMOUNT
	Auto Loan Broker Commission Amount	The commission amount that has to be paid to AUTO loan broker. Note: This column is a derived column and not found in the source system. Derivation Rule: Auto Loan Amount ".01
	Auto Loan Identifier	This column identifies the Auto VIN Number
	Borrower Full Name	The full name of the borrower. Note: This column is a derived column and not found in the source system. Derivation Rule: SOURCE_AUTO_LOAN_BY_WEB.(BOR_FST_NAME concatenated with BOR_LAST_NAME)
	DataTimeStamp	The data on which the record has been created or updated.

Definitions in Business Metadata

Many business decisions are made (and later regretted) due to a misunderstanding of the data, and what the data element used in a report is signifying. Some of these accidents and misunderstandings are large enough to be reported in the media.

Context is everything. The English language is full of meaning nuances; a word may have multiple meanings based upon the context that it is used.

Business metadata is all about adding context to data. A Dictionary or Glossary is part of business metadata, and it is all about making meaning explicit and providing definitions to business terms, data elements, acronyms and abbreviations.

Components of a Definition

Here are the components of a well-written definition. The actual definition text is comprised of items 3, 4 and 5 below.

1. The name of the term being defined.
2. Part of speech (optional; can be helpful). Examples: noun, verb.
3. Broader term (BT): general class to which the thing belongs; sometimes this is implied. In object modeling parlance this is called an "IS-A" relationship. Example: "A spoon is a utensil". Note that some definitions may be explaining things in the past, which would be "WAS-A" instead of "IS-A".
4. Distinguishing Characteristics, otherwise known as pertinent attributes with specific values. In object modeling parlance this is called a "HAS-A" relationship. Example: "A spoon has a small bowl attached to the end". Note that some definitions may be explaining things in the past, which would be "HAD-A" instead of "HAS-A".
5. Function Qualifier, describing how the thing being defined is used; this usually involves one or more verbs. We would extend the CV structure to include USED-FOR, but this term is not to be confused with USE-FOR, described below. As in the last two components, the Function Qualifier may be describing something in the past, but USE-FOR is already taken, so past may have to be implied or made explicit in the text.
6. Narrower Term (NT) refers to the classes below the term being defined. For example, if the term being defined is Spoon, then pertinent narrow terms of interest could be Soup, Tea, and Serving.
7. Related term (RT) refers to a term that has relevance to the term being defined but is not a synonym. For example: Can opener is related to can but not a synonym. Dictionaries, indexes and search engines often have a "SEE ALSO" section that lists RTs.
8. Synonyms, or terms that mean nearly the same thing as the term being defined. CVs often handle synonyms using a synonym ring, defining one term as the (PT) or Preferred Term.
9. Examples: Example of the term; an instance of the term as it is seen in everyday life. Example (of the example!): An example of an employee is Mary Jones.
10. Usage refers to using the term in a sentence. The example can incorporate sentence usage, but it doesn't have to. Example: A Spoon is defined as an eating utensil that has a small bowl at the end. Usage: Mary gracefully lifted her spoon to her mouth to sample the soup.
11. Source refers to where the definition came from. If it came from a document or manual, pertinent reference information may be important (date of the document, author, etc.)
12. Dates may be important. Create, modify date should always be recorded which track inserts and changes to the glossary. In addition, sometimes dates that indicate the validity of the definition if governance is used may be necessary such as Effective Date and Expiry date.

13. Replaced by: Sometimes you may want to keep "legacy" terms in your glossary, especially if re-engineering has occurred or a migration to a different system that uses different terms. You may want to indicate that the term is legacy and has been replaced by some other term. Alternatively, you can use Synonyms, but Replaced by indicates you should not use the legacy term in common usage.
14. Approval information can be added to track the governance trail, for such things as when the definition was approved, by whom, etc.

Definition Text Structure

As noted above, the three major parts of the definition text are indicated in 3, 4 and 5 above. They are:

- IS-A (class)
- HAS-A (attribute discrimination)
- USED-FOR (function)

A good, sound definition must make explicit two out of three of these components. The following example incorporates A and C:

A : A sleeve is a part of a shirt that

B: goes over the arm.

Note that "a part of" indicates the broader term or class: Shirt. "Goes over the arm" illustrates a distinguishing characteristic that is a function or use of the sleeve.

PART-OF and TYPE-OF are terms that indicate a broader class relationship. Often the class relationship denoted by IS-A is implied. Sometimes these types of implications can be important to make explicit, sometimes not.

Enumerated and Multiple Meanings

Sometimes a definition can include more than one meaning. This is common in a typical dictionary, and our language is full of such cases. The meaning that the term is used must be derived from the context of the sentence. The multiple meanings are enumerated in a definition description as follows:

1-<definition text>

2-<definition text>

There are search tools that prompt the user with "DO you mean..." and lists each possibility corresponding to the different definitions, and assist the user to direct the search.

Technical Metadata

Technical metadata (ETL process metadata, back room metadata, transformation metadata) is a representation of the ETL process. It stores data mapping and transformations from source systems to the data warehouse and is mostly used by data warehouse developers, specialists and ETL modellers.

Most commercial ETL applications provide a metadata repository with an integrated metadata management system to manage the ETL process definition.

The definition of technical metadata is usually more complex than the business metadata and it sometimes involves multiple dependencies.

The technical metadata can be structured in the following way:

- Source Database - or system definition. It can be a source system database, another data warehouse, file system, etc.
- Target Database - Data Warehouse instance.
- Source Tables - one or more tables which are input to calculate a value of the field.
- Source Columns - one or more columns which are input to calculate a value of the field.
- Target Table - target DW table and column are always single in a metadata repository.
- Target Column - target DW column.
- Transformation - the descriptive part of a metadata entry. It usually contains a lot of information, so it is important to use a common standard throughout the organization to keep the data consistent.

Technical Metadata Example

Table Name	Column Name	Column Null	Column Datatype	Primary Key	Foreign Key
SOURCE_AUTO_ LOAN_BY_WEB		NOT NULL	VARCHAR2(20)	Yes	No
		NOT NULL	NUMBER(11)	No	No
		NOT NULL	VARCHAR2(16)	No	No
		NOT NULL	VARCHAR2(20)	No	No
		NOT NULL	VARCHAR2(20)	No	No
		NOT NULL	DATE	No	No
TARGET_AUTO_ LOAN_BY_WEB		NOT NULL	VARCHAR2(20)	Yes	No
		NOT NULL	NUMBER(11)	No	No
		NOT NULL	NUMBER	No	No
		NOT NULL	VARCHAR2(20)	No	No
		NOT NULL	VARCHAR2(40)	No	No
		NOT NULL	DATE	No	No

Operational Metadata

Organizations that use a metadata repository can add an additional layer of detail to their data warehouse and ETL processes by incorporating operational metadata into their architecture and design, providing increased capabilities in data acquisition and maintenance, along with opportunities for data consumer reconciliation and data warehouse audit functions.

Operational metadata offers a connection between the metadata repository and the data warehouse by adding physical database columns to the data warehouse tables, enabling easier use for business and technical consumers.

The main benefits of operational metadata can be summarized in these points:

- Operational metadata, unlike information stored in the metadata repository, is referenced at a row level of granularity in the data warehouse.
- Operational metadata provides a detailed row level explanation of actual information content in the data warehouse.

Incorporation of Operational Meta Data

A variety of formats can be used in data warehouse design to enhance the automation of its support and maintenance. Data warehouse requirements will vary, and the inclusion of specific metadata will be determined by the requirements, but certain operational metadata has been found to be useful for all data warehouse implementations.

- Current Flag Indicator.
- Load Date.
- Load Cycle Identifier.
- Update Date.
- Operational System(s) Identifier.
- Active in Operational System Flag.
- Confidence Level Indicator.

Current Flag Indicator

The current flag indicator column is used to identify the latest version of a row in a table. It facilitates rapid identification of the latest version of a row, rather than performing date comparison calculations. This flag is especially useful for managing the processing of slowly changing dimensions (SCD), type 2, where history of a production record must be maintained.

Load Date

Load date column is the most commonly used and best understood operational metadata field in data warehouse design. This attribute indicates the date and/or time when data instance (row) was loaded into the data warehouse, or in some business cases, when the data was extracted from the operational source system. This snapshot date is used to maintain the temporal integrity of the data in the warehouse since new information is added during each refresh cycle. The column can be referenced by warehouse administrators to identify candidate rows for archival or purge processing. Data consumers and data stewards can use this column to reconcile and audit information in the data warehouse against the operational source systems to confirm the validity of the data found in the data warehouse.

Load Cycle Identifier

The load cycle identifier is a column assigned during each load cycle to the data warehouse regardless of the refresh frequency. It is a sequential identifier, and it can be used to remove data from a particular load cycle run if data corruption or other data quality issues are discovered. Typically, the load cycle identifier is used in conjunction with a static reference table or a metadata repository table that describes other operational statistics about the load cycle.

Update Date

Another extremely common operational metadata column is the update date. This column indicates when a row was last updated in the warehouse during a refresh cycle. This column, like load date, is used to maintain the temporal integrity of information in the data warehouse. It is used in almost all dimension table designs that implement SCD type 1, 2 or 3 processing methods to identify when the row was refreshed, and can serve as important metadata for data consumers and data stewards. The column, like load date, can be employed in administration activities such as archival / purge processing or reconciliation / audit by data consumers.

Operational System(s) Identifier

One of the most useful operational metadata attributes for the warehouse administrator and the data consumer is the operational system(s) identifier. This column is used to track the origination source or sources of an instance (row) in the data warehouse.

In cases where a row of data was integrated from more than one operational source system, a column value indicating the combination of these systems can be assigned. It can be used by data consumers who question the quality and/or validity of data in the warehouse to trace back information to the operational source system that furnished the information.

In certain cases, this column can be used by administrators to identify and remove corrupt data from a particular operational source system(s).

Active Operational System Flag

This column is used to indicate if the production keys in a dimension table are still active in the originating operational system. The active operational system flag provides a variety of analytical alternatives to queries posed to the data warehouse. Data stewards and other analysts can use this metadata effectively to identify dormant data or data that should be constrained in reporting (e.g., out of bounds results, products no longer supported, previous customers, etc.)

Confidence Level Indicator

One of the more controversial operational metadata attributes is the confidence level indicator. This column is used to indicate how business rules or assumptions were applied during the ETL processes for a particular data instance (row). This field provides a way for the data consumer and data steward to indicate the credibility level of an instance (data row) based on the transformation processing action.

Often used to identify potential problems with data quality from operational source systems and to facilitate correcting these issues, each organization's data warehouse team and data governance program will vary in the approach and implementation of this operational metadata attribute.

Use of Operational Metadata in Moderation

Organizations should not incorporate operational metadata columns universally (to every table) and without a clear, justifiable need. In some cases, these attributes do not make a positive contribution to the architecture or design of the data warehouse and its ETL processes:

- For an aggregation table, use of a load cycle identifier and / or an operational system identifier would not be beneficial since the context of the operational metadata would be lost.
- For a fact table, the use of current flag indicator on a row would not be useful since the concept of slowly changing dimensions does not apply to a fact.
- In very simple cases, the identification of an operational system may provide little value to a data consumer or data steward due to a very limited number of sources with insignificant integration requirements.

Metadata Repository

The Metadata Repository provides a single—albeit often logical—repository for gathering, integrating, storing, sharing, and visualizing metadata and its incumbent capabilities and structures. The repository within which metadata resides provides key functions:

- Identify and sanction origins of business data and metadata.
- Hold the metadata in a form that can be analyzed, manipulated, and promoted.
- Ensure traceability and lineage of business definitions and derivations from their origin to the point of consumption or obsolescence.
- Manage and administer the Metadata Repository tool(s) as a common structure across entities and domains, ensuring data integrity and consistency.
- Define and implement standard operating processes and precepts, including those for Data Governance.
- Offer unencumbered availability and easy access for business users.
- Build branding, communication, and adoption of Metadata and the Metadata Repository to encourage usage.
- Establish accountability.

The Metadata Catalog

The Metadata Catalog (Repository) provides a structure within which to effectively manage and organize Metadata for easy retrieval and use. The Metadata Catalog organizes resources being allocated to various Metadata Management View, Abstraction, Implementation, and Infrastructure areas to identify elements, dependencies, priorities, efficiencies, and opportunities to leverage and reuse resources.

The Metadata Catalog:

- Illustrates the state of Metadata structures across the enterprise, including how various systematic events interrelate.
- Organizes projects, programs, and initiatives to synchronize efforts and identify essential Metadata Management capability elements to address.
- Serves as a common frame of reference to communicate Information Technology requirements and limitations between the Information Technology providers and the operational data consumers.
- Holds the requisite characteristics of Metadata organized by use or function to enable clearly articulated governance, responsibilities, relationships, meanings, orchestrations, and other constructs that augment the veracity of data used for decision making and allow for the garnering of insight from Advanced Analytics.

The Metadata Repository Services

Proper construction of the Metadata Repository enables a variety of very important services. Most importantly, the structural and organization components of the Metadata Repository enable representation of Metadata in meta-models that promote many business-critical services:

- Create, load, change, manage, and navigate Metadata models.

- Aggregate and stitch Metadata models from disparate sources.
- Run queries and reports on repository content.
- Transform Metadata models into standard meta-models.
- Export Metadata models into different formats.
- Collaboration facilitation.
- Logical stores for partitioning Metadata models.
- Metadata model versioning and comparison.
- Access control for security and role focus simplicity.
- Web application for universal access.

Metadata Domains

A variety of Metadata Domains allow for the categorization of Metadata elements into meaningful subjects for effective management.

Domain	Example
KPIs & Metrics	Business Rules (e.g., Privacy)
Security	Access Rights & Permission, Authorization, Encryption, Mask
Audit	Version
Data Model	Logical, Physical, Schema, Attribute
Governance	Policy
Lineage	Source, Target, Intermediary, Mappings
Traceability	Derivations, Manipulation, History, provenance
Taxonomy	Codification, Patterns, Classification Schemes, Category
Orchestration	People, Process, Technology
Ontology	Dictionary, Lexicon, Glossary
Semantics	Business perspectives and views
Technological	Infrastructure, Operating System, DBMS, table, table space, server, node, views
Business	Glossary, Rules, Functions, Unit, Process
Location	Geography, Region, Territory
Application	Component, Package

Organization of the Metadata Repository

The Metadata Repository holds entries into domain-specific subsets of metadata that make visible business-specific metadata along with its associated glossary, processing, and supporting capabilities in a holistic, self-contained environment within which to operate. Key components of the Metadata Repository include:

- Glossary, Dictionary, Lexicon, Ontology, Language.

- Taxonomy, Classification schemes, Domains.
- Views (support competing perspectives).

The prototypical Meta-Model for Metadata Management relies on a 5-tier model:

1. Business Viewpoint
2. Application Viewpoint
3. Component Viewpoint
4. Technology Viewpoint
5. Deployment Viewpoint

The Meta-Model must address 2 Primary Concerns:

1. Behavior
2. Information

In addition, the Meta-Model may address numerous Secondary Concerns

- Roles
- Security
- Governance
- Analytics
- Collaboration
- Compliance

Enterprise Meta-Model (Metadata Framework)

The prototypical Enterprise-Meta Model encompasses multiple layers of abstraction, process, roles, and management. The Meta-Model may be extended using periods of time to enable historical change management.

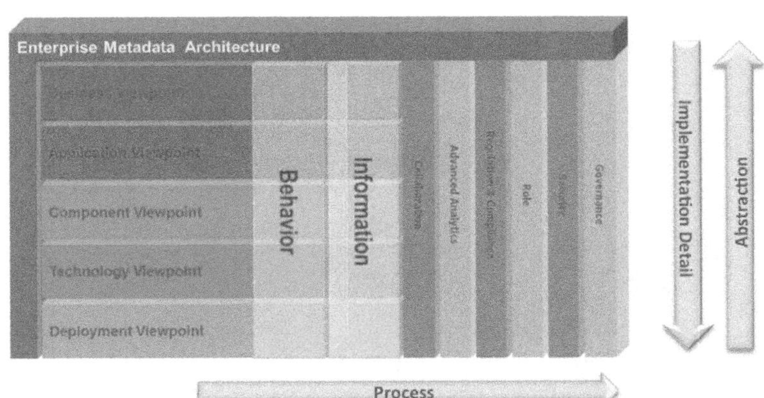

The Metadata Repository Model

To take a step further, a prototypical Meta-Model of the Metadata Repository emerges. The Metadata Repository Model encompasses various services, capabilities, and orchestrations that enable executing Metadata Management for each business perspective, even those competing for data services.

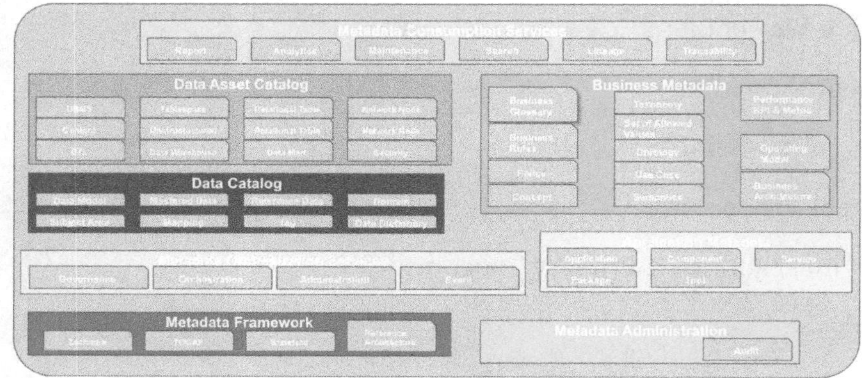

- The Metadata Repository holds a variety of types of metadata:
    - Operational metadata supporting reporting requirements.
    - Federated integration aspects to facilitate data virtualization or reporting capabilities across multiple locations and domains.
    - Runtime metadata completes historical and lineage requests.
- Front-end applications provide the Metadata Consumption Services, such as the catalog and glossary, for easy consistent access across the Metadata Repository.
    - For example, business-specific front-end tools pull a very focused set of data out of the Metadata Repository to help folks do their work.

Metadata Repository Capabilities

To delve deeper into the capabilities of the Metadata Repository consider:

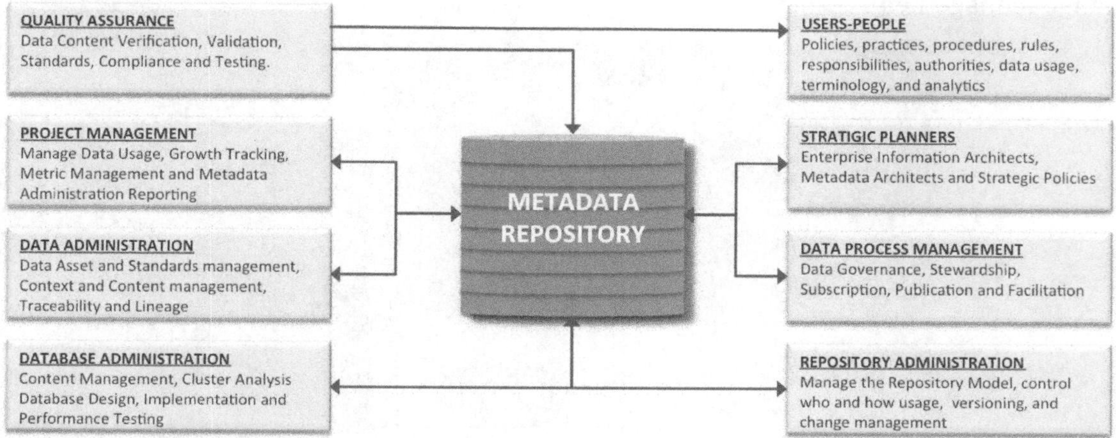

Measure

Dimensional modeling is made up of both logical and physical modeling. Measures are the core of the dimensional model and are data elements that can be summed, averaged, or mathematically manipulated. Fact tables are at the center of the star schema (which is a physically implemented dimensional model), and data marts are made up of multiple fact tables.

Dimensional vs. ER Modeling

Dimensional modeling is a logical design technique. Unlike ER modeling, which consists of conceptual, logical, and physical data modeling, dimensional modeling is made up of only logical and physical modeling.

There are sharp contrasts between ER and dimensional modeling. ER modeling is a design discipline that seeks to represent business rules as highly detailed relationships between business elements that are materialized as database tables. You can extrapolate the business rules from the types and cardinalities of the relationships in an ER model. The primary goal of ER modeling is to remove all non-key data redundancy.

Dimensional modeling, however, seeks to represent data in a logical, understandable manner. In dimensional modeling, you can control data redundancy by conforming dimension and fact tables. A table that's been conformed can be used in more than one dimensional data model and is the same no matter how it's used. The relationships in a dimensional model don't represent business rules; instead, they're navigational paths used to help write reports or create graphs.

Many data modeling software packages support dimensional modeling. Some even let you generate SQL Data Definition Language (DDL) scripts so that all you have to do to create a data warehouse/data mart is run those scripts.

Determining the Facts

In the world of BI, data elements that can be summed, averaged, or otherwise mathematically manipulated are called *measures*. A dimensional model is designed to deliver numbers to BI users, and measures are the core of the model. Measures are data elements such as Order Quantity, Discount Amount, and Tax Amount that are used to determine all types of statistical information, such as the percentage of sales that were discounted or the total sales tax collected per region. Like foreign keys in an ER diagram (ERD), keys in a dimensional model are expressions of a relationship to a dimension table. In contrast to foreign keys in an ERD, however, the relationship isn't intended to enforce referential integrity; after all, the data has already been through the extraction, transformation, and loading (ETL) process, having been scrubbed and validated before being loaded into the data warehouse. Instead, the relationship's function is to associate keys in the fact table with the expanded definitions, which are found in the dimension tables.

In a data warehouse environment, you rarely retrieve just one record. Typically, hundreds, thousands, or even millions of records are retrieved in a single query, and the most logical thing to do with record sets that large is to perform a mathematical process on their data. That's why the section of a fact table that contains the numeric and additive columns is arguably the most important section.

You can start your dimensional design by reviewing the ER model of the transactional data source (the operational database). You can usually identify potential fact tables by locating the associative tables that represent the many-to-many (M:N) relationship in an ER model. An ER model will break down into multiple dimensional diagrams: The number of diagrams is determined by the number of functions in the organization and the organization's BI reporting needs.

To create a dimensional model from an ER model, first separate the ER model into its discrete business processes. Each business process can be expressed as a *data mart*—a modular, highly focused, richly detailed, incrementally designed component of the enterprise data warehouse. Although there are many ways to approach and implement an enterprise data warehouse, the data mart approach lets you tackle the data warehouse project business-process-by-business-process and produce deliverables for your user community.

If this is your first excursion into dimensional modeling, start with a single-source data mart; don't try to tackle multiple-source data marts until you've acquired the skill set necessary to design a complex data warehouse. Examples of single-source data marts include retail sales, purchase orders, shipments, and payments. An example of a multiple-source data mart is customer profitability, which combines revenue and costs that often come from separate transactional sources (e.g., the sales database and the inventory database, respectively).

For each preliminary data mart, identify the M:N relationships from the transactional model that are comprised of numeric and additive non-key data. These relationships will most likely be the associative tables in the ER model. Designate these as fact tables. It's not unusual for a large ER model to produce a dimensional model that has from 10 to 25—or even more—fact tables.

Understandability and Performance

The dimensional model, which becomes a star schema when physically implemented, is a lean, mean performance machine. When faced with a star schema, the database optimizer can depend on heuristics (i.e., rules) rather than on more time-consuming cost-based algorithms to resolve a query. First, the optimizer can constrain the dimension tables referenced in the query. Then, using the filtered key values from the dimension tables, the optimizer can resolve the many-way join to the fact table in a single sort-merge pass.

We know that SSAS uses thin-client architecture to minimize the load on the client computer, ensuring that SSAS will have scalable performance. The SSAS calculation engine is entirely server-based, so all queries are resolved on the server, optimizing the use of the corporate network. Each query, regardless of its complexity, requires just one round trip between the client and the server.

The dimensional model is extensible and expandable; it can accommodate changes in user behavior, new data elements, and new ways of analyzing the data. You can easily change a fact table in place by executing the ALTER TABLE command—the table doesn't have to be dropped and recreated and the data doesn't have to be reloaded. You can add new (and unanticipated) columns to the fact table as long as they're consistent with the fact table's existing grain.

Going with the Grain

The *grain* of a fact table is the level of detail that the table captures. When designing a fact table, choose the grain very carefully—don't aggregate (i.e., summarize) prematurely. For example, a fact table whose records contain weekly sales summaries rather than individual sale amounts is a coarse-grained, aggregated fact table that doesn't support reports on individual sales.

If you aggregate prematurely, you won't be able to gracefully accommodate new sources of data. Design your table to have the finest possible granularity of data: the finer the granularity, the more robust the design.

Finely grained data consists of unsummarized detail records from an operational data source. Individual line items in a sales transaction, individual deposits and withdrawals in a banking transaction, individual line items on a shipping invoice, and individual attendance at an event can all be considered fine-grained data.

For performance reasons, you might find it useful to aggregate fact table records, and that's fine. Just remember that summarized or aggregated versions of the individual fact records are separate records that need to be stored in different fact tables that have a coarser grain. It's important not to mix detail and summary records in the same table: Store them separately. You'll be rewarded when you start using BI query and reporting tools that combine the facts along various dimensions.

Data Marts and Fact Tables

A single fact table does not a data mart make—at least, not usually. Most data marts consist of multiple coordinated fact tables that have similar structures because they're all derived from one business supply chain or value chain. An example of a manufacturing supply chain would be ingredient purchasing, ingredient inventory, bill of materials, manufacturing process control and costs, packaging, and finished goods inventory. Many companies have software systems that manage the flow of control through the supply chain. Usually, there's a data source for each step of the supply chain. Each data source can translate into a set of data marts and has at least one fact table. After the manufacturing step, the flow of control is called a *value chain*. An example of a retail value chain is ship from manufacturing, reseller inventory, reseller shipments, retail inventory, and retail sales.

The purpose of the data warehouse is to provide BI end users with a single source of information regarding supply and value chains so they can follow the data as it flows through the business cycle from beginning to end.

When doing dimensional designs, it helps to understand what kinds of information you can request from the data. For example, from fine-grained fact tables such as Reseller_Sales, you can analyze behavior and frequencies and perform behavior counts, such as the number of times a customer places an order on the date of a storewide inventory sale. You can do time-of-day analysis (e.g., determine whether online sales increase during the lunch hour) and queue analysis (e.g., determine highway capacity and traffic flow, packet traffic on IP networks, and customer movement within an online store). You might be able to do some sequential behavior analysis (e.g., does action A always result in action B?), which could in turn warn you of possible fraud or customer cancellation intent (e.g., this reseller is planning to drop out of your company's partner program). Finally, every retail data mart should lend itself to basket analysis (e.g., do people really buy more beer if it's placed near the baby diapers?) and missing-basket analysis (e.g., what didn't work the way we thought it would and why?). These are all valuable measures that can be derived only with the assistance of a fine-grained fact table containing records at the individual transaction level.

Building a User-Friendly Data Structure

A dimensional model lets you build a user-friendly data structure that makes data access intuitive. The fact table is the core of the dimensional model and contains keys from the dimension tables and the raw numbers that BI users will turn into information. Constructing the fact table so that it contains the finest grain of transactional data available will let you expand and extend your data warehouse as necessary. The dimensional model conforms easily as you coalesce multiple data marts into an enterprise data warehouse and supports a very wide variety of analytical questions that will help you determine your next move in the business world.

Metadata Management

Metadata management is the administration of data that describes other data. It involves establishing policies and processes that ensure information can be integrated, accessed, shared, linked, analyzed and maintained to best effect across the organization.

Metadata is generated whenever data is created, acquired, added to, deleted from, or updated. For example, document metadata in Microsoft Word includes the file size, date of document creation, the name(s) of the author and most recent modifier, the dates of any changes and the total edit time. Further metadata can be added, including title, tags and comments.

The goal of metadata management is to make it easier for a person or program to locate a specific data asset. This requires designing a metadata repository, populating the repository and making it easy to use information in the repository.

Benefits of metadata management include:

- Consistency of definitions of metadata so that terminology variations don't cause data retrieval problems.
- Less redundancy of effort and greater consistency across multiple instances of data because data can be reused appropriately.
- Maintenance of information across the organization that is not dependent on a particular employee's knowledge.
- Greater efficiency, leading to faster product and project delivery.

Good Metadata Management

Creating or pointing more Metadata does not make the information more useful. Good Metadata Management does that. Properly managed Metadata, whether from an old- fashioned card catalog or a computer application, simplifies resource descriptions and provides vocabularies to link contexts.

Good Metadata Management makes for quality Metadata for enterprise content:

> "Not evidently immediately, but cumulatively. Over time, consistently applied Metadata will yield greater and greater returns, while lack of such Metadata will progressively compound retrieval issues and further stress organizational efficacy."

Key components of Metadata Management include Metadata Strategy, Metadata Capture and Storage, Metadata Integration & Publication and Metadata Management & Governance:

- Metadata Strategy

  According to the research report Emerging Trends in Metadata Management only 13.59% of those surveyed have a clearly defined Metadata Strategy and for most it is a piece of another strategy. A Metadata Strategy "ensures actionable, consistent and relevant control of an enterprise's data ecosystem." A good Metadata Strategy needs to include why should the business track Metadata, in addition to gaining feedback from business stakeholders and prioritizing key data components. Key considerations in implementing a Metadata strategy also include business drivers and motivation, Metadata Management maturity, and Metadata sources and technologies.

- Metadata Capture and Storage

  Good Metadata Management requires identification of all external and external Metadata sources and what the business is trying to capture. Using a combination of Metadata solutions, including Data Modeling, Metadata Repositories, and Data Governance tools can help business people evaluate and specify Metadata Captured. Metadata from IoT promises to be helpful. Two research groups, the Thing to Thing Research Group (T2TRG) and the Web of Things (WoT-IG) are exploring Hypermedia. "Hypermedia is the descriptive Metadata about how to exchange state information between applications and resources." This standard will make diverse Metadata from IoT more interoperable.

- Metadata Integration and Publication

  Metadata Integration and Publication describes how to communicate Metadata Strategies and Management to stakeholders and to whom. Prioritizing field standards, using an established external Metadata standard, and emphasizing cohesion among diverse types of Metadata, makes Metadata Integration and Publication easier. The Jet Propulsion Laboratory (JPL) accomplished this using the Dublin Core Specifications. Two templates, also used, include the Business Glossary and Data Lineage.

  - Business Glossary: Firms use a Business Glossary as a common way to publish business terms and their definitions The Metadata managed in a Business Glossary becomes a backbone for a common business vocabulary and accountability for its terms and definitions. This resulting Metadata layer, enhances shared communication, exchange, and understanding of the Business Glossary. Consequently the Business Glossary enables collaboration around business data, resulting in a focused entry point.

- Data Lineage: Publishing Data Lineage describes information on the what, when, where, why, and how of business data, enhancing regulatory compliance and problem solving. Data Lineage especially helps in showing the interrelationship of diverse types of Metadata, clarifying customer's relationships to businesses and information security. "This Data Lineage can be tracked in most Data Modeling tools," or businesses may consider using a Metadata Management tool to stich Metadata together providing "understanding and validation" of data usage and risks that need to be mitigated. Using web-based reporting makes it easy for users to explore Metadata, by drilling-down to each data source and investigate further lineage.

Metadata Management and Governance

Enterprises need holistic Data Governance to make informed business decisions, including Metadata Governance: Metadata Governance involves looking at Metadata roles responsibilities, standards, lifecycles, and statistics, in addition to how operational activities and related Data Management projects integrate Metadata.

Although firms acknowledge Metadata's value, about 50% of organizations have no Metadata standards in place, a crucial piece of Metadata Governance. Formal roles, such as an Executive Sponsor or champion assist stakeholders in understanding the importance of standards and Metadata Management. Finding ways to track and view Metadata quality through completeness, accuracy, currency/timeline, consistency, accountability, integrity, privacy, and usability can show strengths and improvements needed in Metadata management.

Effectively governed Metadata provides a view into the flow of data, the ability to perform an impact analysis, and finally an audit trail for compliance, ensuring trust in a firm's data. Good Metadata Management becomes central to holistic Data Governance.

"Just Enough" Metadata Management

Give "just enough" consideration to Metadata Management. Spending too little resources on Metadata Management "will progressively compound retrieval issues and further stress organizational efficacy". Throw too much at Metadata Management and product fundamentals and business stakeholders suffer. Consider cost and relevancy.

- Cost: Too much or too little Metadata management results in increasing costs. Beware of using the greatest new shiniest data processing paradigm. Businesses can spend hours and dollars inventorying their data across various computer files or in the latest Cloud environments, to the expense of product development and meeting customer needs. Don't focus on compiling data about data to achieve a particular function at the expense of directing Metadata creation and usage. The latter will give the best bang for the buck.
- Irrelevant: Nothing can be more disheartening than to create a Business Glossary or another type of Metadata publication and having it become obsolete. Internal and external users then ignore the firm's Metadata relegating it to the dusty corners of a book shelf or the dark recesses of a distant computer's memory. Without commitment to knowing data's inventory, lifecycle, characteristics, relationships and roles within a business, and the resulting Metadata Management becomes an academic exercise with little use.

References

- Metadata-definition-and-examples-1019177: lifewire.com, Retrieved 11 April 2018
- Business-metadata: learndatamodeling.com, Retrieved 18 May 2018
- Business-metadata-how-to-write-definitions-5239: tdan.com, Retrieved 16 June 2018
- Technical-metadata: learndatamodeling.com, Retrieved 10 March 2018
- Data-warehousing-measuring-facts, microsoft-sql-server: itprotoday.com, Retrieved 17 March 2018
- Toward-a-better-understanding-of-metadata-repository-20255: tdan.com, Retrieved 28 May 2018

4

Data Mining

The process which involves methods of machine learning, database systems and mining to discover different patterns in large data sets is referred to as data mining. All the diverse principles of data mining such as structure mining, data dredging, affinity analysis, etc. have been carefully analyzed in this chapter.

The storing information in a data warehouse does not provide the benefits an organization is seeking. To realize the value of a data warehouse, it is necessary to extract the knowledge hidden within the warehouse. However, as the amount and complexity of the data in a data warehouse grows, it becomes increasingly difficult, if not impossible, for business analysts to identify trends and relationships in the data using simple query and reporting tools.

Data mining is one of the best way to extract meaningful trends and patterns from huge amounts of data. Data mining discovers .information within data warehouse that queries and reports cannot effectively reveal.

The process of extracting valid, previously unknown, comprehensible, and actionable information from large databases and using it to make crucial business decisions is know as Data Mining.

Data mining is concerned with the analysis of data and the use of software techniques for finding hidden and unexpected patterns and relationships in sets of data. The focus of data mining is to find the information that is hidden and unexpected.

Data mining can provide huge paybacks for companies who have made a significant investment in data warehousing. Although data mining is still a relatively new technology, it is already used in a number of industries. Table lists examples of applications of data mining in retail/marketing, banking, insurance, and medicine.

Examples of data mining applications

• Retail marketing ◦ Identify buying patterns of customers. ◦ Finding associations among customer demographics characteristics. ◦ Predicting response to mailing campaigns market basket analysis.
• Banking ◦ Detecting patterns of fraudulent credit and use. ◦ Identifying loyal customers. ◦ Predicting customers likely to change their credit card affiliation. ◦ Determining credit card spending by customer group.

• Insurance ◦ Claim analysis. ◦ Predicting which customers will be new polices.
• Medicine ◦ Characterizing patient behavior to predict surgery visits. ◦ Identifying successful medical therapies for different illnesses.

Data Mining Techniques

There are four main operations associated with data mining techniques which include:

- Predictive modeling.
- Database segmentation.
- Link analysis.
- Deviation detection.

Techniques are specific implementations of the· data mining operations. However, each operation has its own strengths and weaknesses. With this in mind, data mining tools sometimes offer a choice of operations to implement a technique.

Predictive Modeling

It is designed on a similar pattern of the human learning experience in using observations to form a model of the important characteristics of some task. It corresponds to the 'real world'. It 'is developed using a supervised learning approach, which has to phases: training and testing. Training phase is based on a large sample of historical data called a training set, while testing involves trying out the model on new, previously unseen data to determine its accuracy and physical performance characteristics.

It is commonly used in customer retention management, credit approval, cross-selling, and direct marketing. There are two techniques associated with predictive modeling. These are:

- Classification.
- Value prediction.

Classification

Classification is used to classify the records to form a finite set of possible class values. There are two specializations of classification: tree induction and neural induction. An example of classification using tree induction is shown in figure.

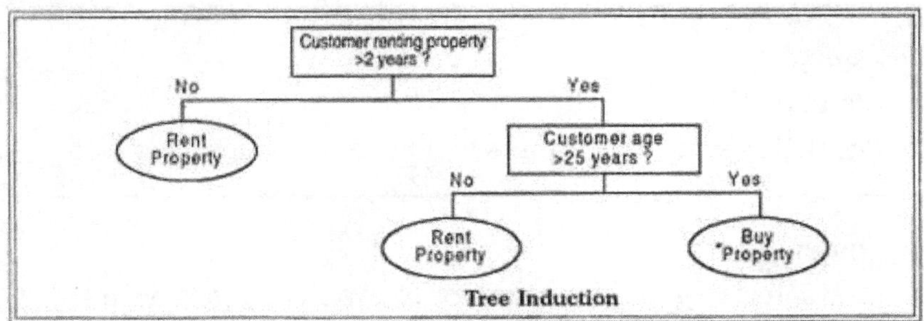

Tree Induction

In this example, we are interested in predicting whether a customer who is currently renting property is likely to be interested in buying property. A predictive model has determined that only two variables are of interest: the length· of the customer has rented property and the age of the customer. The model predicts that those customers who have rented for more than two years and are over 25 years old are the most likely to .be interested in buying property. An example of classification using neural induction is shown in Figure.

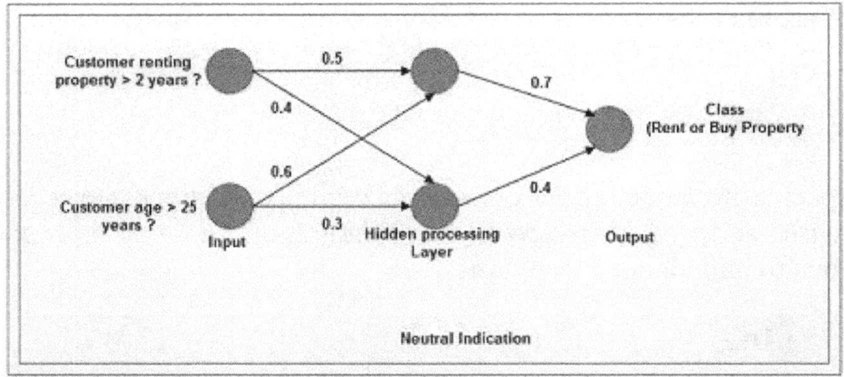

Neutral Indication

A neural network contains collections of connected nodes with input, output, and processing at each node. Between the visible input and output layers may be a number of hidden processing layers. Each processing unit (circle) in one layer is connected to each processing unit in the next layer by a weighted value, expressing the strength of the relationship. This approach is an attempt to copy the way the human brain works· in recognizing patterns by arithmetically combining all the variables associated with a given data point.

Value Prediction

It uses the traditional statistical techniques of linear regression and nonlinear regression. These techniques are easy to use and understand. Linear regression attempts to fit a straight line through a plot of the data, such that the line is the best representation of the average of all observations at that point in the plot. The problem with linear regression is that the technique only works well with linear data and is sensitive to those data values which do not conform to the expected norm. Although nonlinear regression avoids the main problems of linear regression, it is still not flexible enough to handle all possible shapes of the data plot. This is where the traditional statistical analysis methods and data mining methods begin to diverge. Applications of value prediction include credit card fraud detection and target mailing list identification.

Database Segmentation

Segmentation is a group of similar records that share a number of properties. The aim of database segmentation is to partition a database into an unknown number of segments, or clusters.

This approach uses unsupervised learning to discover homogeneous sub-populations in a database to improve the accuracy of the profiles. Applications of database segmentation include customer profiling, direct marketing, and cross-selling.

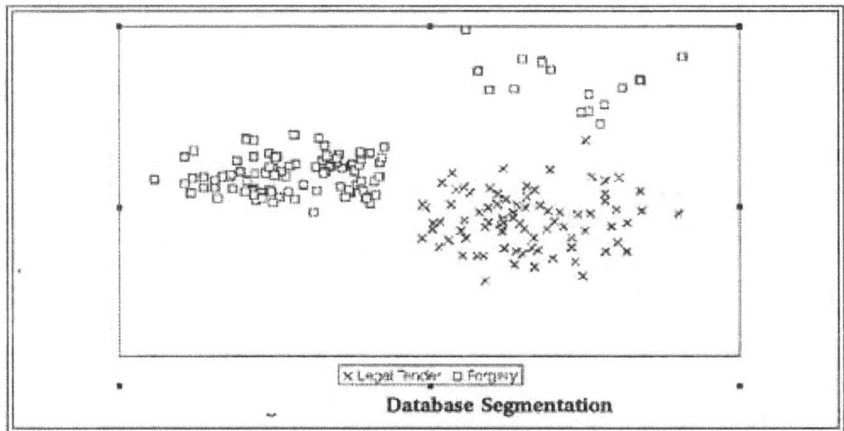

Database Segmentation

As shown in figure, using database segmentation, we identify the cluster that corresponds to legal tender and forgeries. Note that there are two clusters of forgeries, which is attributed to at least two gangs of forgers working on falsifying the banknotes.

Link Analysis

Link analysis aims to establish links, called associations, between the individual record sets of records, in a database. There are three specializations of link analysis. These are:

- Associations discovery.
- Sequential pattern discovery.
- Similar time sequence discovery.

Association's discovery finds items that imply the presence of other items in the same event. There are association rules which are used to define association. For example, 'when a customer rents property for more than two years and is more than 25 years old, in 40% of cases, the customer will buy a property. This association happens in 35% of all customers who rent properties'.

Sequential pattern discovery finds patterns between events such that the presence of one set of item is followed by another set of items in a database of events over a period of the. For example, this approach can be used to understand long-term customer buying behavior.

Time sequence discovery is used in the discovery of links between two sets of data that are time-dependent. For example, within three months of buying property, new home owners will purchase goods such as cookers, freezers, and washing machines.

Applications of link analysis include product affinity analysis, direct marketing, and stock price movement.

Deviation Detection

Deviation detection is a relatively new technique in terms of commercially available data mining tools. However, deviation detection is often a source of true discovery because it identifies outliers, which express deviation from some previously known expectation "and norm. This operation can be performed using statistics and visualization techniques.

Applications of deviation detection include fraud detection in the use of credit cards and insurance claims, quality control, and defects tracing.

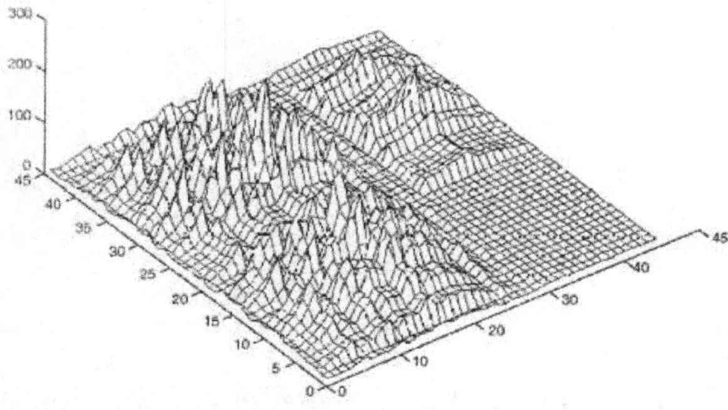

Visual detection of deviation

Data Mining and Data Warehousing

Data mining requires a single, separate, clean, integrated, and self-consistent source of data. A data warehouse is well equipped for providing data for mining for the following reasons:

- Data mining requires data quality and consistency of input data and data warehouse provides it.
- It is advantageous to mine data from multiple sources to discover as many interrelationships as possible. Data warehouse contain data from a number of sources.
- Query capabilities of the data warehouse helps in selecting the relevant information.

Uses of Data Mining

Data mining is a powerful tool that can help you find patterns and relationships within your data. But data mining does not work by itself. It does not eliminate the need to know your business, to understand your data, or to understand analytical methods. Data mining discovers hidden information in your data, but it cannot tell you the value of the information to your organization.

You might already be aware of important patterns as a result of working with your data over time. Data mining can confirm or qualify such empirical observations in addition to finding new patterns that may not be immediately discernible through simple observation.

It is important to remember that the predictive relationships discovered through data mining are not necessarily *causes* of an action or behavior. For example, data mining might determine that males with incomes between $50,000 and $65,000 who subscribe to certain magazines are likely to buy a given product. You can use this information to help you develop a marketing strategy. However, you should not assume that the population identified through data mining will buy the product because they belong to this population.

Asking the Right Questions

Data mining does not automatically discover solutions without guidance. The patterns you find through data mining will be very different depending on how you formulate the problem.

To obtain meaningful results, you must learn how to ask the right questions. For example, rather than trying to learn how to "improve the response to a direct mail solicitation," you might try to find the characteristics of people who have responded to your solicitations in the past.

Understanding your Data

To ensure meaningful data mining results, you must understand your data. Data mining algorithms are often sensitive to specific characteristics of the data: outliers (data values that are very different from the typical values in your database), irrelevant columns, columns that vary together (such as age and date of birth), data coding, and data that you choose to include or exclude. Oracle Data Mining can automatically perform much of the data preparation required by the algorithm. But some of the data preparation is typically specific to the domain or the data mining problem. At any rate, you need to understand the data that was used to build the model in order to properly interpret the results when the model is applied.

Data Mining Process

Figure illustrates the phases, and the iterative nature, of a data mining project. The process flow shows that a data mining project does not stop when a particular solution is deployed. The results of data mining trigger new business questions, which in turn can be used to develop more focused models.

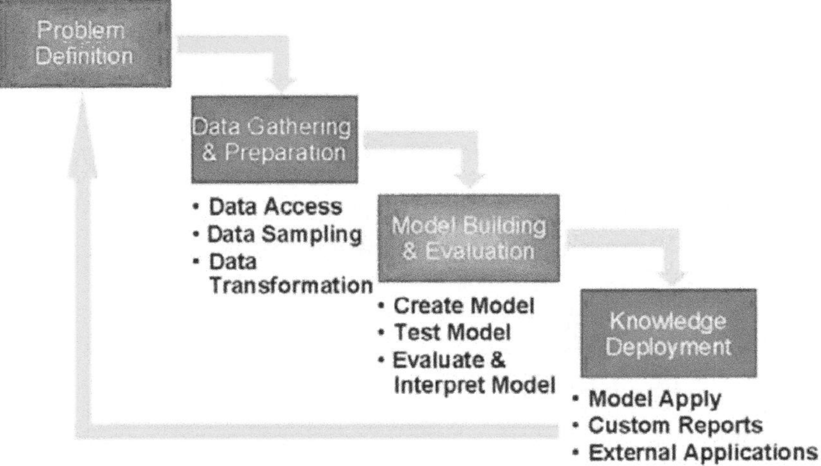

Figure: The Data Mining Process

Problem Definition

This initial phase of a data mining project focuses on understanding the project objectives and requirements. Once you have specified the project from a business perspective, you can formulate it as a data mining problem and develop a preliminary implementation plan.

For example, your business problem might be: "How can I sell more of my product to customers?" You might translate this into a data mining problem such as: "Which customers are most likely to purchase the product?" A model that predicts who is most likely to purchase the product must be built on data that describes the customers who have purchased the product in the past. Before building the model, you must assemble the data that is likely to contain relationships between customers who have purchased the product and customers who have not purchased the product. Customer attributes might include age, number of children, years of residence, owners/renters, and so on.

Data Gathering and Preparation

The data understanding phase involves data collection and exploration. As you take a closer look at the data, you can determine how well it addresses the business problem. You might decide to remove some of the data or add additional data. This is also the time to identify data quality problems and to scan for patterns in the data.

The data preparation phase covers all the tasks involved in creating the case table you will use to build the model. Data preparation tasks are likely to be performed multiple times, and not in any prescribed order. Tasks include table, case, and attribute selection as well as data cleansing and transformation. For example, you might transform a *DATE_OF_BIRTH* **column to** *AGE*; you might insert the average income in cases where the *INCOME* **column is null.**

Additionally you might add new computed attributes in an effort to tease information closer to the surface of the data. For example, rather than using the purchase amount, you might create a new attribute: "Number of Times Amount Purchase Exceeds $500 in a 12 month time period." Customers who frequently make large purchases may also be related to customers who respond or don't respond to an offer.

Thoughtful data preparation can significantly improve the information that can be discovered through data mining.

Model Building and Evaluation

In this phase, you select and apply various modeling techniques and calibrate the parameters to optimal values. If the algorithm requires data transformations, you will need to step back to the previous phase to implement them.

In preliminary model building, it often makes sense to work with a reduced set of data (fewer rows in the case table), since the final case table might contain thousands or millions of cases.

At this stage of the project, it is time to evaluate how well the model satisfies the originally-stated business goal (phase 1). If the model is supposed to predict customers who are likely to purchase a product, does it sufficiently differentiate between the two classes? Is there sufficient lift? Are the trade-offs shown in the confusion matrix acceptable? Would the model be improved by adding text data? Should transactional data such as purchases (market-basket data) be included? Should costs associated with false positives or false negatives be incorporated into the model?

Knowledge Deployment

Knowledge deployment is the use of data mining within a target environment. In the deployment phase, insight and actionable information can be derived from data.

Deployment can involve scoring (the application of models to new data), the extraction of model details (for example the rules of a decision tree), or the integration of data mining models within applications, data warehouse infrastructure, or query and reporting tools.

Structure Mining

The mining structure defines the data from which mining models are built: it specifies the source data view, the number and type of columns, and an optional partition into training and testing sets. A single mining structure can support multiple mining models that share the same domain. The following diagram illustrates the relationship of the data mining structure to the data source, and to its constituent data mining models.

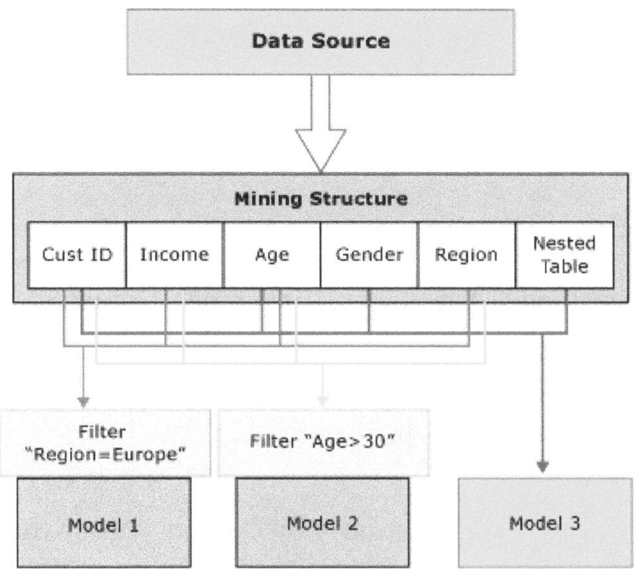

The mining structure in the diagram is based on a data source that contains multiple tables or views, joined on the CustomerID field. One table contains information about customers, such as the geographical region, age, income and gender, while the related nested table contains multiple rows of additional information about each customer, such as products the customer has purchased. The diagram shows that multiple models can be built on one mining structure, and that the models can use different columns from the structure.

Model 1: Uses CustomerID, Income, Age, Region, and filters the data on Region.

Model 2: Uses CustomerID, Income, Age, Region and filters the data on Age.

Model 3: Uses CustomerID, Age, Gender, and the nested table, with no filter.

Because the models use different columns for input, and because two of the models additionally restrict the data that is used in the model by applying a filter, the models might have very different results even though they are based on the same data. Note that the CustomerID column is required in all models because it is the only available column that can be used as the case key.

Setting up a data mining structure includes the following steps:

- Define a data source.
- Select columns of data to include in the structure (not all columns need to be added to the model) and defining a key.
- Define a key for the structure, including the key for the bested table, if applicable.
- Specify whether the source data should be separate into a training set and testing set. This step is optional.
- Process the structure.

Data Sources for Mining Structures

When you define a mining structure, you use columns that are available in an existing data source view. A data source view is a shared object that lets you combine multiple data sources and use them as a single source. The original data sources are not visible to client applications, and you can use the properties of the data source view to modify data types, create aggregations, or alias columns.

If you build multiple mining models from the same mining structure, the models can use different columns from the structure. For example, you can create a single structure and then build separate decision tree and clustering models from it, with each model using different columns and predicting different attributes.

Moreover, each model can use the columns from the structure in different ways. For example, your data source view might contain an Income column, which you can bin in different ways for different models.

The data mining structure stores the definition of the data source and the columns in it in the form of bindings to the source data. However, note that you can also create a data mining structure without binding it to a specific data source by using the DMX CREATE MINING STRUCTURE (DMX) statement.

Mining Structure Columns

The building blocks of the mining structure are the mining structure columns, which describe the data that the data source contains. These columns contain information such as data type, content type, and how the data is distributed. The mining structure does not contain information about how columns are used for a specific mining model, or about the type of algorithm that is used to build a model; this information is defined in the mining model itself.

A mining structure can also contain nested tables. A nested table represents a one-to-many relationship between the entity of a case and its related attributes. For example, if the information that describes the customer resides in one table, and the customer's purchases reside in another table, you can use nested tables to combine the information into a single case. The customer identifier is the entity, and the purchases are the related attributes. To create a data mining model in SQL Server Data Tools (SSDT), you must first create a data mining structure. The Data Mining wizard walks you through the process of creating a mining structure, choosing data, and adding a mining model.

If you create a mining model by using Data Mining Extensions (DMX), you can specify the model and the columns in it, and DMX will automatically create the required mining structure.

Dividing the Data into Training and Testing Sets

When you define the data for the mining structure, you can also specify that some of the data be used for training, and some for testing. Therefore, it is no longer necessary to separate your data in advance of creating a data mining structure. Instead, while you create your model, you can specify that a certain percentage of the data be held out for testing, and the rest used for training, or you can specify a certain number of cases to use as the test data set. The information about the training and testing data sets is cached with the mining structure, and as a result, the same test set can be used with all models that are based on that structure.

Enabling Drillthrough

You can add columns to the mining structure even if you do not plan to use the column in a specific mining model. This is useful if, for example, you want to retrieve the e-mail addresses of customers in a clustering model, without using the e-mail address during the analysis process. To ignore a column during the analysis and prediction phase, you add it to the structure but do not specify a usage for the column, or set the usage flag to Ignore. Data flagged in this way can still be used in queries if drillthrough has been enabled on the mining model, and if you have the appropriate permissions. For example, you could review the clusters resulting from analysis of all customers, and then use a drillthrough query to get the names and e-mail addresses of customers in a particular cluster, even though those columns of data were not used to build the model.

Processing Mining Structures

A mining structure is just a metadata container until it is processed. When you process a mining structure, Analysis Services creates a cache that stores statistics about the data, information about how any continuous attributes are discretized, and other information that is later used by mining models. The mining model itself does not store this summary information, but instead references the information that was cached when the mining structure was processed. Therefore, you do not need to reprocess the structure each time you add a new model to an existing structure; you can process just the model.

You can opt to discard this cache after processing, if the cache is very large or you want to remove detailed data. If you do not want the data to be cached, you can change the CacheMode property of the mining structure to ClearAfterProcessing. This will destroy the cache after any models are processed. Setting the CacheMode property to ClearAfterProcessing will disable drillthrough from the mining model.

However, after you destroy the cache, you will not be able to add new models to the mining structure. If you add a new mining model to the structure, or change the properties of existing models, you would need to reprocess the mining structure first.

Viewing Mining Structures

You cannot use viewers to browse the data in a mining structure. However, in SQL Server Data Tools (SSDT), you can use the Mining Structure tab of Data Mining Designer to view the structure columns and their definitions.

If you want to review the data in the mining structure, you can create queries by using Data Mining Extensions (DMX). For example, the statement SELECT * FROM <structure>.CASES returns all the data in the mining structure. To retrieve this information, the mining structure must have been processed, and the results of processing must be cached.

The statement SELECT * FROM <model>.CASES returns the same columns, but only for the cases in that particular model.

Using Data Mining Models with Mining Structures

A data mining model applies a mining model algorithm to the data that is represented by a mining structure. A mining model is an object that belongs to a particular mining structure, and the model inherits all the values of the properties that are defined by the mining structure. The model can use all the columns that the mining structure contains or a subset of the columns. You can add multiple copies of a structure column to a structure. You can also add multiple copies of a structure column to a model, and then assign different names, or *aliases*, to each structure column in the model.

Sequential Pattern Mining

"What is sequential pattern mining?" Sequential pattern mining is the mining of frequently occurring ordered events or subsequences as patterns. An example of a sequential pattern is "Customers who buy a Canon digital camera are likely to buy an HP color printer within a month." For retail data, sequential patterns are useful for shelf placement and promotions. This industry, as well as telecommunications and other businesses, may also use sequential patterns for targeted marketing, customer retention, and many other tasks. Other areas in which sequential patterns can be applied include Web access pattern analysis, weather prediction, production processes, and network intrusion detection. Notice that most studies of sequential pattern mining concentrate on categorical.

Let's establish some vocabulary for our discussion of sequential pattern mining. Let $I = \{I_1, I_2, ..., I_p\}$ be the set of all items. An itemset is a nonempty set of items. A sequence is an ordered list of events. A sequence s is denoted $\langle e_1\ e_2\ e_3 \cdots e_l \rangle$, where event e_1 occurs before e_2, which occurs before e_3, and so on. Event e_j is also called an element of s. In the case of customer purchase data, an event refers to a shopping trip in which a customer bought items at a certain store. The event is thus an itemset, that is, an unordered list of items that the customer purchased during the trip. The itemset (or event) is denoted $(x_1x_2 \cdots x_q)$, where x_k is an item. For brevity, the brackets are omitted if an element has only one item that is element (x) is written as x. Suppose that a customer made several shopping trips to the store. These ordered events form a sequence for the customer. That is, the customer first bought the items in s_1, then later bought the items in s_2, and so on. An item can occur at most once in an event of a sequence, but can occur multiple times in different events of a sequence. The number of instances of items in a sequence is called the length of the sequence. A sequence with length l is called an l-sequence. A sequence $\alpha = \langle a_1\ a_2 \ldots a_n \rangle$ is called a subsequence of another sequence $\beta = \langle b_1b_2 \cdots b_m \rangle$, and β is a super sequence of α, denoted as $\alpha \subseteq \beta$, if there exist integers $1 \le j_1 < j_2 < \cdots < j_n \le m$ such that $a_1 \subseteq b_{j1}, a_2 \subseteq b_{j2}, \ldots, a_n \subseteq b_{jn}$. For example, if $\alpha = \langle (ab), d \rangle$ and $\beta = \langle (abc), (de) \rangle$, where $a, b, c, d,$ and e are items, then α is a subsequence of β and β is a super sequence of α.

A sequence database, S, is a set of tuples, $\langle SID, s \rangle$ where SID is a sequence ID and s is a sequence. For our example, S contains sequences for all customers of the store. A tuple $\langle SID, s \rangle$ is said to contain a sequence , if α is a subsequence of s. The support of a sequence α in a sequence database S is the number of tuples in the database containing α, that is, $support_S(\alpha) = |\{\langle SID, s \rangle | (\langle SID, s \rangle \in S) \wedge (\alpha \subseteq s)\}|$. It can be denoted as $support_S(\alpha)$ if the sequence database is clear from the context. Given a positive integer min sup as the minimum support threshold, a sequence α is frequent in sequence database S *if* $support_S(\alpha) \ge min\,\text{sup}$. That is, for sequence α to be frequent, it must occur at least min sup times in S. A frequent sequence is called a sequential pattern. A sequential pattern with length l is called an l-pattern. The following example illustrates these concepts.

Example: Sequential patterns. Consider the sequence database S, given in table, which will be used in examples throughout this section. Let min sup = 2. The set of items in the database is $\{a, b, c, d, e, f, g\}$. The database contains four sequences.

Let's look at sequence 1, which is $\langle a(abc)(ac)d(cf) \rangle$. It has five events, namely (a), (abc), (ac), (d), and (c f), which occur in the order listed. Items a and c each appear more than once in different events of the sequence. There are nine instances of items in sequence 1; therefore, it has a length of nine and is called a 9-sequence. Item a occurs three times in sequence 1 and so contributes three to the length of the sequence. However, the entire sequence contributes only one to the support of $\langle a \rangle$ Sequence $\langle a(bc)df \rangle$ is a subsequence of sequence 1 since the events of the former are each subsets of events in sequence 1, and the order of events is preserved. Consider sub sequence $s = \langle (ab)c \rangle$. Looking at the sequence database, S, we see that sequences 1 and 3 are the only ones that contain the subsequence s. The support of s is thus 2, which satisfies minimum support.

Sequence ID	Sequence
1	$\langle a(abc)(ac)d(cf) \rangle$
2	$\langle (ad)c(bc)(ae) \rangle$

3	$\langle (ef)(ab)(df)cb \rangle$
4	$\langle eg(af)cbc \rangle$

Table: A sequence database

Therefore, s is frequent, and so we call it a sequential pattern. It is a 3-pattern since it is a sequential pattern of length three.

This model of sequential pattern mining is an abstraction of customer-shopping sequence analysis. Many other sequential pattern mining applications may not be covered by this model. For example, when analyzing Web clickstream sequences, gaps between clicks become important if one wants to predict what the next click might be. In DNA sequence analysis, approximate patterns become useful since DNA sequences may contain (symbol) insertions, deletions, and mutations. Such diverse requirements can be viewed as constraint relaxation or enforcement.

Scalable Methods for Mining Sequential Patterns

Sequential pattern mining is computationally challenging because such mining may generate and/or test a combinatorially explosive number of intermediate subsequences.

"How can we develop efficient and scalable methods for sequential pattern mining?" Recent developments have made progress in two directions:

(1) Efficient methods for mining the full set of sequential patterns, and

(2) Efficient methods for mining only the set of closed sequential patterns, where a sequential pattern s is closed if there exists no sequential pattern s o where s' is a proper super sequence of s, and s' has the same (frequency) support as s.

Because all of the subsequences of a frequent sequence are also frequent, mining the set of closed sequential patterns may avoid the generation of unnecessary subsequences and thus lead to more compact results as well as more efficient methods than mining the full set. We will first examine methods for mining the full set and then study how they can be extended for mining the closed set. In addition, we discuss modifications for mining multilevel, multidimensional sequential patterns (i.e., with multiple levels of granularity).

The major approaches for mining the full set of sequential patterns are similar to those introduced for frequent itemset mining. Here, we discuss three such approaches for sequential pattern mining, represented by the algorithms GSP, SPADE, and PrefixSpan, respectively.

SPADE adopts a candidate generate and-test approach using vertical data format (where the data are represented as $\langle itemset : (sequence\_ID,\ event\_ID) \rangle$). The vertical data format can be obtained by transforming from a horizontally formatted sequence database in just one scan. PrefixSpan is a pattern growth method, which does not require candidate generation.

All three approaches either directly or indirectly explore the Apriori property, stated as follows: every nonempty subsequence of a sequential pattern is a sequential pattern. (Recall that for a pattern to be called sequential, it must be frequent. That is, it must satisfy minimum support.)

The Apriori property is antimonotonic (or downward-closed) in that, if a sequence cannot pass a test (e.g., regarding minimum support), all of its super sequences will also fail the test. Use of this property to prune the search space can help make the discovery of sequential patterns more efficient.

SPADE: An Apriori-Based Vertical Data Format Sequential Pattern Mining Algorithm The Apriori-like sequential pattern mining approach (based on candidate generate-andtest) can also be explored by mapping a sequence database into vertical data format. In vertical data format, the database becomes a set of tuples of the form $\langle itemset\ :\ (sequence\ ID,\ event\ ID)\rangle$. That is, for a given itemset, we record the sequence identifier and corresponding event identifier for which the itemset occurs. The event identifier serves as a timestamp within a sequence. The event ID of the ith itemset (or event) in a sequence is i. Note than an itemset can occur in more than one sequence. The set of (sequence ID, event ID) pairs for a given itemset forms the ID list of the itemset. The mapping from horizontal to vertical format requires one scan of the database. A major advantage of using this format is that we can determine the support of any k-sequence by simply joining the ID lists of any two of its (k −1)-length subsequences. The length of the resulting ID list (i.e., unique sequence ID values) is equal to the support of the k-sequence, which tells us whether the sequence is frequent.

SPADE (Sequential PAttern Discovery using Equivalent classes) is an Apriori-based sequential pattern mining algorithm that uses vertical data format. As with GSP, SPADE requires one scan to find the frequent 1-sequences. To find candidate 2-sequences, we join all pairs of single items if they are frequent (therein, it applies the Apriori property), share the same sequence identifier, and their event identifiers follow a sequential ordering. That is, the first item in the pair must occur as an event before the second item, where both occur in the same sequence. Similarly, we can grow the length of itemsets from length 2 to length 3, and so on. The procedure stops when no frequent sequences can be found or no such sequences can be formed by such joins. The following example helps illustrate the process.

Example

SPADE: Candidate generate-and-test using vertical data format

Let $min\_sup\ \equiv\ 2$. Our running example sequence database, S, of table is in horizonal data format. SPADE first scans S and transforms it into vertical format. Each itemset (or event) is associated with its ID list, which is the set of SID (sequence_ID) and EID (event_ID) pairs that contain the itemset. The ID list for individual items, a, b, and so on. For example, the ID list for item b consists of the following (SID, EID) pairs: $\{(1,\ 2),\ (2,\ 3),\ (3,\ 2),\ (3,\ 5),\ (4,\ 5)\}$, where the entry (1, 2) means that b occurs in sequence 1, event 2, and so on. Items a and b are frequent. They can be joined to form the length-2 sequence, ha, bi. We find the support of this sequence as follows. We join the ID_lists of a and b by joining on the same sequence_ID wherever, according to the event IDs, a occurs before b. That is, the join must preserve the temporal order of the events involved. The result of such a join for a and b is shown in the ID_list for ab of figure. For example, the ID_list for 2-sequence ab is a set of triples, (SID, EID(a), EID(b)), namely $\{(1,\ 1,\ 2),\ (2,\ 1,\ 3),\ (3,\ 2,\ 5),\ (4,\ 3,\ 5)\}$. The entry (2, 1, 3), for example, shows that both a and b occur in sequence 2, and that a (event 1 of the sequence) occurs before b (event 3), as required. Furthermore, the frequent 2- sequences can be joined (while considering the Apriori pruning heuristic that the (k1)-subsequences of a candidate k-sequence must be frequent) to form 3-sequences. The process terminates when no frequent sequences can be found or no candidate sequences can be formed. Additional details of the method can be found in Zaki.

The use of vertical data format, with the creation of ID lists, reduces scans of the sequence database. The ID_lists carry the information necessary to find the support of candidates. As the length of a frequent sequence increases, the size of its ID_list decreases, resulting in very fast joins. However, the basic search methodology of SPADE and GSP is breadth-first search (e.g., exploring 1-sequences, then 2-sequences, and so on) and Apriori pruning. Despite the pruning, both algorithms have to generate large sets of candidates in breadth-first manner in order to grow longer sequences. Thus, most of the difficulties suffered in the GSP algorithm recur in SPADE as well.

PrefixSpan: Prefix-Projected Sequential Pattern Growth

Pattern growth is a method of frequent-pattern mining that does not require candidate generation. The technique originated in the FP-growth algorithm for transaction databases, presented. The general idea of this approach is as follows: it finds the frequent single items, then compresses this information into a frequent-pattern tree, or FP-tree.

SID	*EID*	*itemset*
1	1	a
1	2	abc
1	3	ac
1	4	d
1	5	cf
2	1	ad
2	2	c
2	3	bc
2	4	ae
3	1	ef
3	2	ab
3	3	df
3	4	c
3	5	b
4	1	e
4	2	g
4	3	af
4	4	c
4	5	b
4	6	c

(a) vertical format database

a		b		...
SID	*EID*	*SID*	*EID*	...
1	1	1	2	
1	2	2	3	
1	3	3	2	
2	1	3	5	
2	4	4	5	
3	2			
4	3			

(b) ID_lists for some 1-sequences

ab			ba			...
SID	*EID(a)*	*EID(b)*	*SID*	*EID(b)*	*EID(a)*	...
1	1	2	1	2	3	
2	1	3	2	3	4	
3	2	5				
4	3	5				

(c) ID_lists for some 2-sequences

aba				...
SID	*EID(a)*	*EID(b)*	*EID(a)*	...
1	1	2	3	
2	1	3	4	

(d) ID_lists for some 3-sequences

Figure: The SPADE mining process: (a) vertical format database; (b) to (d) show fragments of the ID lists for 1-sequences, 2-sequences, and 3-sequences, respectively

The FP-tree is used to generation a set of projected databases, each associated with one frequent item. Each of these databases is mined separately. The algorithm builds prefix patterns, which it concatenates with suffix patterns to find frequent patterns, avoiding candidate generation. Here, we look at PrefixSpan, which extends the pattern-growth approach to instead mine sequential patterns.

Suppose that all the items within an event are listed alphabetically. For example, instead of listing the items in an event as, say, (bac), we list them as (abc) without loss of generality. Given a sequence $\alpha = \langle e_1 e_2 \ldots e_n \rangle$ (where each e_i corresponds to a frequent event in a sequence database, S) a sequence $\beta = \langle e_1' e_2' \ldots e_m' \rangle (m \le n)$ is called a prefix of α if and only if

(1) $e_i' = e_i$ for $(i \le m-1)$;

(2) $e_m' \subseteq e_m$;

(3) all the frequent items in $(e_m - e_m')$ are alphabetically after those in e_m' Sequence $\gamma = \langle e_m'' e_{m+1} \cdots e_n \rangle$ is called the suffix of α with respect to prefix β, denoted as $\gamma = \alpha / \beta$, where $e_m'' = (e_m - e_m')$. We also denote $\alpha = \beta \cdot \gamma$. Note if β is not a subsequence of α, the suffix of α with respect to β is empty.

We illustrate these concepts with the following example.

Example: Prefix and suffix. Let sequence $s = \langle a(abc)(ac)d(cf) \rangle$, which corresponds to sequence 1 of our running example sequence database. $\langle a \rangle, \langle aa \rangle, \langle a(ab) \rangle$, and $\langle a(abc) \rangle$ are four prefixes of s. $\langle (abc)(ac)d(cf) \rangle$ is the suffix of s with respect to the prefix $\langle a \rangle$; $\langle (\_bc)(ac)d(cf) \rangle$ is its suffix with respect to the prefix $\langle aa \rangle$; $\langle (\_c)(ac)d(cf) \rangle \langle a(ab) \rangle$ is its suffix with respect to the prefix $\langle a(ab) \rangle$.

Based on the concepts of prefix and suffix, the problem of mining sequential patterns can be decomposed into a set of subproblems as shown:

1. Let $\{\langle x_1 \rangle, \langle x_2 \rangle, \ldots, \langle x_n \rangle\}$ be the complete set of length-1 sequential patterns in a sequence database, S. The complete set of sequential patterns in S can be partitioned into n disjoint subsets. The ith subset $(1 \le i \le n)$ is the set of sequential patterns with prefix $\langle x_i \rangle$.
2. Let α be a length-l sequential pattern and $\{\beta 1, \beta 2, \ldots, \beta m\}$ be the set of all length- (l + 1) sequential patterns with prefix α. The complete set of sequential patterns with prefix α, except for α itself, can be partitioned into m disjoint subsets. The jth subset $(1 \le j \le m)$ is the set of sequential patterns prefixed with β_j.

Based on this observation, the problem can be partitioned recursively. That is, each subset of sequential patterns can be further partitioned when necessary. This forms a divide-and-conquer framework. To mine the subsets of sequential patterns, we construct corresponding projected databases and mine each one recursively.

Let's use our running example to examine how to use the prefix-based projection approach for mining sequential patterns.

Example

PrefixSpan: A pattern-growth approach

Using the same sequence database, S, of table with $min\_sup \equiv 2$, sequential patterns in S can be mined by a prefix-projection method in the following steps.

1. Find length-1 sequential patterns. Scan S once to find all of the frequent items in sequences. Each of these frequent items is a length-1 sequential pattern. They are $\langle a\rangle:4, \langle b\rangle:4, \langle c\rangle:4, \langle d\rangle:3, \langle e\rangle:3$, and $\langle f\rangle:3$, where the notation "$\langle pattern\rangle$: count" represents the pattern and its associated support count.

prefix	*projected database*	*sequential patterns*
$\langle a\rangle$	$\langle(abc)(ac)d(cf)\rangle$, $\langle(\_d)c(bc)(ae)\rangle$, $\langle(\_b)(df)eb\rangle$, $\langle(\_f)cbc\rangle$	$\langle a\rangle$, $\langle aa\rangle$, $\langle ab\rangle$, $\langle a(bc)\rangle$, $\langle a(bc)a\rangle$, $\langle aba\rangle$, $\langle abc\rangle$, $\langle(ab)\rangle$, $\langle(ab)c\rangle$, $\langle(ab)d\rangle$, $\langle(ab)f\rangle$, $\langle(ab)dc\rangle$, $\langle ac\rangle$, $\langle aca\rangle$, $\langle acb\rangle$, $\langle acc\rangle$, $\langle ad\rangle$, $\langle adc\rangle$, $\langle af\rangle$
$\langle b\rangle$	$\langle(\_c)(ac)d(cf)\rangle$, $\langle(\_c)(ae)\rangle$, $\langle(df)cb\rangle$, $\langle c\rangle$	$\langle b\rangle$, $\langle ba\rangle$, $\langle bc\rangle$, $\langle(bc)\rangle$, $\langle(bc)a\rangle$, $\langle bd\rangle$, $\langle bdc\rangle$, $\langle bf\rangle$
$\langle c\rangle$	$\langle(ac)d(cf)\rangle$, $\langle(bc)(ae)\rangle$, $\langle b\rangle$, $\langle bc\rangle$	$\langle c\rangle$, $\langle ca\rangle$, $\langle cb\rangle$, $\langle cc\rangle$
$\langle d\rangle$	$\langle(cf)\rangle$, $\langle c(bc)(ae)\rangle$, $\langle(\_f)cb\rangle$	$\langle d\rangle$, $\langle db\rangle$, $\langle dc\rangle$, $\langle dcb\rangle$
$\langle e\rangle$	$\langle(\_f)(ab)(df)cb\rangle$, $\langle(af)cbc\rangle$	$\langle e\rangle$, $\langle ea\rangle$, $\langle eab\rangle$, $\langle eac\rangle$, $\langle eacb\rangle$, $\langle eb\rangle$, $\langle ebc\rangle$, $\langle ec\rangle$, $\langle ecb\rangle$, $\langle ef\rangle$, $\langle efb\rangle$, $\langle efc\rangle$, $\langle efcb\rangle$.
$\langle f\rangle$	$\langle(ab)(df)cb\rangle$, $\langle cbc\rangle$	$\langle f\rangle$, $\langle fb\rangle$, $\langle fbc\rangle$, $\langle fc\rangle$, $\langle fcb\rangle$

Table: Projected databases and sequential patterns

2. Partition the search space. The complete set of sequential patterns can be partitioned into the following six subsets according to the six prefixes: (1) the ones with prefix $\langle a\rangle$, (2) the ones with prefix $\langle b\rangle$, ..., and (6) the ones with prefix $\langle f\rangle$.

3. Find subsets of sequential patterns. The subsets of sequential patterns mentioned in step 2 can be mined by constructing corresponding projected databases and mining each recursively. The projected databases, as well as the sequential patterns found in them, are listed in table, while the mining process is explained as follows:

   a) Find sequential patterns with prefix $\langle a\rangle$ Only the sequences containing $\langle a\rangle$ should be collected. Moreover, in a sequence containing $\langle a\rangle$, only the subsequence prefixed with the first occurrence of $\langle a\rangle$ should be considered. For example, in sequence $\langle(ef)(ab)(df)cb\rangle$ only the subsequence $\langle(\_b)(df)cb\rangle$ should be considered for mining sequential patterns prefixed with $\langle a\rangle$ Notice that $(\_b)$ means that the last event in the prefix, which is a together with b, form one event.

   The sequences in S containing $\langle a\rangle$ are projected with respect to $\langle a\rangle$ to form the $\langle a\rangle$- *projected database*, which consists of four suffix sequences: $\langle(abc)(ac)d(cf)\rangle$ $\langle(\_b)c(bc)(ae)\rangle$,$\langle(\_b)(df)cb\rangle$,and$\langle(_f)cbc\rangle$. By scanning the $\langle a\rangle$- projected database once, its locally frequent items are a :2 b : 4, b : 2, c : 4, d : 2, *and* f : 2.

Thus all the length-2 sequential patterns prefixed with $\langle a\rangle$ are found, and they are: $\langle aa\rangle:2, \langle ab\rangle:4, \langle(ab)\rangle:2, \langle ac\rangle:4, \langle ad\rangle:2, \text{and} \langle ad\rangle:2$.

Recursively, all sequential patterns with prefix $\langle a\rangle$ can be partitioned into six subsets:

(1) Those prefixed with $\langle aa\rangle$,

(2) Those with $\langle ab\rangle$, and finally (6) those with $\langle af\rangle$ These subsets can be mined by constructing respective projected databases and mining each recursively as follows:

- The $\langle aa\rangle$-projected database consists of two nonempty (suffix) subsequences prefixed with $\{\langle(\_bc)(ac)d(cf)\rangle, \{\langle(\_e)\rangle\}\}$ Because there is no hope of generating any frequent subsequence from this projected database, the processing of the $\langle aa\rangle$ -projected database terminates.
- The $\langle ab\rangle$ - projected database consists of three suffix sequences: $\langle(\_c)(ac)d(cf)\rangle$, $\langle(\_c)a\rangle$ and $\langle c\rangle$ Recursively mining the $\langle ab\rangle$ -projected database returns four sequential patterns: $\langle(\_c)\rangle, \langle(\_c)a\rangle, \langle a\rangle, \text{and} \langle c\rangle$ (*i.e.*, $\langle a(bc)\rangle, \langle a(bc)a\rangle, \langle aba\rangle, \text{and} \langle abc\rangle$ They form the complete set of sequential pat terns prefixed with $\langle ab\rangle$.
- The $\langle(ab)\rangle$ -projected database contains only two sequences: $\langle(\_c)(ac)d(cf)\rangle \text{and} \langle(df)cb\rangle$, which leads to the finding of the following sequential patterns prefixed with $\langle(ab)\rangle: \langle c\rangle, \langle d\rangle, \langle f\rangle, \text{and} \langle dc\rangle$.
- The $\langle ac\rangle - \langle ad\rangle -, \text{and} \langle af\rangle -$ projected databases can be constructed and recursively mined in a similar manner.

b) Find sequential patterns with prefix $\langle b\rangle, \langle c\rangle, \langle d\rangle, \langle e\rangle, \text{and} \langle f\rangle$. respectively. This can be done by constructing the $\langle b\rangle -, \langle c\rangle -, \langle d\rangle -, \langle e\rangle, \text{and} \langle f\rangle -$.-projected databases and mining them respectively. The projected databases as well as the sequential patterns found are also shown in table.

The set of sequential patterns is the collection of patterns found in the above recursive mining process.

The method described above generates no candidate sequences in the mining process. However, it may generate many projected databases, one for each frequent prefix subsequence. Forming a large number of projected databases recursively may become the major cost of the method, if such databases have to be generated physically. An important optimization technique is pseudo-projection, which registers the index (or identifier) of the corresponding sequence and the starting position of the projected suffix in the sequence instead of performing physical projection. That is, a physical projection of a sequence is replaced by registering a sequence identifier and the projected position index point. Pseudo-projection reduces the cost of projection substantially when such projection can be done in main memory. However, it may not be efficient if the pseudo-projection is used for disk-based accessing because random access of disk space is costly. The suggested approach is that if the original sequence database or the projected databases are too big to fit in memory, the physical projection should be applied; however, the execution should be swapped to pseudo-projection once the projected databases can fit in memory. This methodology is adopted in the PrefixSpan implementation.

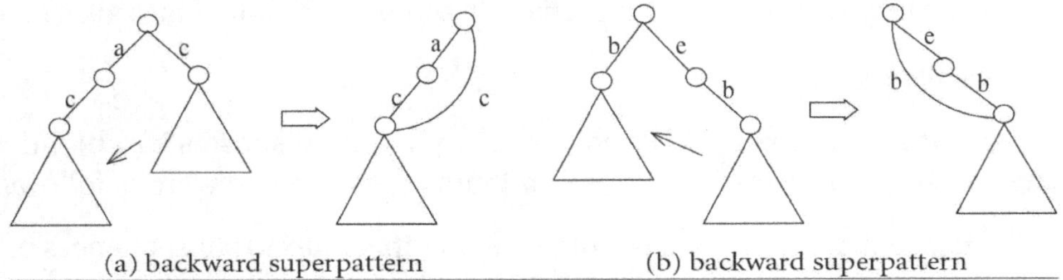

(a) backward superpattern (b) backward superpattern

A backward subpattern and a backward superpattern.

A performance comparison of GSP, SPADE, and PrefixSpan shows that PrefixSpan has the best overall performance. SPADE, although weaker than PrefixSpan in most cases, outperforms GSP. Generating huge candidate sets may consume a tremendous amount of memory, thereby causing candidate generate-and-test algorithms to become very slow. The comparison also found that when there is a large number of frequent subsequences, all three algorithms run slowly. This problem can be partially solved by closed sequential pattern mining.

Mining Closed Sequential Patterns

Because mining the complete set of frequent subsequences can generate a huge number of sequential patterns, an interesting alternative is to mine frequent closed subsequences only, that is, those containing no super sequence with the same support. Mining closed sequential patterns can produce a significantly less number of sequences than the full set of sequential patterns. Note that the full set of frequent subsequences, together with their supports, can easily be derived from the closed subsequences. Thus, closed subsequences have the same expressive power as the corresponding full set of subsequences. Because of their compactness, they may also be quicker to find.

CloSpan is an efficient closed sequential pattern mining method. The method is based on a property of sequence databases, called equivalence of projected databases, stated as follows: Two projected sequence databases $S|_\alpha = S|_\beta$, $\alpha \subseteq \beta$ (*i.e.,α is a subsequence of* β), are equivalent if and only if the total number of items in $S|_\alpha$ is equal to the total number of items in $S|\beta$.

Based on this property, CloSpan can prune the nonclosed sequences from further consideration during the mining process. That is, whenever we find two prefix-based projected databases that are exactly the same, we can stop growing one of them. This can be used to prune backward subpatterns and backward superpatterns.

Mining Sequence Patterns in Transactional Databases

After such pruning and mining, a post processing step is still required in order to delete non closed sequential patterns that may exist in the derived set. A later algorithm called BIDE (which performs a bidirectional search) can further optimize this process to avoid such additional checking

Empirical results show that CloSpan often derives a much smaller set of sequential patterns in a shorter time than PrefixSpan, which mines the complete set of sequential patterns.

Mining Multidimensional and Multilevel Sequential Patterns

Sequence identifiers (representing individual customers, for example) and sequence items (such as products bought) are often associated with additional pieces of information. Sequential pattern mining should take advantage of such additional information to discover interesting patterns in multidimensional, multilevel information space. Take customer shopping transactions, for instance. In a sequence database for such data, the additional information associated with sequence IDs could include customer age, address, group, and profession. Information associated with items could include item category, brand, model type, model number, place manufactured, and manufacture date. Mining multidimensional, multilevel sequential patterns is the discovery of interesting patterns in such a broad dimensional space, at different levels of detail.

- Example: Multidimensional, multilevel sequential patters

The discovery that "Retired customers who purchase a digital camera are likely to purchase a color printer within a month" and that "Young adults who purchase a laptop are likely to buy a flash drive within two weeks" are examples of multidimensional, multilevel sequential patterns. By grouping customers into "retired customers" and "young adults" according to the values in the age dimension, and by generalizing items to, say, "digital camera" rather than a specific model, the patterns mined here are associated with additional dimensions and are at a higher level of granularity.

"Can a typical sequential pattern algorithm such as PrefixSpan be extended to efficiently mine multidimensional, multilevel sequential patterns?" One suggested modification is to associate the multidimensional, multilevel information with the sequence ID and item ID, respectively, which the mining method can take into consideration when finding frequent subsequences. For example, (Chicago, middle aged, business) can be associated with sequence_ID_1002 (for a given customer), whereas (Digital camera, Canon, Supershot, SD400, Japan, 2005) can be associated with item_ID_543005 in the sequence. A sequential pattern mining algorithm will use such information in the mining process to find sequential patterns associated with multidimensional, multilevel information.

Constraint-Based Mining of Sequential Patterns

Mining that is performed without user- or expert-specified constraints may generate numerous patterns that are of no interest. Such unfocused mining can reduce both the efficiency and usability of frequent-pattern mining. Thus, we promote constraint-based mining, which incorporates user-specified constraints to reduce the search space and derive only patterns that are of interest to the user.

Constraints can be expressed in many forms. They may specify desired relationships between attributes, attribute values, or aggregates within the resulting patterns mined. Regular expressions can also be used as constraints in the form of "pattern templates," which specify the desired form of the patterns to be mined. The general concepts introduced for constraint-based frequent pattern mining apply to constraint-based sequential pattern mining as well. The key idea to note is that these kinds of constraints can be used during the mining process to confine the search space, thereby improving (1) the efficiency of the mining and (2) the interestingness of the resulting patterns found. This idea is also referred to as "pushing the constraints deep into the mining process."

We now examine some typical examples of constraints for sequential pattern mining. First, constraints can be related to the duration T, of a sequence. The duration may be the maximal or minimal length of the sequence in the database, or a user-specified duration related to time, such as the year 2005. Sequential pattern mining can then be confined to the data within the specified duration, T.

Constraints relating to the maximal or minimal length (duration) can be treated as antimonotonic or monotonic constraints, respectively. For example, the constraint $T \leq 10$ is antimonotonic since, if a sequence does not satisfy this constraint, then neither will any of its super sequences (which are, obviously, longer). The constraint $T > 10$ is monotonic. This means that if a sequence satisfies the constraint, then all of its super sequences will also satisfy the constraint. We have already seen several examples in this chapter of how antimonotonic constraints (such as those involving minimum support) can be pushed deep into the mining process to prune the search space. Monotonic constraints can be used in a way similar to its frequent-pattern counterpart as well.

Constraints related to a specific duration, such as a particular year, are considered succinct constraints. A constraint is succinct if we can enumerate all and only those sequences that are guaranteed to satisfy the constraint, even before support counting begins. Suppose, here, $T \equiv 2005$. By selecting the data for which $year \equiv 2005$, we can enumerate all of the sequences guaranteed to satisfy the constraint before mining begins. In other words, we don't need to generate and test. Thus, such constraints contribute toward efficiency in that they avoid the substantial overhead of the generate-and-test paradigm.

Durations may also be defined as being related to sets of partitioned sequences, such as every year, or every month after stock dips, or every two weeks before and after an earthquake. In such cases, periodic patterns can be discovered.

Second, the constraint may be related to an event folding window, w. A set of events occurring within a specified period can be viewed as occurring together. If w is set to be as long as the duration, T, it finds time-insensitive frequent patterns—these are essentially frequent patterns, such as "In 1999, customers who bought a PC bought a digital camera as well" (i.e., without bothering about which items were bought first). If w is set to 0 (i.e., no event sequence folding), sequential patterns are found where each event occurs at a distinct time instant, such as "A customer who bought a PC and then a digital camera is likely to buy an SD memory chip in a month. If w is set to be something in between (e.g., for transactions occurring within the same month or within a sliding window of 24 hours), then these transactions are considered as occurring within the same period, and such sequences are "folded" in the analysis Third, a desired (time) gap between events in the discovered patterns may be specified as a constraint. Possible cases are:

(1) $gap = 0$ (no gap is allowed), which is to find strictly consecutive sequential patterns like $a_{i-1}a_ia_{i+1}$. For example, if the event folding window is set to a week, this will find frequent patterns occurring in consecutive weeks;

(2) $min\_gap \leq gap \leq max\_gap$ which is to find patterns that are separated by at least min_gap but at most min_gap such as "If a person rents movie A it is likely she will rent movie B within 30 days" implies s $gap \leq 30$ (days); and

(3) $gap = c\ 6 \neq 0$ which is to find patterns with an exact gap, c.

It is straightforward to push gap constraints into the sequential pattern mining process. With minor modifications to the mining process, it can handle constraints with approximate gaps as well.

Finally, a user can specify constraints on the kinds of sequential patterns by providing "pattern templates" in the form of serial episodes and parallel episodes using regular expressions. A serial episode is a set of events that occurs in a total order, whereas a parallel episode is a set of events whose occurrence ordering is trivial. Consider the following example.

- Example: Specifying serial episodes and parallel episodes with regular expressions

  Let the notation $(E,\ t)$ represent event type E at time tt. Consider the data $(A,\ 1)$, $(C,\ 2)$, and $(B,\ 5)$ with an event folding window width of $w = 2$ where the serial episode $A \rightarrow B$ and the parallel episode $A\ \&\ C$ both occur in the data. The user can specify constraints in the form of a regular expression, such as $(A|B)C\ *\ (D|E)$ which indicates that the user would like to find patterns where event A and B first occur (but they are parallel in that their relative ordering is unimportant), followed by one or a set of events C followed by the events D and E E (where D can occur either before or after E). Other events can occur in between those specified in the regular expression.

  A regular expression constraint may antimonotonic nor monotonic. In such cases, we cannot use it to prune the search space in the same ways as described above. However, by modifying the PrefixSpan-based pattern-growth approach, such constraints can be handled elegantly. Let's examine one such example.

- Example: Constraint-based sequential pattern mining with a regular expression constraint

  Suppose that our task is to mine sequential patterns, again using the sequence database, S , of table. This time, however, we are particularly interested in patterns that match the regular expression constraint, $C = \langle a * \{bb|(bc)d|dd\}\rangle$ with minimum support. Such a regular expression constraint is neither antimonotonic, nor monotonic, nor succinct. Therefore, it cannot be pushed deep into the mining process. Nonetheless, this constraint can easily be integrated with the pattern-growth mining process as follows.

  First, only the $\langle a\rangle$ -projected database, $S|_{\langle a\rangle}$ needs to be mined since the regular expression constraint C starts with a Retain only the sequences in $S|_{\langle a\rangle}$ that contain items within the set $\{b,\ c,\ d\}$. Second, the remaining mining can proceed from the suffix. This is essentially the Suffix-Span algorithm, which is symmetric to PrefixSpan in that it grows suffixes from the end of the sequence forward. The growth should match the suffix as the constraint, $\langle\{bb\,|\,(bc)d\,|\,dd\}\rangle$ For the projected databases that match these suffixes, we can grow sequential patterns either in prefix- or suffix-expansion manner to find all of the remaining sequential patterns.

Data Dredging

Data dredging, also called as data snooping or data fishing, refers to the practice of misusing data mining techniques to show misleading scientific 'research'.

Data dredging is usually followed by the researcher who wants to try and 'prove' a point of view that might not hold or might not be shown in by the actual data. There are a number of reasons for data snooping and it is a matter of grave concern as it uses statistical principles for the purpose of drawing misleading and false conclusions.

The Way Data Snooping Works is as Follows

Suppose there is a given data set and there are a huge number of hypotheses about this data set. If the data is totally random, then say all the hypotheses are actually false. However, owing to the sheer number of hypotheses on a limited data set, it is possible to see some very highly correlated data that are statistically significant. In such cases, data dredging is said to have taken place. Industries that are heavy on data mining are many times involved in data dredging

For example, a drug company might spend millions of dollars on a drug but it may not show the kind of results that were initially expected. However, it needs to market the drug in order to make profits from it. Therefore the company uses data snooping to project claims that are not actually true, even though the data confirms the claim. This is done by taking a representative sample and collecting huge number of parameters related to the test subjects, so that the drug can be claimed and correlated to the problem in some form or the other.

Data fishing can also be done by narrowing down the sample size to include those results that bear out the intended hypothesis. Thus the drug might be tested on 1000 patients and the results might not show a statistically significant positive result for a given problem. However, by narrowing down the study to 500 people and using a selection bias towards those who showed favorable results by using the drug, the company can claim something that is not actually true.

If there is no effect between variables and your confidence level is at .05 (5%), 1 of 20 tests will show that there is an effect even though this is not true, due to random error.

However, most data dredging is intentional. Many times, researchers are simply misled by the apparent correlations that they see. This happens most frequently when the researchers themselves are not sure what exactly they are looking for. Therefore it is important to form a hypothesis before starting and conducting the experiment in order to prevent any accidental cases of data dredging.

If not, the researchers might stumble upon some correlation that doesn't actually exist but shows strongly in their data. Thus researchers working in data mining need to be aware of this as it can be a serious mislead and divert valuable resources to some claims that are not really true.

Affinity Analysis

Association Rule Mining is a powerful tool in Data Mining. In large databases, it is used to identifying correlation or pattern between objects. Market basket analysis is one of the ways to derive associations by examining the buying habits of the customers in their baskets. Market Basket Analysis is a mathematical modeling technique based upon the theory that if you buy a certain group of items, you are likely to buy another group of items. It is used to analyze the customer purchasing behavior and helps in increasing the sales and maintain inventory by focusing on the point of sale transaction data.

Affinity analysis and association rule learning encompasses a broad set of analytics techniques aimed at uncovering the associations and connections between specific objects. These might be visitors to a website such as customers or audience, products in a store, or content items on a media site. Of this market basket analysis is perhaps the most famous example. Market Basket Analysis(MBA) uncovers associations between products by looking for combinations of products that frequently co-occur in transactions. For example, may be people who buy flour and casting sugar, also tend to buy eggs because a high proportion of them are planning on baking a cake.

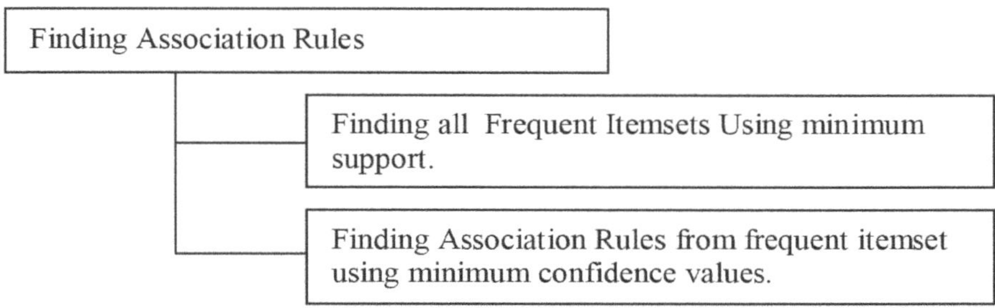

A retailer can use this information to inform:

- Store layout, which put products that co-occur together close to one another, to improve the customer shopping experience.
- Marketing such as target customers who buy flour with offers on eggs, to encourage them to spend more on their shopping basket.
- Online retailers and publishers can use this type of analysis to:
- Inform the placement of content items on their media sites, or products in their catalogue.
- Drive recommendation engines like Amazon's customers who bought this product also bought these products.
- Deliver targeted marketing e.g. emailing customers who bought products specific products with other products and offers on those products that are likely to be interesting to them.

A. Market Basket Analysis

Market basket analysis explains the combinations of products that frequently co-occur in transactions. For example, people who buy bread and eggs, also tend to buy butter as many of them are planning to make an omelette. Marketing team should target customers who buy bread and eggs with offers on butter, to encourage them to spend more on their shopping basket. It is also known as "Affinity Analysis" or "Association Rule Mining".

B. Basics of Market Basket Analysis

For example, In a retail shop 400 customers had visited in last month to buy products. It was observed that out of 400 customers, 200 of them bought Product A, 160 of them bought Product B and 100 of them buy both Product A and Product B; we can say 50%(200 out of 400) of the customer buy Product A, 40%(160 out of 400) customers buy Product B and 25% (100 out of 400) buy Product A and B. some terminologies to be discussed,

1. Items (Products)

   Items are the objects that we are identifying associations between. For an online retailer, each item is a product in the shop. A group of items is an item sets(set of products.)

2. Support

   The support of a product or set of products is the fraction of transactions in our data set that contain that product or set of products.

   In our example,

   - Support(Product A)=50%
   - Support(Product B)=40%
   - Support(Product A and B)=25%

3. Confidence

   Confidence is a conditional probability that customer buy product A will also buy product B. Out of 200 customers who bought Product A, 100 bought Product B too.

   Confidence (Product A, Product B) = 100/200=50%

   It implies if someone buys product A, they are 50% likely to buy Product B too. Confidence (A==>B)=Support(A and B)/Support (A)

4. Lift

   If someone buys product A, what % of chance of buying product B would increase. A lift greater than 1 indicates that the presence of A has increased the probability that the product B will occur on this transaction. A lift smaller than 1 indicates that the presence of A has decreased the probability that the product B will occur on this transaction.

   Lift (A==>B)= Confidence(A==>B)/Support(B)

% increase of chance of buying other product(s)=(Lift-1)*100

A lift value of 1.25 implies that chance of buying product B(on the right hand side) would increase by 25%.

5. Desired outcome

In market basket analysis, we pick rules with a lift of more than one because the presence of one product increases the probability of the other product(s) on the same transaction. Rules with higher confidence are ones where the probability of an item appearing on the RHS is high given the presence of the items on the LHS.

The formulas to calculate them are:

Support(A=>B)=P(AUB

Confidence(A=>B) = P(B|A)

= P(AUB)/P(A)

Lift(A=>B)=Confidence(A=>B)/P(B)

= P(AUB)/P(A)P(B)

Where P(A) is the percentage(or Probability) of cases containing A.

In this proposed system, we analyzed the transactional dataset with summarized information on buying status according to item details of ID, Products, Quality, Status. To make it suitable for association rule mining, we reconstruct the raw data as new raw, where each row represents a product.

Example of Affinity Analysis with Code

- Assume there are 100 customers.
- 10 of them bought milk, 8 bought butter and 6 bought both of them.
- Bought milk => bought butter.
- Support = P(Milk & Butter) = 6/100 = 0.06.
- Confidence = support/P(Butter) = 0.06/0.08 = 0.75.
- Lift = confidence/P(Milk) = 0.75/0.10 = 7.5.

What Time Do People Often Purchase Online?

In order to find the answer to this question, we need to extract "hour" from the time column.

```
retail$Time <- as.factor(retail$Time)

a <- hms(as.character(retail$Time))

retail$Time = hour(a)
```

```
retail %>%
  ggplot(aes(x=Time)) +
  geom_histogram(stat="count",fill="indianred")
```

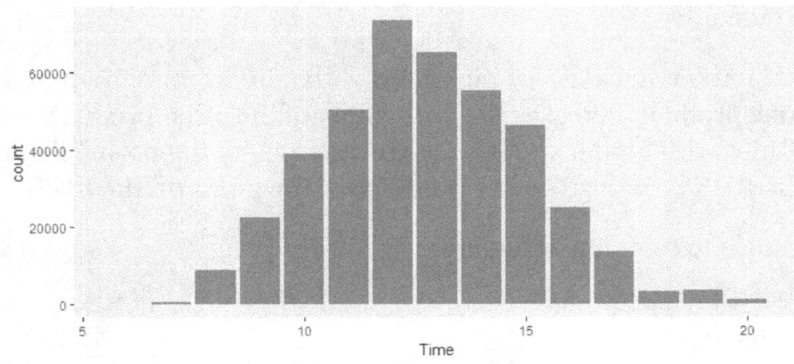

Figure: Shopping time distribution

There is a clear bias between the hour of day and order volume. Most orders happened between 10:00–15:00.

How Many Items Each Customer Buy?

```
detach("package:plyr", unload=TRUE)

retail %>%
  group_by(InvoiceNo) %>%
  summarize(n_items = mean(Quantity)) %>%
  ggplot(aes(x=n_items))+
  geom_histogram(fill="indianred", bins = 100000) +
  geom_rug()+
  coord_cartesian(xlim=c(0,80))
```

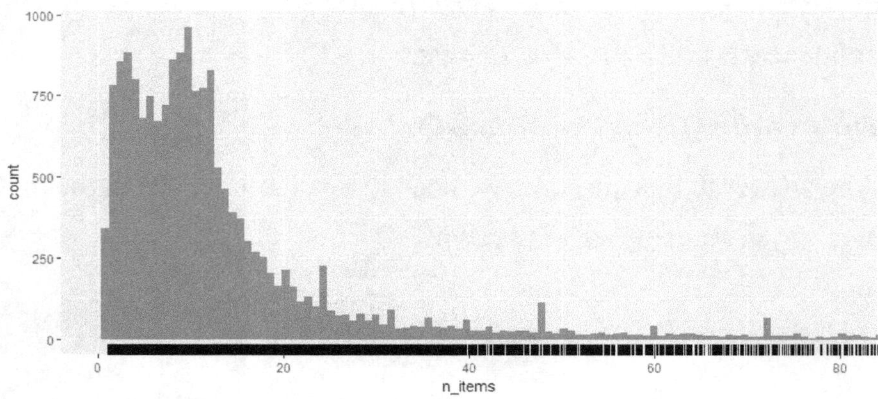

Figure: Number of items per invoice distribution

People mostly purchased less than 10 items (less than 10 items in each invoice).

Top 10 best sellers

```
tmp <- retail %>%
  group_by(StockCode, Description) %>%
  summarize(count = n()) %>%
  arrange(desc(count))
tmp <- head(tmp, n=10)
tmp

tmp %>%
  ggplot(aes(x=reorder(Description,count), y=count))+
  geom_bar(stat="identity",fill="indian red")+
  coord_flip()
```

```
> tmp
# A tibble: 10 x 3
# Groups:   StockCode [10]
   StockCode                        Description count
       <chr>                             <fctr> <int>
 1    85123A WHITE HANGING HEART T-LIGHT HOLDER  2070
 2     22423           REGENCY CAKESTAND 3 TIER  1905
 3    85099B            JUMBO BAG RED RETROSPOT  1662
 4     84879      ASSORTED COLOUR BIRD ORNAMENT  1418
 5     47566                      PARTY BUNTING  1416
 6     20725            LUNCH BAG RED RETROSPOT  1358
 7     22720  SET OF 3 CAKE TINS PANTRY DESIGN   1232
 8      POST                            POSTAGE  1196
 9     20727            LUNCH BAG  BLACK SKULL.  1126
10     21212    PACK OF 72 RETROSPOT CAKE CASES  1080
>
```

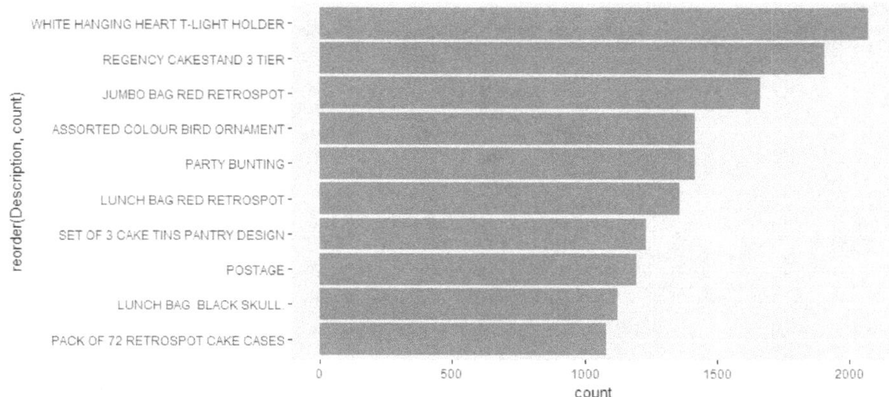

Figure: Top 10 best sellers

Association Rules for Online Retailer

Before using any rule mining algorithm, we need to transform the data from the data frame format, into transactions such that we have all the items bought together in one row. For example, this is the format we need:

	1..Item1	Item2	Item3	Item4
1	Road-250	Road Bottle Cage		
2	Touring-2000	Sport-100		
3	Mountain-200	Mountain Bottle Cage	Water Bottle	
4	Road-250	HL Road Tire	Road Tire Tube	All-Purpose E
5	Road-250	Road Bottle Cage	Water Bottle	Sport-100
6	Road-250	Road Tire Tube	HL Road Tire	Sport-100
7	Road-350-W	Long-Sleeve Logo Jersey		

```
retail_sorted <- retail[order(retail$CustomerID),]
library(plyr)
itemList <- ddply(retail,c("CustomerID","Date"),
                        function(df1)paste(df1$Description,
                        collapse = ","))
```

The function ddply() accepts a data frame, splits it into pieces based on one or more factors, computes on the pieces, and then returns the results as a data frame. We use "," to separate different items.

We only need item transactions, so remove customerID and Date columns.

```
itemList$CustomerID <- NULL
itemList$Date <- NULL
colnames(itemList) <- c("items")
```

Write the data fram to a csv file and check whether our transaction format is correct.

```
write.csv(itemList,"market_basket.csv", quote = FALSE, row.names = TRUE)
```

	A	B	C	D	E	F	G	H	I	J	K	L	M	N	O	P	Q	R	S	T	U
1	MEDIUM C	MEDIUM CERAMIC TOP STORAGE JAR																			
2	BLACK CA	AIRLINE B	COLOUR G	MINI PAIN	CLEAR DR	PINK DRA	GREEN DR	RED DRAW	PURPLE DI	BLUE DRA	ALARM CL	ALARM CL	ALARM CL	ALARM CL	ALARM CL	FOUR HOO	BLACK GR	BATHROO	LARGE HE	BOX OF 6	BLUE
3	PINK NEW	BLUE NEW	BLACK CA	WOODLAN	AIRLINE B	AIRLINE B	SANDWIC	ALARM CL	ALARM CL	ALARM CL	ALARM CL	ALARM CL	SMALL HE	72 SWEETI	60 TEATIM	PACK OF 6	PACK OF 6	TEA TIME	RED RETRO	RED RETRO	SET/2
4	AIRLINE B	AIRLINE B	AIRLINE B	AIRLINE B	RED RETR	ICE CREAM	VINTAGE	HOLIDAY F	TREASURE	WATERIN	RED DRAW	LARGE HE	SMALL HE	PACK OF 6	RED RETR	REGENCY	ROSES RE	RED TOAD	MINI PAIN	3D SHEET	3D SH
5	RABBIT NI	REGENCY	REGENCY	REGENCY	REGENCY	REGENCY	REGENCY	REGENCY	AIRLINE B	AIRLINE B	VICTORIA	NAMASTE	TRIPLE HO	SMALL HE	3D DOG PI	FEATHER	COAL BLA	ALARM CL	ALARM CLOCK BAKELIKE CH		
6	SET OF 60	SET 40 HE	AIRLINE B	AIRLINE B	AIRLINE B	AIRLINE B	AIRLINE B	WOODLAN	WOODLAN	ALARM CL	TRIPLE HO	SINGLE AN	TEA TIME	72 SWEETI	60 TEATIM	PACK OF 6	REGENCY	REGENCY	3D DOG PI	REVOLVER	VINTA
7	MINI LIGH	PINK GOO	MADRAS	AIRLINE B	AIRLINE B	AIRLINE B	AIRLINE B	BIRDCAGE	CHRISTMA	REGENCY	REGENCY	TEA TIME	TEA TIME	TEA TIME	PINK REGE	GREEN RE	3D DOG PI	RABBIT NI	RED TOAD	TREASURE	VINTA
8	CLASSIC C	BICYCLE P	BOOM BO	PINK NEW	RED TOAD	RABBIT NI	WOODLAN	PINK GOO	CHRISTMA	MINI PLAY	MINI PLAYING CARDS DOLLY GIRL										
9	72 SWEETI	60 CAKE C	60 TEATIM	60 TEATIM	PACK OF 7	PACK OF 7	PACK OF 1	PACK OF 1	PACK OF 1	SWEETIES	SET OF 72	SET OF 72	60 CAKE C	60 CAKE C	PACK OF 6	PACK OF 6	POSTAGE				
10	PACK OF 1	PACK OF 1	MULTI HE	PACK OF 1	PACK OF 1	POSTAGE															
11	DOUGHNU	ICE CREAM	ICE CREAM	SET OF 9 B	POSTAGE																
12	DOUGHNU	ICE CREAM	POSTAGE																		
13	PARISIEN	SWEETHE	PINK HEA	GINGHAM	RED HEAR	FOOD CO	LARGE HE	DOORMA	HANGING	BROCANT	PLASTERS	PANTRY M	RECIPE BO	SET OF 3 C	JAM MAKI	SET OF 6 S	PANTRY C	DOORMA	16 PIECE C	SMALL WH	BLACK
14	CHOCOLA	METAL SIG	RETRO MO	RETRO PL	TEA BAG P	PINK/PUR	PLASTERS	PLASTERS	CHOCOLA	RED HARM	4 TRADITI	BATHROO	POSTAGE	UNION JA	UNION JA	BLUE POL	BLUE POLKADOT PASSPORT COVER				
15	WOODEN	PINK DOU	STRAWBE	CERAMIC	WOODEN	REGENCY	DELUXE SE	WELCOME	LOVE BUIL	BATH BUIL	HOME BUI	CAT BOWL	BIG DOUG	DOLLY GIR	LIGHT GARLAND BUTTERFILES PINK						
16	POSTAGE	DELUXE SE	PINK HEA	BAKING SE	VINTAGE	Manual	Manual	Manual	Manual	Manual	Manual										
17	CERAMIC	CERAMIC	BLUE HAR	PINK DOG	PINK HEA	LANTERN	METAL SIGN TAKE IT OR LEAVE IT														
18	PINK HEA	CERAMIC	LANTERN	PINK DOG	CERAMIC	METAL SIG	BLUE HAR	POSTAGE	PINK HEA	CERAMIC	LANTERN	PINK DOG	CERAMIC	METAL SIG	BLUE HARMONICA IN BOX						
19	ANTIQUE	PANTRY M	PANTRY S	SET OF 3 R	SMALL GL	DOORMA	SET OF 4 P	PANTRY W	BAKING SE	IVORY KIT	SET OF 3 C	REGENCY	WOODEN	LIGHT GAR	FAIRY CAK	SPOTTY BU	SET OF 4 E	POSTAGE			
20	OPEN CLO	SET OF 6 S	SET OF 3 R	RED TOAD	CHILDS BR	CHILDS BR	SET OF 3 C	SET OF TE	LOVE BUIL	HOLIDAY F	BATH BUIL	WOODEN	LIGHT GAR	POSTAGE							
21	PETIT TRA	PANTRY R	PANTRY P	WOODLAN	PINK BAB	MINT KITC	SET 12 CO	ZINC HEA	VICTORIA	IVORY KIT	GLASS BO	BLUE STRI	SET 12 CO	CHILDS BR	POSTAGE						

market_basket

Now we have our transaction dataset, and it shows the matrix of items being bought together. We don't actually see how often they are bought together, and we don't see rules either. But we are going to find out.

Let's have a closer look at how many transactions we have and what they are.

```
tr <- read.transactions('market_basket.csv', format = 'basket', sep=',')
tr
summary(tr)
```

```
transactions in sparse format with
 19296 transactions (rows) and
 7881 items (columns)
> summary(tr)
transactions as itemMatrix in sparse format with
 19296 rows (elements/itemsets/transactions) and
 7881 columns (items) and a density of 0.002200461

most frequent items:
WHITE HANGING HEART T-LIGHT HOLDER            REGENCY CAKESTAND 3 TIER
                              1772                                1667
           JUMBO BAG RED RETROSPOT                       PARTY BUNTING
                              1445                                1279
     ASSORTED COLOUR BIRD ORNAMENT                             (Other)
                              1239                              327226

element (itemset/transaction) length distribution:
sizes
   1    2    3    4    5    6    7    8    9   10   11   12   13   14   15   16
2247 1177  848  762  724  660  614  595  584  553  574  507  490  507  503  504
  17   18   19   20   21   22   23   24   25   26   27   28   29   30   31   32
 452  415  474  420  383  309  311  271  236  253  223  204  226  218  174  146
  33   34   35   36   37   38   39   40   41   42   43   44   45   46   47   48
 139  145  130  112  116   88  104   94   91   86   94   60   68   74   68   65
  49   50   51   52   53   54   55   56   57   58   59   60   61   62   63   64
  52   50   60   51   41   53   51   36   23   40   37   30   31   23   22   24
  65   66   67   68   69   70   71   72   73   74   75   76   77   78   79   80
  17   27   32   22   17   25   17   20   18   12   13   19   14    7    9   18
  81   82   83   84   85   86   87   88   89   90   91   92   93   94   95   96
  17   11   10    8   12   10   15    7    7    9    6    7    8    5    4    5
  97   98   99  100  101  102  103  104  105  106  107  108  109  110  111  112
   5    3    3    3    5    5    5    2    3    3    8    5    6    3    3    1
 113  114  115  116  117  118  119  120  121  122  123  125  126  127  131  132
   2    2    1    4    6    3    1    2    1    3    3    4    2    1    1    1
```

We see 19,296 transactions, and this is the number of rows as well. There are 7,881 items—remember items are the product descriptions in our original dataset. Transactions here are the collections or subsets of these 7,881 items.

The summary gives us some useful information:

- Density: The percentage of non-empty cells in the sparse matrix. In another words, the total number of items that are purchased divided by the total number of possible items in that matrix. We can calculate how many items were purchased using density like so: *19296 X 7881 X 0.0022.*
- The most frequent items should be the same as our results in figure.
- Looking at the size of the transactions: 2247 transactions were for just 1 item, 1147 transactions for 2 items, all the way up to the biggest transaction: 1 transaction for 420 items. This indicates that most customers buy a small number of items in each transaction.

```
   Min. 1st Qu.  Median    Mean 3rd Qu.    Max.
   1.00    4.00   12.00   17.34   23.00  420.00

includes extended item information - examples:
                   labels
1                1 HANGER
2      10 COLOUR SPACEBOY PEN
3 12 COLOURED PARTY BALLOONS
>
```

- The distribution of the data is right skewed.

Let's have a look at the item frequency plot, which should be in aligned with figure.

```
itemFrequencyPlot(tr, topN=20, type='absolute')
```

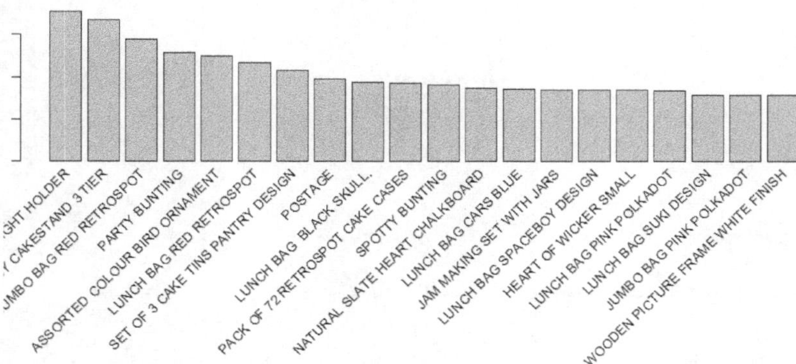

Figure: A bar plot of the support of the 20 most frequent items bought.

Create Some Rules

- We use the Apriori algorithm in Arules library to mine frequent itemsets and association rules. The algorithm employs level-wise search for frequent itemsets.
- We pass supp=0.001 and conf=0.8 to return all the rules that have a support of at least 0.1% and confidence of at least 80%.
- We sort the rules by decreasing confidence.
- Have a look at the summary of the rules.

```
rules <- apriori(tr, parameter = list(supp=0.001, conf=0.8))
rules <- sort(rules, by='confidence', decreasing = TRUE)
summary(rules)
```

```
> summary(rules)
set of 89697 rules

rule length distribution (lhs + rhs):sizes
    2     3     4     5     6     7     8     9    10
  103  3206  9909 26451 31144 14599  3464   700   121

   Min. 1st Qu.  Median    Mean 3rd Qu.    Max.
  2.000   5.000   6.000   5.641   6.000  10.000

summary of quality measures:
    support           confidence          lift              count
 Min.   :0.001036   Min.   :0.8000   Min.   :  8.711   Min.   : 20.00
 1st Qu.:0.001088   1st Qu.:0.8333   1st Qu.: 19.052   1st Qu.: 21.00
 Median :0.001192   Median :0.8750   Median : 24.495   Median : 23.00
 Mean   :0.001382   Mean   :0.8827   Mean   : 49.558   Mean   : 26.67
 3rd Qu.:0.001503   3rd Qu.:0.9231   3rd Qu.: 42.265   3rd Qu.: 29.00
 Max.   :0.018242   Max.   :1.0000   Max.   :622.452   Max.   :352.00

mining info:
 data ntransactions support confidence
   tr         19296   0.001        0.8
>
```

The summary of the rules gives us some very interesting information:

- The number of rules: 89,697.
- The distribution of rules by length: a length of 6 items has the most rules.
- The summary of quality measures: ranges of support, confidence, and lift.

- The information on data mining: total data mined, and the minimum parameters we set earlier.

We have 89,697 rules. I don't want to print them all, so let's inspect the top 10.

```
inspect(rules[1:10])
```

```
> inspect(rules[1:10])
     lhs                          rhs                  support     confidence
[1]  {WOBBLY CHICKEN}          => {DECORATION}         0.001451078 1
[2]  {WOBBLY CHICKEN}          => {METAL}              0.001451078 1
[3]  {DECOUPAGE}               => {GREETING CARD}      0.001191957 1
[4]  {BILLBOARD FONTS DESIGN}  => {WRAP}               0.001502902 1
[5]  {WOBBLY RABBIT}           => {DECORATION}         0.001762023 1
[6]  {WOBBLY RABBIT}           => {METAL}              0.001762023 1
[7]  {BLACK TEA}               => {SUGAR JARS}         0.002332090 1
[8]  {BLACK TEA}               => {COFFEE}             0.002332090 1
[9]  {CHOCOLATE  SPOTS}        => {SWISS ROLL TOWEL}   0.002176617 1
[10] {ART LIGHTS}              => {FUNK MONKEY}        0.002021144 1
     lift      count
[1]  385.92000 28
[2]  385.92000 28
[3]  344.57143 23
[4]  622.45161 29
[5]  385.92000 34
[6]  385.92000 34
[7]  212.04396 45
[8]   61.06329 45
[9]  410.55319 42
[10] 494.76923 39
>
```

The interpretation is pretty straight forward:

- 100% customers who bought "WOBBLY CHICKEN" also bought "DECORATION".
- 100% customers who bought "BLACK TEA" also bought "SUGAR JAR".

And plot these top 10 rules.

```
topRules <- rules[1:10]
plot(topRules)
```

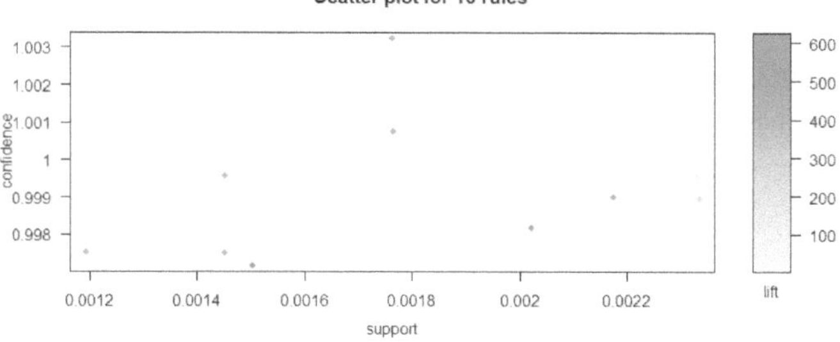


```
plot(topRules, method="graph")
```

Graph for 10 rules

size: support (0.001 - 0.002)
color: lift (61.063 - 622.452)

SWISS ROLL TOWEL
SUGAR JARS
CHOCOLATE SPOTS
WRAP
BLACK TEA
BILLBOARD FONTS DESIGN
COFFEE
FUNK MONKEY
GREETING CARD
DECOUPAGE
ART LIGHTS
DECORATION
WOBBLY RABBIT
WOBBLY CHICKEN
METAL

```
plot(topRules, method = "grouped")
```

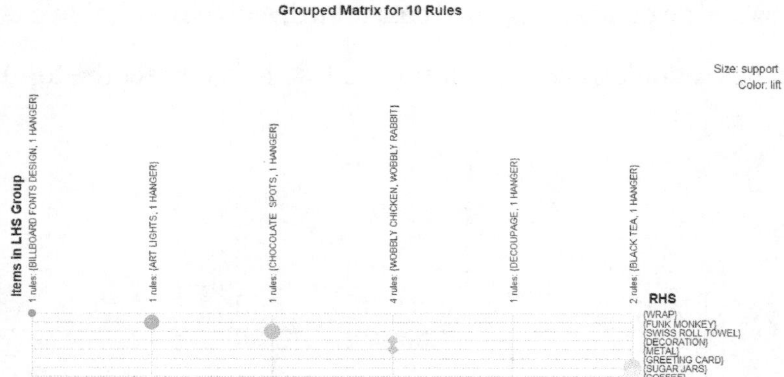

Anomaly Detection

Anomaly detection is a technique used to identify unusual patterns that do not conform to expected behavior, called outliers. It has many applications in business, from intrusion detection (identifying strange patterns in network traffic that could signal a hack) to system health monitoring (spotting a malignant tumor in an MRI scan), and from fraud detection in credit card transactions to fault detection in operating environments.

Anomaly detection can be approached in many ways depending on the nature of data and circumstances. Following is a classification of some of those techniques.

Static Rules Approach

The most simple, and maybe the best approach to start with, is using static rules. The Idea is to identify a list of known anomalies and then write rules to detect those anomalies. Rules identification is done by a domain expert, by using pattern mining techniques, or a by combination of both.

Static rules are used with the hypothesis that anomalies follow the 80/20 rule where most anomalous occurrences belong to few anomaly types. If the hypothesis is true, then we can detect most anomalies by finding few rules that describe those anomalies.

Implementing those rules can be done using one of three following methods:

1. If they are simple and no inference is needed, you can code them using your favorite programming language.
2. If decisions need inference, then you can use a rule-based or expert system (e.g. Drools).
3. If decisions have temporal conditions, you can use a Complex Event Processing System (e.g. WSO2 CEP, Esper).

Although simple, static rules-based systems tend to be brittle and complex. Furthermore, identifying those rules is often a complex and subjective task. Therefore, statistical or machine learning based approach, which automatically learns the general rules, are preferred to static rules.

When We have Training Data

Anomalies are rare under most conditions. Hence, even when training data is available, often there will be few dozen anomalies exists among millions of regular data points. The standard classification methods such as SVM or Random Forest will classify almost all data as normal because doing that will provide a very high accuracy score (e.g. accuracy is 99.9 if anomalies are one in thousand).

Generally, the class imbalance is solved using an ensemble built by resampling data many times. The idea is to first create new datasets by taking all anomalous data points and adding a subset of normal data points (e.g. as 4 times as anomalous data points). Then a classifier is built for each data set using SVM or Random Forest, and those classifiers are combined using ensemble learning. This approach has worked well and produced very good results.

If the data points are auto correlated with each other, then simple classifiers would not work well. We handle those use cases using time series classification techniques or Recurrent Neural networks.

When There is no Training Data

If you do not have training data, still it is possible to do anomaly detection using unsupervised learning and semi-supervised learning. However, after building the model, you will have no idea how well it is doing as you have nothing to test it against. Hence, the results of those methods need to be tested in the field before placing them in the critical path.

No Training Data: Point Anomalies

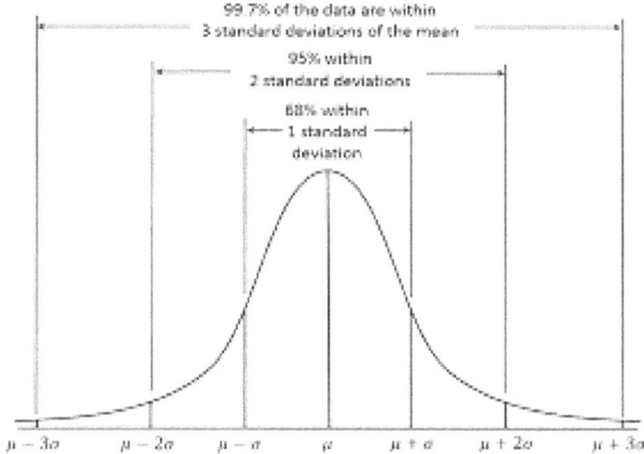

Point anomalies will only have one field in the data set. We use percentiles to detect point anomalies with numeric data and histograms to detect Detecting point anomalies in categorical data. Either case, we find rare data ranges or field values from the data and predict those as anomalies if it happens again. For example, if 99.9 percentile of my transaction value is 800$, one can guess any transaction greater than that value as the potential anomaly. When building models, often we use moving averages instead of point values when possible as they are much more stable to noise.

No Training Data: Univariate Collective Outliers

Time series data are the best examples of collective outliers in a univariate dataset. In this case, anomalies happen because values occur in unexpected order. For example: the third heart beat might be anomalous not because values are out of range, but they happen in a wrong order.

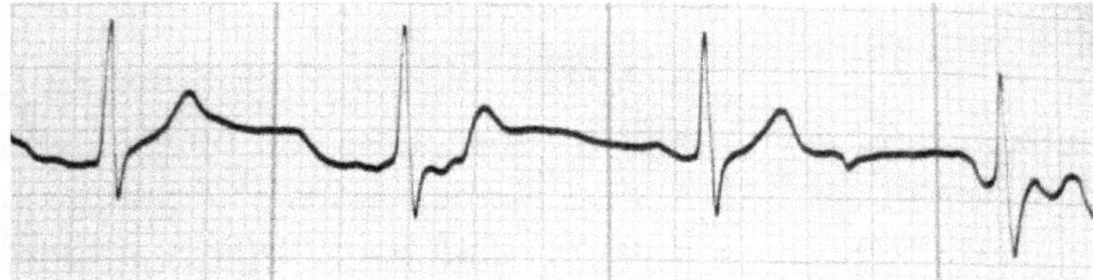

There are three several approaches to handle these use cases.

Solution 1: build a predictor and look for outliers using residues: This is based on the heuristic that the values not explained by the model are anomalies. Hence we can build a model to predict the next value, and then apply percentiles on the error (predicted value – actual value) as described before. The model can be built using regression, time series models, or Recurrent Neural Networks.

Solution 2: Markov chains and Hidden Markov chains can measure the probability of a sequence of events happening. This approach builds a Markov chain for the underline process, and when a sequence of events has happened, we can use the Markov Chain to measure the probability of that sequence occurring and use that to detect any rare sequences.

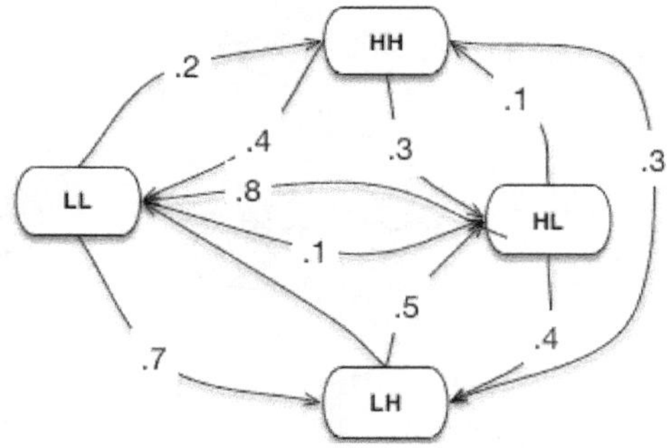

For example, let's consider credit card transactions. To model the transactions using Markov chains, let's represent each transaction using two values: transaction value (L, H) and time since the last transaction (L, H). Since Markov chain's states have to be finite, we will choose two values Low (L), High (H) to represent variable values. Then Markov chains would represent by states LL, LH, HL, HH and each transaction would be a transition from one state to another state. We can build the Markov chain using historical data and use the chain to calculate sequence probabilities. Then, we can find the probability of any new sequence happening and then mark rare sequences as anomalies.

No Training Data: Multivariate Collective Outliers (Unordered)

Here data have multiple reading but does not have an order. For example, vitals collected from many people are such a multi-variate but not ordered dataset. For example, higher temperatures and slow heartbeats might be an anomaly even though both temperature and heartbeats by itself are in a normal range.

Approach 1: Clustering: The underline assumption in the first approach is that if we cluster the data, normal data will belong to clusters while anomalies will not belong to any clusters or belong to small clusters.

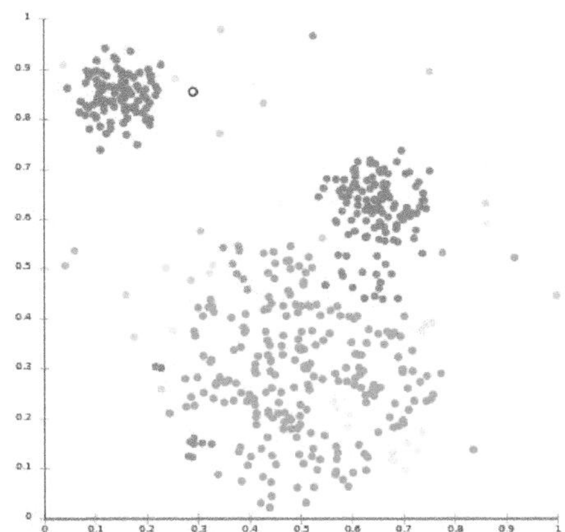

Then to detect anomalies we will cluster the data, and calculate the centroids and density of each cluster found. When we receive a new data point, we calculate the distance from the new data point to known large clusters and if it is too far, then decide it as an anomaly.

Furthermore, we can improve upon the above approach by first manually inspecting ranges of each cluster and labeling each cluster as anomalous or normal and use that while doing anomaly check for a data point.

Approach 2: Nearest neighbor techniques: The underline assumption is new anomalies are closer to known anomalies. This can be implemented by using distance to k-anomalies or using the relative density of other anomalies near the new data point. While calculating the above, with numerical data, we will break the space into hypercubes, and with categorical data, we will break the space into bins using histograms.

No Training Data: Multivariate Collective Outliers (Ordered)

This class is most general and consider ordering as well as value combinations. For example, consider a series of vital readings taken from the same patient. Some reading may be normal in combination but anomalous as combinations happen in wrong order. For example, given a reading that has the blood pressure, temperature, and heart beat frequency, each reading by itself may be normal, but not normal if it oscillates too fast in a short period of time.

Combine Markov Chains and Clustering – This method combines clustering and Markov Chains by first clustering the data, and then using clusters as the states in a Markov Chain and building a Markov Chain. Clustering will capture common value combinations and Markov chains will capture their order.

Other Techniques

There are several other techniques that have been tried out, and following are some of them.

- Information Theory: The main idea is that anomalies have high information content due to irregularities, and this approach tries to find a subset of data points that have highest irregularities.
- Dimension Reduction: The main idea is that after applying dimension reduction, a normal data can be easily expressed as a combination of dimensions while anomalies tend to create complex combinations.
- Graph Analysis: Some processes would have interaction between different players. For example, money transfers would create a dependency graph among participants. Flow analysis of such graphs might show anomalies. On some other use cases such as insurance, stock markets, corporate payment fraud etc., similarities between player's transactions might suggest anomalous behavior.

Building a Simple Detection Solution Using a Low-Pass Filter

Here we will focus on building a simple anomaly-detection package using moving average to identify anomalies in the number of sunspots per month in a sample dataset, which can be downloaded using the following command:

```
wget -c -b http://www-personal.umich.edu/~mejn/cp/data/sunspots.txt
```

The file has 3,143 rows, which contain information about sunspots collected between the years 1749-1984. Sunspots are defined as dark spots on the surface of the sun. The study of sunspots helps scientists understand the sun's properties over a period of time; in particular, its magnetic properties.

Moving Average Using Discrete Linear Convolution

Convolution is a mathematical operation that is performed on two functions to produce a third function. Mathematically, it could be described as the integral of the product of two functions, after one is reversed and shifted: $f*g(t) = \int_{-\infty}^{\infty} f(T)*g(t-T)dT$, where *f(T)* **is an input function containing the quantity of interest (e.g. sunspot count at time** *T*). *g(t —T)* **is the weighting function shifted by an amount** *t*. This way as *t* **changes, different weights are assigned to the input function** *f(T)*. In our case, *f(T)* **represents the sunspot counts at time T.** *g(t —T)* **is the moving average kernel.**

```
from __future__ import division

from itertools import izip, count

import matplotlib.pyplot as plt

from numpy import linspace, loadtxt, ones, convolve

import numpy as np

import pandas as pd
```

```
import collections
from random import randint
from matplotlib import style
style.use('fivethirtyeight')
%matplotlib inline
# 1. Download sunspot dataset and upload the same to dataset directory
#    Load the sunspot dataset as an Array
!mkdir -p dataset
!wget -c -b http://www-personal.umich.edu/~mejn/cp/data/sunspots.txt -P data-
set
data = loadtxt("dataset/sunspots.txt", float)

# 2. View the data as a table
data_as_frame = pd.DataFrame(data, columns=['Months', 'SunSpots'])
data_as_frame.head()
```

	Months	SunSpots
0	0.0	58.0
1	1.0	62.6
2	2.0	70.0
3	3.0	55.7
4	4.0	85.0

```
# 3. Lets define some use-case specific UDF(User Defined Functions)

def moving_average(data, window_size):
    """ Computes moving average using discrete linear convolution of two one
dimensional sequences.
    Args:
    -----
            data (pandas.Series): independent variable
            window_size (int): rolling window size
```

```
    Returns:
    --------
            ndarray of linear convolution

    References:
    ------------
    [1] Wikipedia, "Convolution", http://en.wikipedia.org/wiki/Convolution.
     [2] API Reference: https://docs.scipy.org/doc/numpy/reference/generated/
numpy.convolve.html

    """
    window = np.ones(int(window_size))/float(window_size)
    return np.convolve(data, window, 'same')


def explain_anomalies(y, window_size, sigma=1.0):
  """ Helps in exploring the anamolies using stationary standard deviation
    Args:
    -----
        y (pandas.Series): independent variable
        window_size (int): rolling window size
        sigma (int): value for standard deviation

    Returns:
    --------
        a dict (dict of 'standard_deviation': int, 'anomalies_dict': (index:
value))
        containing information about the points indentified as anomalies

    """
    avg = moving_average(y, window_size).tolist()
    residual = y - avg
```

```
    # Calculate the variation in the distribution of the residual
    std = np.std(residual)
    return {'standard_deviation': round(std, 3),
            'anomalies_dict': collections.OrderedDict([(index, y_i) for
                                                index, y_i, avg_i in
izip(count(), y, avg)
              if (y_i > avg_i + (sigma*std)) | (y_i < avg_i - (sigma*std))])}


def explain_anomalies_rolling_std(y, window_size, sigma=1.0):
    """ Helps in exploring the anamolies using rolling standard deviation
    Args:
    -----
        y (pandas.Series): independent variable
        window_size (int): rolling window size
        sigma (int): value for standard deviation

    Returns:
    --------
        a dict (dict of 'standard_deviation': int, 'anomalies_dict': (index:
value))
        containing information about the points indentified as anomalies
    """
    avg = moving_average(y, window_size)
    avg_list = avg.tolist()
    residual = y - avg
    # Calculate the variation in the distribution of the residual
    testing_std = pd.rolling_std(residual, window_size)
    testing_std_as_df = pd.DataFrame(testing_std)
    rolling_std = testing_std_as_df.replace(np.nan,
                              testing_std_as_df.ix[window_size - 1]).
round(3).iloc[:,0].tolist()
    std = np.std(residual)
```

```
    return {'stationary standard_deviation': round(std, 3),
            'anomalies_dict': collections.OrderedDict([(index, y_i)
                                                        for index, y_i, avg_i,
rs_i in izip(count(),
                                                                              y,
avg_list, rolling_std)
                    if (y_i > avg_i + (sigma * rs_i)) | (y_i < avg_i - (sigma *
rs_i))])}
.


# This function is repsonsible for displaying how the function performs on the
given dataset.
def plot_results(x, y, window_size, sigma_value=1,
                  text_xlabel="X Axis", text_ylabel="Y Axis", applying_roll-
ing_std=False):
    """ Helps in generating the plot and flagging the anamolies.
        Supports both moving and stationary standard deviation. Use the 'ap-
plying_rolling_std' to switch
        between the two.
    Args:
    -----
        x (pandas.Series): dependent variable
        y (pandas.Series): independent variable
        window_size (int): rolling window size
        sigma_value (int): value for standard deviation
        text_xlabel (str): label for annotating the X Axis
        text_ylabel (str): label for annotatin the Y Axis
        applying_rolling_std (boolean): True/False for using rolling vs sta-
tionary standard deviation
    """
    plt.figure(figsize=(15, 8))
    plt.plot(x, y, "k.")
    y_av = moving_average(y, window_size)
    plt.plot(x, y_av, color='green')
    plt.xlim(0, 1000)
    plt.xlabel(text_xlabel)
```

```
    plt.ylabel(text_ylabel)

    # Query for the anomalies and plot the same
    events = {}
    if applying_rolling_std:
           events = explain_anomalies_rolling_std(y, window_size=window_size,
sigma=sigma_value)
    else:
       events = explain_anomalies(y, window_size=window_size, sigma=sigma_val-
ue)

     x_anomaly = np.fromiter(events['anomalies_dict'].iterkeys(), dtype=int,
count=len(events['anomalies_dict']))
   y_anomaly = np.fromiter(events['anomalies_dict'].itervalues(), dtype=float,
                                              count=len(events['anomalies_dict']))
    plt.plot(x_anomaly, y_anomaly, "r*", markersize=12)

    # add grid and lines and enable the plot
    plt.grid(True)
    plt.show()



# 4. Lets play with the functions
x = data_as_frame['Months']
Y = data_as_frame['SunSpots']

# plot the results
plot_results(x, y=Y, window_size=10, text_xlabel="Months", sigma_value=3,
             text_ylabel="No. of Sun spots")
events = explain_anomalies(y, window_size=5, sigma=3)

# Display the anomaly dict
print("Information about the anomalies model:{}".format(events))
```

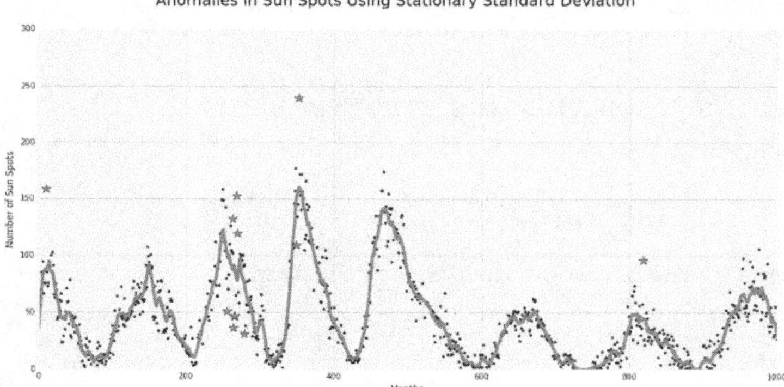

Let's see if the above anomaly detection function could be used for another use case. Let's assume that we generate a random dataset that hypothetically relates to Company A's stock value over a period of time. The x axis represents time in days (since 2013) and the y axis represents the value of the stock in dollars.

```
# Convenience function to add noise
def noise(yval):
    """ Helper function to generate random points """
    np.random.seed(0)
    return 0.2*np.asarray(yval)*np.random.normal(size=len(yval))

# Generate a random dataset
def generate_random_dataset(size_of_array=1000, random_state=0):
    """ Helps in generating a random dataset which has a normal distribution
    Args:
    -----
        size_of_array (int): number of data points
        random_state (int): to initialize a random state

    Returns:
    --------
        a list of data points for dependent variable, pandas.Series of inde-
pendent variable
    """
    np.random.seed(random_state)
    y = np.random.normal(0, 0.5, size_of_array)
```

```
    x = range(0, size_of_array)
    y_new = [y_i + index**((size_of_array - index)/size_of_array) +  noise()
     for index, y_i in izip(count(), y)]
    return x, pd.Series(y_new)


# Lets play
x1, y1 = generate_random_dataset()
# Using stationary standard deviation over a continuous sample replicating
plot_results(x1, y1, window_size=12, title_for_plot="Statinoary Standard De-
viation",
            sigma_value=2, text_xlabel="Time in Days", text_ylabel="Value in $")


# using rolling standard deviation for
x1, y1 = generate_random_dataset()
plot_results(x1, y1, window_size=50, title_for_plot="Using rolling standard
deviation",
               sigma_value=2, text_xlabel="Time in Days", text_ylabel="Value in
$", applying_rolling_std=True)
```

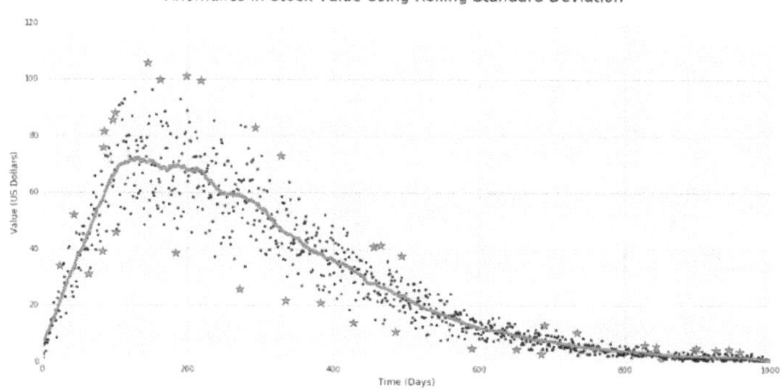

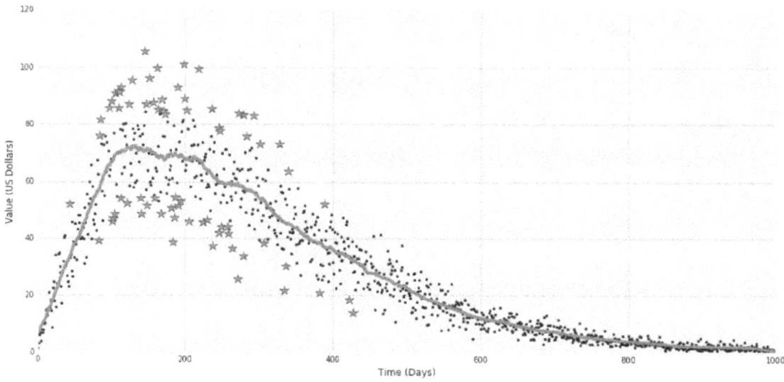

Looks like our anomaly detector is doing a decent job. It is able to detect data points that are 2 sigma away from the fitted curve. Depending on the distribution of a use case in a time-series setting, and the dynamicity of the environment, you may need to use stationary (global) or non-stationary (local) standard deviation to stabilize a model. The mathematical function around the standard deviation could be modified very easily to use a customized formulation.

K-optimal Pattern Discovery

Most data-mining techniques seek a single model that optimizes an objective function with respect to the data. In many real-world applications several models will equally optimize this function. However, they may not all equally satisfy a user's preferences, which will be affected by background knowledge and pragmatic considerations that are infeasible to quantify into an objective function.

Thus, the program may make arbitrary and potentially suboptimal decisions. In contrast, methods for exploratory pattern discovery seek all models that satisfy user defined criteria. This allows the user select between these models, rather than relinquishing control to the program. Association rule discovery is the best known example of this approach. However, it is based on the minimum-support technique, by which patterns are only discovered that occur in the data more than a user-specified number of times. While this approach has proved very effective in many applications, it is subject to a number of limitations.

- It creates an arbitrary discontinuity in the interestingness function by which one more or less case supporting a pattern can transform its assessment from uninteresting to most interesting.
- Sometimes the most interesting patterns are very rare.
- Minimum support may not be relevant to whether a pattern is interesting.
- It is often difficult to find a minimum support level that results in sufficient but not excessive numbers of patterns being discovered.
- It cannot handle dense data.
- It limits the ability to efficiently prune the search space on the basis on constraints that are neither monotone nor anti-monotone with respect to support.

K-optimal pattern discovery is an exploratory technique that finds the k patterns that optimize a user-selected objective function while respecting other user-specified constraints. This strategy avoids the above problems while empowering the user to select between preference criteria and to directly control the number of patterns that are discovered. It also supports statistically sound exploratory pattern discovery.

K-Optimal Rule Discovery (KORD)

K-optimal rule discovery (KORD) follows the idea of generating association rules with respect to a well-defined measure, instead of first finding all frequent itemsets and then generating all possible rules. The algorithm only calculates the top-k rules according to that measure. The size of the right hand side (RHS) of those rules is restricted to one. Futhermore, the KORD implementation generates only non-redundant rules.

The algorithm's search strategy is based on the so-called OPUS search. While the search space of all possible LHSs is traversed in a depth-first manner, the information about all qualified RHSs of the rules for a given LHS is propagated further to the deeper search levels. KORD does not build a real tree search structure; instead it traverses the LHSs in a specific order, which allows the pruning of the search space by simply not visiting those itemsets subsequently. In this way it is possible to use pruning rules which restrict the possible LHSs and RHSs at different rule generation stages.

Prerequisites

- There are no duplicated items in each transaction.
- The input data does not contain null value. The algorithm will issue errors when encountering null values.

KORD

Procedure Generation

```
CALL SYS.AFLLANG_WRAPPER_PROCEDURE_CREATE('AFLPAL', 'KORD', '<schema_name>',
'<procedure_name>', <signature_table
```

The signature table should contain the following records:

Position	Schema Name	Table Type Name	Parameter Type
1	<schema_name>	<TRANSACTION table type>	IN
2	<schema_name>	<PARAMETER table type>	IN
3	<schema_name>	<Rules OUTPUT table type>	OUT
4	<schema_name>	<Antecedent table type>	OUT
5	<schema_name>	<Consequent table type>	OUT

Procedure Calling

```
CALL <schema_name>.<procedure_name>(<transaction_table>, <parameter_table>,
<rules_output_table>, <antecedent_output_table>, <consequent_output_table>)
with overview;
```

The procedure name is the same as specified in the procedure generation.

The input, parameter, and output tables must be of the types specified in the signature table.

Signature

Transaction Table

Table	Column	Column Data Type	Description
Data	1st column	Integer, varchar, or nvarchar	Transaction ID
	2nd column	Integer, varchar, or nvarchar	Item ID

PAL will use its default value.

ame	Data Type	Default Value	Description	Dependency
TOPK	Integer	10	Specifies the number (k) of top rules.	
MAX_ANTECENDENT	Integer	4	Specifies the maximum length of antecedent rules.	
MEASURE_TYPE	Integer	0	Specifies the measure that will be used to define the priority of the rules. 0: Leverage 1: Lift	
IS_USE_EPSILON	Integer	0	Controls whether to use epsilon to punish the length of rules: 0: Does not use epsilon 1: Uses epsilon	
THREAD_NUMBER	Integer	1	Specifies the number of threads.	
MIN_SUPPORT	Double	0.0	Specifies the minimum support.	
MIN_CONFIDENCE	Double	0.0	Specifies the minimum confidence.	
MIN_COVERAGE	Double	The value of MIN_SUP-PORT	Specifies the minimum coverage. Default: T	
MIN_MEASURE	Double	0.0	Specifies the minimum measure value for leverage or lift, dependent on the MEASURE_TYPE setting.	
EPSILON	Double	0.0	Epsilon value.	Only valid when IS_USE_EPSILON is 1.

Output Tables

Table	Column	Column Data Type	Description
Rules	1st column	Integer	ID
	2nd column	Double	Support
	3rd column	Double	Confidence
	4th column	Double	Lift
	5th column	Double	Leverage
	6th column	Double	Measure value
Antecedent	1st column	Integer	ID
	2nd column	Varchar or nvarchar	Antecedent items
Consequent	1st column	Integer	ID
	2nd column	Varchar or nvarchar	Consequent items

Example

Assume that:

- DM_PAL is a schema belonging to USER1; and
- USER1 has been assigned the AFLPM_CREATOR_ERASER_EXECUTE role; and
- USER1 has been assigned the AFL__SYS_AFL_AFLPAL_EXECUTE or AFL__SYS_AFL_AFLPAL_EXECUTE_WITH_GRANT_OPTIONrole.

```
SET SCHEMA DM_PAL;

DROP TYPE PAL_KORD_DATA_T;
CREATE TYPE PAL_KORD_DATA_T AS TABLE(
"CUSTOMER" INTEGER,
"ITEM" VARCHAR(20)
);

DROP TYPE PAL_KORD_RULES_T;
CREATE TYPE PAL_KORD_RULES_T AS TABLE(
"ID" INTEGER,
"SUPPORT" DOUBLE,
"CONFIDENCE" DOUBLE,
"LIFT" DOUBLE,
```

```
"LEVERAGE" DOUBLE,
"MEASURE" DOUBLE
);

DROP TYPE PAL_KORD_ANTE_ITEMS_T;
CREATE TYPE PAL_KORD_ANTE_ITEMS_T AS TABLE(
"ID" INTEGER,
"ANTECEDENT" VARCHAR(20)
);
DROP TYPE PAL_KORD_CONS_ITEMS_T;
CREATE TYPE PAL_KORD_CONS_ITEMS_T AS TABLE(
    "ID" INTEGER,
    "CONSEQUENT" VARCHAR(20)
);

DROP TYPE PAL_CONTROL_T;
CREATE TYPE PAL_CONTROL_T AS TABLE(
    "NAME" VARCHAR(100),
    "INTARGS" INTEGER,
    "DOUBLEARGS" DOUBLE,
    "STRINGARGS" VARCHAR (100)
);

DROP TABLE PAL_KORD_PDATA_TBL;
CREATE COLUMN TABLE PAL_KORD_PDATA_TBL(
    "POSITION" INT,
    "SCHEMA_NAME" NVARCHAR(256),
    "TYPE_NAME" NVARCHAR(256),
    "PARAMETER_TYPE" VARCHAR(7)
);
INSERT INTO PAL_KORD_PDATA_TBL VALUES (1, 'DM_PAL', 'PAL_KORD_DATA_T',
'IN');
INSERT INTO PAL_KORD_PDATA_TBL VALUES (2, 'DM_PAL', 'PAL_CONTROL_T', 'IN');
```

```
INSERT INTO PAL_KORD_PDATA_TBL VALUES (3, 'DM_PAL', 'PAL_KORD_RULES_T',
'OUT');
INSERT INTO PAL_KORD_PDATA_TBL VALUES (4, 'DM_PAL', 'PAL_KORD_ANTE_ITEMS_T',
'OUT');
INSERT INTO PAL_KORD_PDATA_TBL VALUES (5, 'DM_PAL', 'PAL_KORD_CONS_ITEMS_T',
'OUT');

CALL "SYS".AFLLANG_WRAPPER_PROCEDURE_DROP('DM_PAL','PAL_KORD_PROC');
call "SYS".AFLLANG_WRAPPER_PROCEDURE_CREATE('AFLPAL', 'KORD', 'DM_PAL',
'PAL_KORD_PROC', PAL_KORD_PDATA_TBL);

DROP TABLE PAL_KORD_DATA_TBL;
CREATE COLUMN TABLE PAL_KORD_DATA_TBL LIKE PAL_KORD_DATA_T;
INSERT INTO PAL_KORD_DATA_TBL VALUES (2, 'item2');
INSERT INTO PAL_KORD_DATA_TBL VALUES (2, 'item3');
INSERT INTO PAL_KORD_DATA_TBL VALUES (3, 'item1');
INSERT INTO PAL_KORD_DATA_TBL VALUES (3, 'item2');
INSERT INTO PAL_KORD_DATA_TBL VALUES (3, 'item4');
INSERT INTO PAL_KORD_DATA_TBL VALUES (4, 'item1');
INSERT INTO PAL_KORD_DATA_TBL VALUES (4, 'item3');
INSERT INTO PAL_KORD_DATA_TBL VALUES (5, 'item2');
INSERT INTO PAL_KORD_DATA_TBL VALUES (5, 'item3');
INSERT INTO PAL_KORD_DATA_TBL VALUES (6, 'item1');
INSERT INTO PAL_KORD_DATA_TBL VALUES (6, 'item3');
INSERT INTO PAL_KORD_DATA_TBL VALUES (0, 'item1');
INSERT INTO PAL_KORD_DATA_TBL VALUES (0, 'item2');
INSERT INTO PAL_KORD_DATA_TBL VALUES (0, 'item5');
INSERT INTO PAL_KORD_DATA_TBL VALUES (1, 'item2');
INSERT INTO PAL_KORD_DATA_TBL VALUES (1, 'item4');
INSERT INTO PAL_KORD_DATA_TBL VALUES (7, 'item1');
INSERT INTO PAL_KORD_DATA_TBL VALUES (7, 'item2');
INSERT INTO PAL_KORD_DATA_TBL VALUES (7, 'item3');
INSERT INTO PAL_KORD_DATA_TBL VALUES (7, 'item5');
```

```
INSERT INTO PAL_KORD_DATA_TBL VALUES (8, 'item1');
INSERT INTO PAL_KORD_DATA_TBL VALUES (8, 'item2');
INSERT INTO PAL_KORD_DATA_TBL VALUES (8, 'item3');

DROP TABLE #PAL_CONTROL_TBL;
CREATE LOCAL TEMPORARY COLUMN TABLE #PAL_CONTROL_TBL(
    "NAME" VARCHAR(100),
    "INTARGS" INTEGER,
    "DOUBLEARGS" DOUBLE,
    "STRINGARGS" VARCHAR (100)
);
INSERT INTO #PAL_CONTROL_TBL VALUES ('THREAD_NUMBER', 2, null, null);
INSERT INTO #PAL_CONTROL_TBL VALUES ('TOPK', 5, null, null);
INSERT INTO #PAL_CONTROL_TBL VALUES ('MEASURE_TYPE', 1, null, null);
INSERT INTO #PAL_CONTROL_TBL VALUES ('MIN_SUPPORT', null, 0.1, null);
INSERT INTO #PAL_CONTROL_TBL VALUES ('MIN_CONFIDENCE', null, 0.2, null);
INSERT INTO #PAL_CONTROL_TBL VALUES ('IS_USE_EPSILON', 0, null, null);
INSERT INTO #PAL_CONTROL_TBL VALUES ('EPSILON', null, 0.1, null);


DROP TABLE PAL_KORD_RULES_TBL;
CREATE COLUMN TABLE PAL_KORD_RULES_TBL LIKE PAL_KORD_RULES_T;

DROP TABLE PAL_KORD_ANTE_ITEMS_TBL;
CREATE COLUMN TABLE PAL_KORD_ANTE_ITEMS_TBL LIKE PAL_KORD_ANTE_ITEMS_T;

DROP TABLE PAL_KORD_CONS_ITEMS_TBL;
CREATE COLUMN TABLE PAL_KORD_CONS_ITEMS_TBL LIKE PAL_KORD_CONS_ITEMS_T;


CALL "DM_PAL".PAL_KORD_PROC(PAL_KORD_DATA_TBL, #PAL_CONTROL_TBL, PAL_KORD_
RULES_TBL, PAL_KORD_ANTE_ITEMS_TBL, PAL_KORD_CONS_ITEMS_TBL) with OVERVIEW;
```

```
SELECT * FROM PAL_KORD_RULES_TBL ORDER BY "MEASURE" DESC;

SELECT * FROM PAL_KORD_ANTE_ITEMS_TBL;

SELECT * FROM PAL_KORD_CONS_ITEMS_TBL;
```

Expected Result

PAL_KORD_RULES_TBL

ID	SUPPORT	CONFIDENCE	LIFT	LEVERAGE	MEASURE
2	0.22222222222...	0.5	2.25	0.12345679012...	2.25
3	0.22222222222...	1	1.5	0.07407407407...	1.5
1	0.22222222222...	0.3333333333333...	1.5	0.07407407407...	1.5
4	0.22222222222...	0.2857142857142...	1.2857142...	0.04938271604...	1.28571428571...
0	0.22222222222...	0.2857142857142...	1.2857142...	0.04938271604...	1.28571428571...

PAL_KORD_ANTE_ITEMS_TBL

ID	ANTECEDENT
0	item2
1	item1
2	item2
2	item1
3	item5
4	item2

PAL_KORD_CONS_ITEMS_TBL

ID	CONSEQUENT
0	item5
1	item5
2	item5
3	item1
4	item4

References

- Data-mining, adv-database, database-system: ecomputernotes.com, Retrieved 14 April 2018
- Data-dredging: explorable.com, Retrieved 29 May 2018
- A-gentle-introduction-on-market-basket-analysis-association-rules: towardsdatascience.com, Retrieved 17 March 2018
- Anomaly-detection-concepts-and-techniques: iwringer.wordpress.com, Retrieved 28 April 2018
- Python-anomaly-detection: datascience.com, Retrieved 09 July 2018

5

Data Mining Algorithms

Data mining is done with the goal of extracting information from a data set and structuring it comprehensively for future use. It also involves data pre-processing, data management, post-processing of structures, etc. This chapter closely examines the diverse algorithms used in data mining such as GSP algorithm, apriori algorithm, WINEPI, etc.

Alpha Algorithm

α Alpha algorithm or α-algorithm is one of the first Process Mining algorithm that discovers Workflow Nets (in form of Petri Nets) from logs.

The process of (re-)discovering a workflow consists of 3 phases:

- Pre-processing
  - Inferring relations between the transitions
- Processing
  - Execution of the alpha algorithm
- Post-processing

Petri Nets

We use a variant of the classic Petri-net model, namely Place/Transition nets.

P/T-nets: An Place/Transition net, or simply P/T-net, is a tuple (P, T, F) where:

1. P is a finite set of places.
2. T is a finite set of transitions such that $P \cap T = \varnothing$, and
3. $F \subseteq (P \times T) \cup (T \times P)$ is a set of directed arcs, called the flow relation.

A marked P/T-net is a pair (N, s), where $N \quad (P, T, F)$ is a P/T -net and where s is a bag over P denoting the marking of the net. The set of all marked P/T -nets is denoted N .

A marking is a *bag* over the set of places P, i.e., it is a function from P to the natural numbers. We use square brackets for the enumeration of a bag, e.g., $[a^2, b, c^3]$ denotes the bag with two a-s, one b, and three c-s. The sum of two bags $(X + Y)$, the difference $(X - Y)$, the presence of an element in a bag $(a \in X)$, and the notion of subbags $(X \leq Y)$ are defined in a straightforward way and they can handle a mixture of sets and bags.

Let $N = (P, T, F)$ be a P/T-net. Elements of $P \cup T$ are called nodes. A node x is an input node of another node y iff there is a directed arc from x to y (i.e., xFy). Node x is an output node of y *iff* yFx. For any $x \in P \cup T$, $\overset{N}{\bullet} x = \{y \| yFx\}$ and $x \overset{N}{\bullet} = \{y \| xFx\}$ the superscript *N* may be omitted if clear from the context.

Figure shows a P/T-net consisting of 7 places and 6 transitions. Transition A has one input place and two output places. Transition A is an AND-split. Transition D has two input places and one output place. Transition D is an AND-join. The black dot in the input place of A and E represents a token. This token denotes the initial marking. The dynamic behavior of such a marked P/T-net is defined by a firing rule.

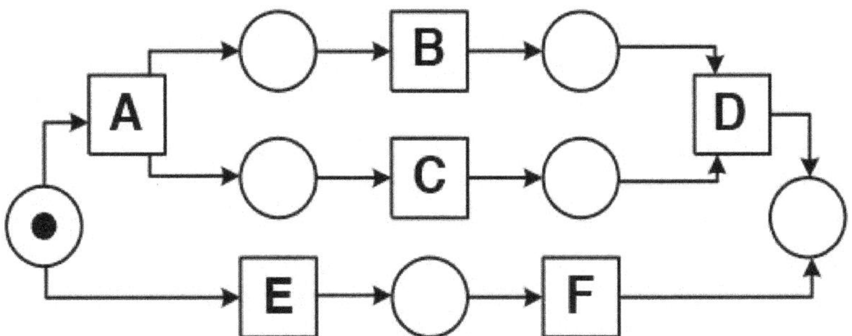

A process model corresponding to the process log

Firing Rule

Let $(N = (P, T, F), s)$ be a marked P/T-net. Transition $t \in T$ is enabled, denoted $(N, s)[t\rangle$, iff $\bullet t \leq s$. The firing rule $-[-\rangle- \subseteq N \times T \times N$ is the smallest relation satisfying for any $(N = (P, T, F), s) \in N$ and any $t \in T$, $(N, s)[t\rangle \Rightarrow (N, s)\ [t\rangle\ (N, s - \bullet t + t \bullet)$.

In the marking shown in figure (i.e., one token in the source place), transitions A and E are enabled. Although both are enabled only one can fire. If transition A fires, a token is removed from its input place and tokens are put in its output places. In the resulting marking, two transitions are enabled: B and C. Note that the firing of B and C are independent.

Reachable Markings

Let (N, s_0) be a marked P/T-net in N. A marking s is reachable from the initial marking s_0 iff there exists a sequence of enabled transitions whose firing leads from s_0 to s. The set of reachable markings of (N, s_0) is denoted $[N, s_0\rangle$.

The marked P/T-net shown in figure has 6 reachable markings. Sometimes it is convenient to know the sequence of transitions that are fired in order to reach some given marking. This paper uses the following notations for sequences. Let A be some alphabet of identifiers. A sequence of length n, for some natural number $n \in \mathbb{N}$, over alphabet A is a function $\sigma : \{0, ..., n - 1\} \rightarrow A$. The sequence of length zero is called the empty sequence and written ε. For the sake of readability, a sequence of positive length is usually written by juxtaposing the function values: For example, a sequence $\sigma = \{(0, a),(1, a),(2, b)\}$, for $a, b \in A$, is written *aab*. The set of all sequences of arbitrary length over alphabet A is written A*.

Firing Sequence

Let (N, s_0) with $N = (P, T, F)$ be a marked P/T net A sequence $\sigma \in T*$ is called a firing sequence of (N, s_0) if and only if, for some natural number $n \in \mathbf{N}$, there exist markings $s_1,...,s_n$ and transitions $t_1,...,t_n \in T$ such that $\sigma = t_1 ...t_n$ and, for all i with $0 \le i < n (N, s_i)[t_{i+1}\rangle$ and $s_{i+1} = s_i - \bullet t_{i+1} + t_{i+1}\bullet$. (Note that n = 0 implies that $\sigma = \varepsilon$ and that ε is a firing sequence of (N, s_0)). Sequence σ is said to be enabled in marking

s_0, denoted $(N, s_0)[\sigma\rangle$. Firing the sequence σ results in a marking s_n, denoted $(N, s_0)[\sigma\rangle (N, s_n)$.

Connectedness

A net N = (P, T, F) is weakly connected, or simply connected, iff, for every two nodes x and y in $P \cup T, x(F \cup F^{-1})^* y$ where R^{-1} is the inverse and $R*$ the reflexive and transitive closure of a relation R. Net N is strongly connected iff, for every two nodes x and y, $xF*y$.

We assume that all nets are weakly connected and have at least two nodes. The P/T-net shown in figure is connected but not strongly connected.

Boundedness, Safeness

A marked net $(N = (P, T, F), s)$ is bounded iff the set of reachable markings $[N, s\rangle$ is finite. It is safe iff, for any $s' \in [N, s\rangle$ and any $p \in P$, $s'(p) \le 1$. Note that safeness implies boundedness.

The marked P/T-net shown in figure is safe (and therefore also bounded) because none of the 6 reachable states puts more than one token in a place.

Dead Transitions, Liveness

Let $(N = (P, T, F), s)$ be a marked P/T-net. A transition $t \in T$ is dead in (N,s) iff there is no reachable marking $s' \in [N, s\rangle$ such that $(N,s')[t\rangle.(N,s)$ is live iff, for every reachable marking $s' \in [N, s\rangle$ and $t \in T$, there is a reachable marking $s'' \in [N, s'\rangle$ such that $(N,s'')[t\rangle$. Note that liveness implies the absence of dead transitions.

None of the transitions in the marked P/T-net shown in figure is dead. However, the marked P/T-net is not live since it is not possible to enable each transition continuously.

Workflow Nets

Most workflow systems offer standard building blocks such as the AND-split, AND-join, OR-split, and OR-join. These are used to model sequential, conditional, parallel and iterative routing (WFMC). Clearly, a Petri net can be used to specify the routing of cases. Tasks are modeled by transitions and causal dependencies are modeled by places and arcs. In fact, a place corresponds to a condition which can be used as pre- and/or post-condition for tasks. An AND-split corresponds to a transition with two or more output places, and an AND-join corresponds to a transition with two or more input places. OR-splits/OR-joins correspond to places with multiple outgoing/ingoing arcs. Given the close relation between tasks and transitions we use the terms interchangeably.

A Petri net which models the control-flow dimension of a workflow, is called a WorkFlow net (WF-net). It should be noted that a WF-net specifies the dynamic behavior of a single case in isolation.

Workflow Nets

Let $N = (P, T, F)$ be a P/T-net and $\bar{t}$ a fresh identifier not in $P \cup T$. N is a workflow net (WF-net) iff:

1. Object creation: P contains an input place i such that $\bullet i = \varnothing$,
2. Object completion: P contains an output place o such that $o\bullet = \varnothing$,
3. Connectedness: is strongly connected, The P/T-net shown in figure is a WF-net. Note that although the net is not strongly connected, the short-circuited net with transition $\bar{t}$ is strongly connected. Even if a net meets all the syntactical requirements stated in Definition 2.8, the corresponding process may exhibit errors such as deadlocks, tasks which can never become active, livelocks, garbage being left in the process after termination, etc. Therefore, we define the following correctness criterion.

Sound

Let $N = (P, T, F)$ be a WF-net with input place I and output place o. N is sound iff:

1. Safeness: $(N, [i])$ is safe,
2. Proper completion: for any marking $s \in [N,[i]\rangle, 0 \in s \textit{ implies } s = [0]$,
3. Option to complete: for any marking $s \in [N,[i]\rangle, [0] \in [N, s\rangle$, and
4. Absence of dead tasks: $(N, [i])$ contains no dead transitions.

The set of all sound WF-nets is denoted W.

The WF-net shown in figure is sound. Soundness can be verified using standard Petri-net-based analysis techniques. In fact soundness corresponds to liveness and safeness of the corresponding short-circuited net. This way efficient algorithms and tools can be applied. An example of a tool tailored towards the analysis of WF-nets is Woflan.

Our process mining research aims at rediscovering WF-nets from event logs. However, not all places in sound WF-nets can be detected. For example places may be implicit which means that they do not affect the behavior of the process. These places remain undetected. Therefore, we limit our investigation to WFnets without implicit places.

Implicit Place

Let $N = (P, T, F)$ be a P/T-net with initial marking s. A place $p \in P$ is called implicit in (N,s) if and only if, for all reachable Markings $s' \in [N, s\rangle$ and transitions $t \in p\bullet$, $s' \geq \bullet t \setminus \{p\} \Rightarrow s' \geq \bullet t$.

Figure contains no implicit places. However, adding a place p connecting transition A and D yields an implicit place. No mining algorithm is able to detect p since the addition of the place does not change the behavior of the net and therefore is not visible in the log.

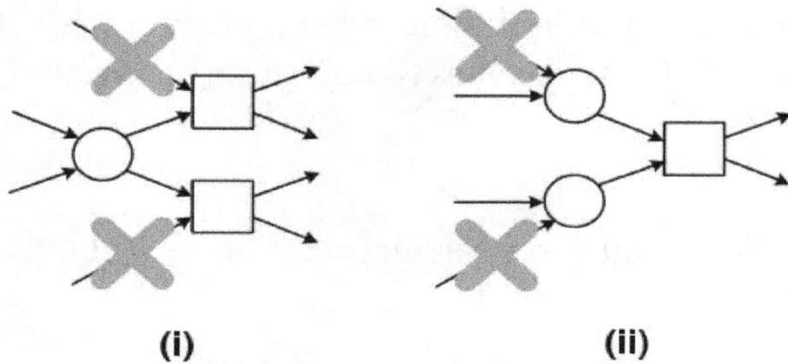

Figure: Constructs not allowed in SWF-nets.

For process mining it is very important that the structure of the WF-net clearly reflects its behavior. Therefore, we also rule out the constructs shown in figure. The left construct illustrates the constraint that choice and synchronization should never meet. If two transitions share an input place, and therefore "fight" for the same token, they should not require synchronization. This means that choices (places with multiple output transitions) should not be mixed with synchronizations. The right-hand construct in figure illustrates the constraint that if there is a synchronization all preceding transitions should have fired, i.e., it is not allowed to have synchronizations directly preceded by an OR-join. WFnets, which satisfy these requirements are named structured workflow nets and are defined as:

SWF-net

A WF-net $N = (P, T, F)$ is an SWF-net (Structured workflow net) if and only if:

1. For all $p \in P$ and $t \in T$ with $(p, t) \in F$: $|p\bullet| > 1$ implies $|\bullet t| = 1$.
2. For all $p \in P$ and $t \in T$ with $(p, t) \in F$: $|\bullet t| > 1$ *implies* $|\bullet p| = 1$.
3. There are no implicit places.

The α^+ - algorithm is based on the α-algorithm, which correctly mines SWF-nets without short loops. In our solution, we first tackle length-two loops and then also length-one loops . While tackling length-two loops only, we do not allow the nets to have length-one loops. That is why we introduce the definition of one-loop-free workflow nets.

One-loop-free workflow nets

Let $N = (P, T, F)$ be a workflow net. *N* is a one-loop-free workflow net if and only if for any $t \in T$, $t \bullet \cap \bullet t = \varnothing$.

The α-Algorithm

Our start point to mine workflows is an event log. A log is a set of traces. Workflow traces and logs are defined as:

Workflow trace, Workflow log

Let T be a set of tasks $\sigma \in T^*$ is a workflow trace and $W \in P(T^*)$ is a workflow log.

From a workflow log, ordering relations between tasks can be inferred. In the case of the α -algorithm, every two tasks in the workflow log must have one of the following four ordering relations: $> w$ (follows), $\rightarrow w$ (causal), $\| w$ (parallel) and $\# w$ (unrelated). These ordering relations are extracted based on local information in the log traces. The ordering relations are defined as:

Log-based Ordering Relations

Let W be a workflow log over T, i.e., $W \in P(T^*)$. Let $a, b \in T$:

- $a >_W b$ and only if there is a trace $\sigma = t_1 t_2 t_3 \ldots t_{n-1}$ and $i \in \{1, \ldots, n-2\}$ such that $\sigma \in W$ and $t_i = a$ and $t_{i+1} = b$,
- $a \rightarrow_W b$ if and only if $a >_W b$ and $b \not>_W a$,
- $a \#_W b$ if and only if $a \not> W b$ and $b \not> W a$, and
- $a \|_W b$ if and only if $a >_W b$ and $b > W a$.

To ensure the workflow log contains the minimal amount of information necessary to mine the workflow, the notion of log completeness is defined as:

Complete Workflow Log

Let $N = (P, T, F)$ be a sound WF-net, i.e., $N \in W$. W is a workflow log of N if and only if $W \in P(T^*)$ and every trace $\sigma \in W$ is a firing sequence of N starting in state [i] and ending in state [o], i.e., $(N, [i])[\sigma\rangle\ (N, [o])$. W is a complete workflow log of N if and only if (1) for any workflow log W' of N: $>W' \subseteq >W$, and (2) for any $t \in T$ there is a $\sigma \in W$ W such that t occurs in σ.

For figure, a possible complete workflow log W is: *abcd, acbd* and *ef.* From this complete log, the following ordering relations are inferred:

- $(follows)$ $a >_W b$, $a >_W c$, $b >_W c$, $b >_W d$, $c >_W b$, $c >_W d$ and $e >_W f$.
- $(causal)$ $a \rightarrow_W b$, $a \rightarrow_W c$, $b \rightarrow_W d$, $c \rightarrow_W d$ and $e \rightarrow_W f$
- $(parallel)$ $b \|_W c$ and $c \|_W b$.

Note that there are no unrelated transitions for the net in figure.

Now we can give the formal definition of the α-algorithm followed by a more intuitive explanation.

Mining Algorithm α

Let W be a workflow log over T. The $\alpha(W)$ is defined as follows.

1. $T_W = \{t \in T \mid \exists_{\sigma \in W} t \in \sigma\}$,
2. $T_I = \{t \in T \mid \exists_{\sigma \in W} t = first(\sigma)\}$,
3. $T_O = \{t \in T \mid \exists_{\sigma \in W} t = last(\sigma)\}$,
4. $X_W = \{(A, B) \mid A \subseteq T_W \wedge B \subseteq T_W \wedge \forall_{a \in A} \forall_{b \in B} a \rightarrow_W b \wedge \forall_{a_1, a_2 \in A} a_1 \#_W a_2 \wedge \forall_{b_1, b_2 \in B} b_1 \#_W b_2\}$,

5. $Y_W = \{(A, B) \in X_W \mid \forall_{(A',B') \in X_W} A \subseteq A' \wedge B \subseteq B' \Longrightarrow (A, B) = (A', B')\}$,
6. $P_W = \{p_{(A,B)} \mid (A, B) \in Y_W\} \cup \{i_W, o_W\}$,
7. $F_W = \{(a, p_{(A,B)}) \mid (A, B) \in Y_W \wedge a \in A\} \cup \{(p_{(A,B)}, b) \mid (A, B) \in Y_W \wedge b \in B\} \cup \{(i_W, t) \mid t \in T_I\} \cup \{(t, o_W) \mid t \in T_O\}$, and
8. $\alpha(W) = (P_W, T_W, F_W)$.

The α -algorithm works as follows. First, it examines the log traces and (Step 1) creates the set of transitions (T_W) in the workflow, (Step 2) the set of output transitions (T_I) of the source place , and (Step 3) the set of the input transitions (T_O) of the sink place3. In steps 4 and 5, the α -algorithm creates sets (X_W and Y_W , respectively) used to define the places of the discovered workflow net. In Step 4, the α-algorithm discovers which transitions are causally related. Thus, for each tuple (A, B) in X_W , each transition in set A causally relates to all transitions in set B, and no transitions within A (or B) follow each other in some firing sequence. These constraints to the elements in sets A and B allow the correct mining of AND-split/join and OR-split/join constructs. Note that the OR-split/join requires the fusion of places. In Step 5, the α -algorithm refines set X_W by taking only the largest elements with respect to set inclusion. In fact, Step 5 establishes the exact amount of places the discovered net has (excluding the source place i_W and the sink place o_W). The places are created in Step 6 and connected to their respective input/output transitions in Step 7. The discovered workflow net is returned in Step 8.

Finally, we define what it means for a WF-net to be rediscovered.

Ability to Rediscover

Let $N = (P, T, F)$ be a sound WFnet, i.e., $N \in \mathcal{W}$ and let α be a mining algorithm which maps workflow logs of N onto sound WF-nets, i.e., $\alpha : P(T^*) \rightarrow \mathcal{W}$. If for any complete workflow log W of N the mining algorithm returns N (modulo renaming of places), then α is able to rediscover N.

Note that no mining algorithm is able to find names of places. Therefore, we ignore place names, i.e., α is able to rediscover N if and only if $\alpha(W) = N$ modulo renaming of places.

GSP Algorithm

The basic structure of the GSP algorithm for finding sequential patterns is as follows. The algorithm makes multiple passes over the data. The first pass determines the support of each item, that is, the number of data-sequences that include the item. At the end of the first pass, the algorithm knows which items are frequent, that is, have minimum support. Each such item yields a 1-element frequent sequence consisting of that item. Each subsequent pass starts with a seed set: the frequent sequences found in the previous pass. The seed set is used to generate new potentially frequent sequences, called candidate sequences. Each candidate sequence has one more item than a seed sequence; so all the candidate sequences in a pass will have the same number of items. The support for these candidate sequences is found during the pass over the data. At the end of the pass, the algorithm determines which of the candidate sequences are actually frequent. These frequent candidates become the seed for the next pass. The algorithm terminates when there are no frequent sequences at the end of a pass, or when there are no candidate sequences generated.

We need to specify two key details:

1. Candidate generation: how candidates sequences are generated before the pass begins. We want to generate as few candidates as possible while maintaining completeness.

2. Counting candidates: how the support count for the candidate sequences is determined.

Our algorithm is not a main-memory algorithm. If the candidates do not fit in memory, the algorithm generates only as many candidates as will fit in memory and the data is scanned to count the support of these candidates. Frequent sequences resulting from these candidates are written to disk, while those candidates without minimum support are deleted. This procedure is repeated until all the candidates have been counted.

Candidate Generation

We refer to a sequence with k items as a k-sequence. (If an item occurs multiple times in different elements of a sequence, each occurrence contributes to the value of k.) Let L_k denote the set of all frequent k-sequences, and C_k the set of candidate k-sequences.

Given L_{k-1}, the set of all frequent $(k-1)$ -sequences, we want to generate a superset of the set of all frequent k-sequences. We first define the notion of a contiguous subsequence.

Given a sequence $s = \langle s_1 s_2 ::: s_n \rangle$ i and a subsequence c, c is a contiguous subsequence of s if any of the following conditions hold:

1. c is derived from s by dropping an item from either s_1 or s_n.

2. c is derived from s by dropping an item from an element s_i which has at least 2 item.

3. c is a contiguous subsequence c', and c' is a contiguous subsequence of s. For example, consider the sequences $s = \langle (1, 2)\ (3, 4)\ (5)\ (6) \rangle$. The sequences $\langle\ (2)\ (3, 4)\ (5) \rangle$, $\langle (1, 2)\ (3)\ (5)\ (6) \rangle$, and $\langle\ (3)\ (5) \rangle$ i are some of the contiguous subsequences of s. However, $\langle (1, 2)\ (3, 4)\ (6) \rangle$ and $\langle (1)(5)(6) \rangle$ are not.

We show that any data-sequence that contains a sequence s will also contain any contiguous subsequence of s. If there is no max-gap constraint, the data-sequence will contain all subsequences of s (including non-contiguous subsequences). This property provides the basis for the candidate generation procedure.

Candidates are generated in two steps:

1. Join Phase: We generate candidate sequences by joining L_{k-1} with L_{k-1}. A sequence s_1 joins with s_2 if the subsequence obtained by dropping the first item of s_1 is the same as the subsequence obtained by dropping the last item of s_2. The candidate sequence generated by joining s_1 with s_2 is the sequence s_1 extended with the last item in s_2. The added item becomes a separate element if it was a separate element in s_2, and part of the last element

of s1 otherwise. When joining L_1 with L_1, we need to add the item in s_2 both as part of an itemset and as a separate element, since both $\langle(x)\ (y)\rangle$ and $\langle(x\ y)\rangle$ give the same sequence $\langle(y)\rangle$ upon deleting the first item. (Observe that s_1 and s_2 are contiguous subsequences of the new candidate sequence).

2. Prune Phase: We delete candidate sequences that have a contiguous $(k-1)$- subsequence whose support count is less than the minimum support. If there is no max-gap constraint, we also delete candidate sequences that have any subsequence without minimum support.

Example: L_3 and C_4 after the join and prune phases. In the join phase, the sequence $\langle(1,\ 2)\ (3)\rangle$ joins with $\langle(2)\ (3,\ 4)\rangle$ i 4) to generate $\langle(1,\ 2)\ (3,\ 4)\rangle$ and with $\langle(2)\ (3)\ (5)\rangle$ to generate $\langle(1,\ 2)\ (3)\ (5)\rangle$. The remaining sequences do not join with any sequence in L_3. For instance, $\langle(1,\ 2)\ (4)\rangle$ does not join with any sequence since there is no sequence of the form $\langle(2)\ (4\ x)\rangle$ or $\langle(2)\ (4)\ (x)\rangle$. In the prune phase, $\langle(1,\ 2)\ (3)\ (5)\rangle$ is dropped since its contiguous subsequence $\langle(1)\ (3)\ (5)\rangle$ is not in L_3.

Counting Candidates

While making a pass, we read one data-sequence at a time and increment the support count of candidates contained in the data-sequence. Thus, given a set of candidate sequences C and a data-sequence d, we need to find all sequences in C that are contained in d. We use two techniques to solve this problem.

1. We use a hash-tree data structure to reduce the number of candidates in C that are checked for a data-sequence.
2. We transform the representation of the data-sequence d so that we can efficiently find whether a specific candidate is a subsequence of d.

Reducing the number of candidates that need to be checked

We adapt the hash-tree data structure for this purpose. A node of the hash-tree either contains a list of sequences (a leaf node) or a hash table (an interior node). In an interior node, each non-empty bucket of the hash table points to another node. The root of the hash-tree is defined to be at depth 1. An interior node at depth p points to nodes at depth p+1.

Adding candidate sequences to the hash-tree: When we add a sequence s, we start from the root and go down the tree until we reach a leaf. At an interior node at depth p, we decide which branch to follow by applying a hash function to the pth item of the sequence. Note that we apply the hash function to the pth item, not the pth element. All nodes are initially created as leaf nodes. When the number of sequences in a leaf node exceeds a threshold, the leaf node is converted to an interior node.

Finding the candidates contained in a data-sequence: Starting from the root node, we find all the candidates contained in a data-sequence d. We apply the following procedure, based on the type of node we are at:

- Interior node, if it is the root: We apply the hash function to each item in d, and recursively apply this procedure to the node in the corresponding bucket. For any sequences contained in the data-sequence d, the first item of s must be in d. By hashing on every item in d, we ensure that we only ignore sequences that start with an item not in d.

- Interior node, if it is not the root: Assume we reached this node by hashing on an item x whose transaction-time is t. We apply the hash function to each item in d whose transaction-time is in [t window-size; t + max(window-size; max-gap)] and recursively apply this procedure to the node in the corresponding bucket.

  To see why this returns the desired set of candidates, consider a candidate sequence s with two consecutive items x and y. Let x be contained in a transaction in d whose transaction-time is t. For d to contain s, the transaction-time corresponding to y must be in [t-window-size; t + window-size] if y is part of the same element as x, or in the interval (t; t + max-gap] if y is part of the next element. Hence if we reached this node by hashing on an item x with transaction-time t, y must be contained in a transaction whose transaction-time is in the interval [t-window-size; t + max(window-size; max-gap)] for the data-sequence to support the sequence. Thus we only need to apply the hash function to the items in d whose transaction-times are in the above interval, and check the corresponding nodes.

- Leaf node: For each sequence s in the leaf, we check whether d contains s, and add s to the answer set if necessary. (We will discuss below exactly how to find whether d contains a specific candidate sequence.) Since we check each sequence contained in this node, we don't miss any sequences.

Checking Whether a Data-sequence Contains a Specific Sequence

Let d be a data-sequence, and let $s = \langle s_1 \ldots s_n \rangle$ be a candidate sequence. We first describe the algorithm for checking if d contains s, assuming existence of a procedure that finds the first occurrence of an element of s in d after a given time, and then describe this procedure.

Contains test: The algorithm for checking if the data-sequence d contains a candidate sequence s alternates between two phases. The algorithm starts in the forward phase from the first element.

- Forward phase: The algorithm finds successive elements of s in d as long as the difference between the end-time of the element just found and the start-time of the previous element is less than max-gap. (Recall that for an element s_i, start-time(s_i) and end-time(s_i) correspond to the first and last transaction-times of the set of transactions that contain s_i.) If the diference is more than max-gap, the algorithm switches to the backward phase. If an element is not found, the data-sequence does not contain *s*.

- Backward phase: The algorithm backtracks and \pulls up" previous elements. If s_i is the current element and end-time $(s_i) = t$, the algorithm finds the first set of transactions containing s_{i-1} whose transaction-times are after t max-gap. The start-time for s_{i-1} (after s_{i-1} is pulled up) could be after the end-time for s_i. Pulling up s_{i-1} may necessitate pulling up s_{i-2} because the max-gap constraint between s_{i-1} and s_{i-2} may no longer be satisfied. The algorithm moves backwards until either the max-gap constraint between the element just pulled up and the previous element is satisfied, or the first element has been pulled up. The algorithm then switches to the forward phase, finding elements of *s* in *d* starting from the element after the last element pulled up. If any element cannot be pulled up (that is, there is no subsequent set of transactions which contain the element), the data-sequence does not contains s.

This procedure is repeated, switching between the backward and forward phases, until all the elements are found. Though the algorithm moves back and forth among the elements of s, it terminates because for any element s_i, the algorithm always checks whether a later set of transactions contains s_i ; thus the transaction-times for an element always increase.

Transaction-Time	Items
10	1, 2
25	4, 6
45	3
50	1, 2
65	3
90	2, 4
95	6

Figure(a): Example Data- structure

Item	Times
1	→ 10 → 50 → NULL
2	→ 10 → 50 → 90 → NULL
3	→ 45 → 65 → NULL
4	→ 25 → 90 → NULL
5	→ NULL
6	→ 25 → 95 → NULL
7	→ NULL

Figure(b): Alternate representation

Example: Consider the data-sequence shown in figure. Consider the case when max-gap is 30, min-gap is 5, and window-size is 0. For the candidate-sequence $\langle(1, 2)\ (3)\ (4)\rangle$, we would first find (1, 2) at transaction-time 10, and then find (3) at time 45. Since the gap between these two elements (35 days) is more than max-gap, we \pull up" (1, 2).

We search for the first occurrence of (1, 2) after time 15, because end-time((3)) = 45 and max-gap is 30, and so even if (1, 2) occurs at some time before 15, it still will not satisfy the max-gap constraint. We nd (1, 2) at time 50. Since this is the first element, we do not have to check to see if the max-gap constraint between (1, 2) and the element before that is satisfied. We now move forward. Since (3) no longer occurs more than 5 days after (1, 2), we search for the next occurrence of (3) after time 55. We find (3) at time 65. Since the max-gap constraint between (3) and (1, 2) is satisfied, we continue to move forward and find (4) at time 90. The max-gap constraint between (4) and (3) is satisfied; so we are done.

Finding a single element: To describe the procedure for finding the first occurrence of an element in a data sequence, we first discuss how to efficiently find a single item. A straightforward approach would be to scan consecutive transactions of the data-sequence until we find the item. A faster alternative is to transform the representation of d as follows.

Create an array that has as many elements as the number of items in the database. For each item in the data-sequence d, store in this array a list of transaction-times of the transactions of d that contain the item. To find the first occurrence of an item after time t, the procedure simply traverses the list corresponding to the item till it finds a transaction-time greater than t. Assuming that the dataset has 7 items, figure (b) shows the tranformed representation of the data-sequence in figure(a). This transformation has a one-time overhead of O (total-number-of-items-in-dataset) over the whole execution (to allocate and initialize the array), plus an overhead of O(no-of-items-in-d) for each data-sequence.

Now, to find the first occurrence of an element after time t, the algorithm makes one pass through the items in the element and finds the first transaction-time greater than t for each item. If the difference between the start-time and end-time is less than or equal to the window-size, we are done. Otherwise, t is set to the end-time minus the window-size, and the procedure is repeated.

Example: Consider the data-sequence shown in figure (a). Assume window-size is set to 7 days, and we have to find the first occurrence of the element (2, 6) after time t = 20. We find 2 at time 50, and 6 at time 25. Since end-time((2,6)) start-time((2,6)) > 7, we set t to 43 (= end-time((2,6)) window-size) and try again. Item 2 remains at time 50, while item 6 is found at time 95. The time gap is still greater than the window-size, so we set t to 88, and repeat the procedure. We now find item 2 at time 90, while item 6 remains at time 95. Since the time gap between 90 and 95 is less than the window size, we are done.

Apriori Algorithm

With the quick growth in e-commerce applications, there is an accumulation vast quantity of data in months not in years. Data Mining, also known as Knowledge Discovery in Databases(KDD), to find anomalies, correlations, patterns, and trends to predict outcomes.

Apriori algorithm is a classical algorithm in data mining. It is used for mining frequent itemsets and relevant association rules. It is devised to operate on a database containing a lot of transactions, for instance, items brought by customers in a store.

It is very important for effective Market Basket Analysis and it helps the customers in purchasing their items with more ease which increases the sales of the markets. It has also been used in the field of healthcare for the detection of adverse drug reactions. It produces association rules that indicates what all combinations of medications and patient characteristics lead to ADRs.

Association Rules

Association rule learning is a prominent and a well-explored method for determining relations among variables in large databases. Let us take a look at the formal definition of the problem of association rules.

Let $I=\{i_1,i_2,i_3,\ldots,i_n\}$ be a set of n attributes called items and $D=\{t_1,t_2,\ldots,t_n\}$ be the set of transactions. It is called database. Every transaction, t_i in D has a unique transaction ID, and it consists of a subset of itemsets in I. A rule can be defined as an implication, $X \to Y$ where X and Y are subsets of $I(X,Y \subseteq I)$, and they have no element in common, i.e., $X \cap Y$. X and Y are the antecedent and the consequent of the rule, respectively.

Let's take an easy example from the supermarket sphere. The example that we are considering is quite small and in practical situations, datasets contain millions or billions of transactions. The set of itemsets, $I=\{Onion,\ Burger,\ Potato,\ Milk,\ Beer\}$ and a database consisting of six transactions. Each transaction is a tuple of 0's and 1's where 0 represents the absence of an item and 1 the presence.

An example for a rule in this scenario would be $\{Onion,\ Potato\}$ => $\{Burger\}$, which means that if onion and potato are bought, customers also buy a burger.

Transaction ID	Onion	Potato	Burger	Milk	Beer
t1	1	1	1	0	0
t2	0	1	1	1	0
t3	0	0	0	1	1
t4	1	1	0	1	0
t5	1	1	1	0	1
t6	1	1	1	1	1

There are multiple rules possible even from a very small database, so in order to select the interesting ones, we use constraints on various measures of interest and significance. We will look at some of these useful measures such as support, confidence, lift and conviction.

Support

The support of an itemset $X, supp(X)$ is the proportion of transaction in the database in which the item X appears. It signifies the popularity of an itemset.

$$supp(X) = \frac{\text{Number of transaction in which X appears}}{\text{Total number of transactions}}$$

In the example above, $supp(Onion) = \frac{4}{6} = 0.66667.$

If the sales of a particular product (item) above a certain proportion have a meaningful effect on profits, that proportion can be considered as the support threshold. Furthermore, we can identify itemsets that have support values beyond this threshold as significant itemsets.

Confidence

Confidence of a rule is defined as follows:

$$conf(X \leftrightarrow Y) = \frac{supp(X \cup Y)}{supp(X)}$$

It signifies the likelihood of item Y being purchased when item X is purchased. So, for the rule $\{Onion,\ Potato\} \ => \ \{Burger\}$,

Undefined control sequence \implies

This implies that for 75% of the transactions containing onion and potatoes, the rule is correct. It can also be interpreted as the conditional probability $P(Y \mid X)$, i.e, the probability of finding the itemset Y in transactions given the transaction already contains X.

It can give some important insights, but it also has a major drawback. It only takes into account the popularity of the itemset X and not the popularity of Y. If Y is equally popular as X then there will be a higher probability that a transaction containing X will also contain Y thus increasing the confidence. To overcome this drawback there is another measure called lift.

Lift

The lift of a rule is defined as:

$$lift(X \rightarrow Y) = \frac{supp(X \cup Y)}{supp(X) * supp(Y)}$$

This signifies the likelihood of the itemset Y being purchased when item X is purchased while taking into account the popularity of Y.

In our example above,

Undefined control sequence \implies

If the value of lift is greater than 1, it means that the itemset Y is likely to be bought with itemset X, while a value less than 1 implies that itemset Y is unlikely to be bought if the itemset X is bought.

Conviction

The conviction of a rule can be defined as:

$$conv(X \rightarrow Y) = \frac{1 - supp(Y)}{1 - conf(X \rightarrow Y)}$$

For the rule $\{onion,\ potato\} => \{burger\}$

Undefined control sequence \implies

The conviction value of 1.32 means that the rule $\{onion,\ potato\} => \{burger\}$ would be incorrect 32% more often if the association between X and Y was an accidental chance.

Working of Apriori algorithm

So far, we learned what the Apriori algorithm is and why is important to learn it.

A key concept in Apriori algorithm is the anti-monotonicity of the support measure. It assumes that:

1. All subsets of a frequent itemset must be frequent.
2. Similarly, for any infrequent itemset, all its supersets must be infrequent too.

Let us now look at the intuitive explanation of the algorithm with the help of the example we used above. Before beginning the process, let us set the support threshold to 50%, i.e. only those items are significant for which support is more than 50%.

Step 1: Create a frequency table of all the items that occur in all the transactions. For our case:

Item	Frequency (No. of transactions)
Onion(O)	4
Potato(P)	5
Burger(B)	4
Milk(M)	4
Beer(Be)	2

Step 2: We know that only those elements are significant for which the support is greater than or equal to the threshold support. Here, support threshold is 50%, hence only those items are significant which occur in more than three transactions and such items are Onion(O), Potato(P), Burger(B), and Milk(M). Therefore, we are left with:

Item	Frequency (No. of transactions)
Onion(O)	4
Potato(P)	5
Burger(B)	4
Milk(M)	4

The table above represents the single items that are purchased by the customers frequently.

Step 3: The next step is to make all the possible pairs of the significant items keeping in mind that the order doesn't matter, i.e., AB is same as BA. To do this, take the first item and pair it with all the others such as OP, OB, OM. Similarly, consider the second item and pair it with preceding items, i.e., PB, PM. We are only considering the preceding items because PO (same as OP) already exists. So, all the pairs in our example are OP, OB, OM, PB, PM, BM.

Step 4: We will now count the occurrences of each pair in all the transactions.

Itemset	Frequency (No. of transactions)
OP	4
OB	3
OM	2

PB	4
PM	3
BM	2

Step 5: Again only those itemsets are significant which cross the support threshold, and those are OP, OB, PB, and PM.

Step 6: Now let's say we would like to look for a set of three items that are purchased together. We will use the itemsets found in step 5 and create a set of 3 items.

To create a set of 3 items another rule, called self-join is required. It says that from the item pairs OP, OB, PB and PM we look for two pairs with the identical first letter and so we get;

- OP and OB, this gives OPB.
- PB and PM, this gives PBM.

Next, we find the frequency for these two itemsets.

Itemset	Frequency (No. of transactions)
OPB	4
PBM	3

Applying the threshold rule again, we find that OPB is the only significant itemset.

Therefore, the set of 3 items that was purchased most frequently is OPB.

The example that we considered was a fairly simple one and mining the frequent itemsets stopped at 3 items but in practice, there are dozens of items and this process could continue to many items. Suppose we got the significant sets with 3 items as OPQ, OPR, OQR, OQS and PQR and now we want to generate the set of 4 items. For this, we will look at the sets which have first two alphabets common, i.e,

- OPQ and OPR gives OPQR.
- OQR and OQS gives OQRS.

In general, we have to look for sets which only differ in their last letter/item.

Now that we have looked at an example of the functionality of Apriori Algorithm, let us formulate the general process.

General Process of the Apriori Algorithm

The entire algorithm can be divided into two steps:

Step 1: Apply minimum support to find all the frequent sets with k items in a database.

Step 2: Use the self-join rule to find the frequent sets with k+1 items with the help of frequent k-itemsets. Repeat this process from k=1 to the point when we are unable to apply the self-join rule.

This approach of extending a frequent itemset one at a time is called the "bottom up" approach.

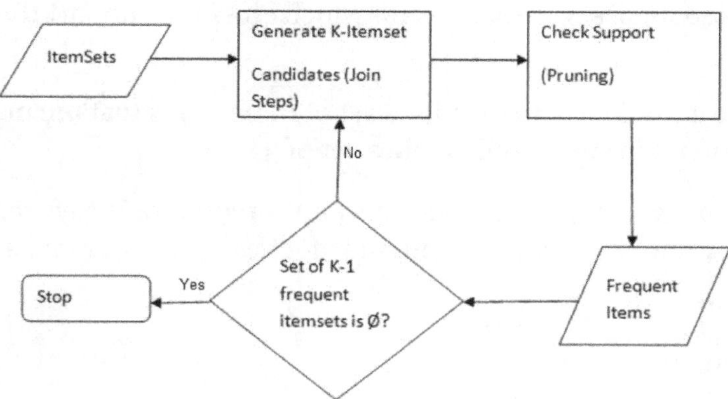

Mining Association Rules

Till now, we have looked at the Apriori algorithm with respect to frequent itemset generation. There is another task for which we can use this algorithm, i.e., finding association rules efficiently.

For finding association rules, we need to find all rules having support greater than the threshold support and confidence greater than the threshold confidence.

But, how do we find these? One possible way is brute force, i.e., to list all the possible association rules and calculate the support and confidence for each rule. Then eliminate the rules that fail the threshold support and confidence. But it is computationally very heavy and prohibitive as the number of all the possible association rules increase exponentially with the number of items.

Given there are n items in the set I, the total number of possible association rules is $3^n - 2^{n+1} + 1$.

We can also use another way, which is called the two-step approach, to find the efficient association rules.

The two-step approach is:

Step 1: Frequent itemset generation: Find all itemsets for which the support is greater than the threshold support.

Step 2: Rule generation: Create rules from each frequent itemset using the binary partition of frequent itemsets and look for the ones with high confidence. These rules are called candidate rules.

Let us look at our previous example to get an efficient association rule. We found that OPB was the frequent itemset. So for this problem, step 1 is already done. So, let' see step 2. All the possible rules using OPB are:

$$OP \rightarrow B,\ OB \rightarrow P,\ PB \rightarrow O,\ B \rightarrow OP,\ P \rightarrow OB,\ O \rightarrow PB$$

If X is a frequent itemset with k elements, then there are $2^k - 2$ candidate association rules.

We will not go deeper into the theory of the Apriori algorithm for rule generation.

Pros of the Apriori algorithm

1. It is an easy-to-implement and easy-to-understand algorithm.
2. It can be used on large itemsets.

Cons of the Apriori Algorithm

1. Sometimes, it may need to find a large number of candidate rules which can be computationally expensive.
2. Calculating support is also expensive because it has to go through the entire database.

R Implementation

The package which is used to implement the Apriori algorithm in R is called *arules*. The function that we will demonstrate here which can be used for mining association rules is

apriori(data, parameter = NULL)

The arguments of the function apriori are:

Data: The data structure which can be coerced into transactions (e.g., a binary matrix or data. frame).

Parameter: It is a named list containing the threshold values for support and confidence. The default value of this argument is a list of minimum support of 0.1, minimum confidence of 0.8, maximum of 10 items (maxlen), and a maximal time for subset checking of 5 seconds (maxtime).

Teiresias Algorithm

The basic idea of Teiresias algorithm is: If a pattern P is a (L, W) pattern occurring in at least K sequences, then its sub patterns are also (L, W) patterns occurring in at least K sequences. (K>=2) That is to say, pattern P is more specific than pattern Q if we can get Q from P by removing several characters from P and/or replacing several non-wildcard characters with wildcard characters. For example: pattern "A.BC" is more specific than pattern "A..C". Definitely, we can convert this idea and get the algorithm's framework: First use the scan phase to discover the elementary patterns, and then extend them to get the final results.

The Teiresias algorithm operates in two phases: "Scan" and "Convolution". Firstly, scan the input sequences, identify all the elementary patterns and then select the elementary patterns which satisfy the minimum support; secondly sort the element patterns and extract useful prefixes and suffixes. Finally in the convolution phase, by convolving the elementary patterns, the maximal length and composition of the motifs will be detected.

Scan Phase

The output for the scan phase is a set of "elementary patterns". The elementary pattern should contain L residues, has a maximum length of W, and appear in at least K (K>=2) of the sequences in the population under study.

In the following example, there are four sequences, we give the parameters as: K=2; L=3; W=5. The string "AST" can be found in three sequences (>K); its length is 3 (=L). So it can be an elementary pattern.

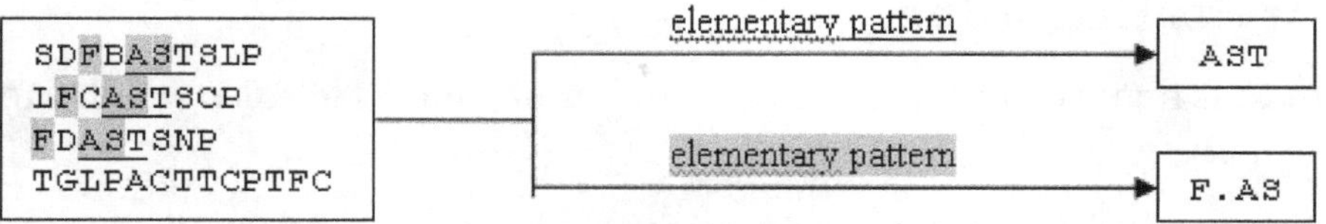

Figure: Elementary pattern

Figure shows the flow chart of the scan phase. An "Extend" procedure is designed here to extend the elementary patterns step by step. First empty the stack of elementary patterns. Then for each letter in the alphabet, count how many sequences contain this letter. If less than K sequences contain this letter, ignore it. Or the program will extend it until it is ignored or it is accepted.

In the extend procedure, the given string will be added by all possible suffixes consisting a set of dot and then followed by a letter. If there are enough supports on the extended sequence, then accept or continue extending; otherwise it will be ignored.

In our implementation, the patterns are represented as objects. Each pattern consists two parts, one is the pattern string itself, the other is an offset list which contains all pairs (x, y) such that string x matches pattern *p* at position y.

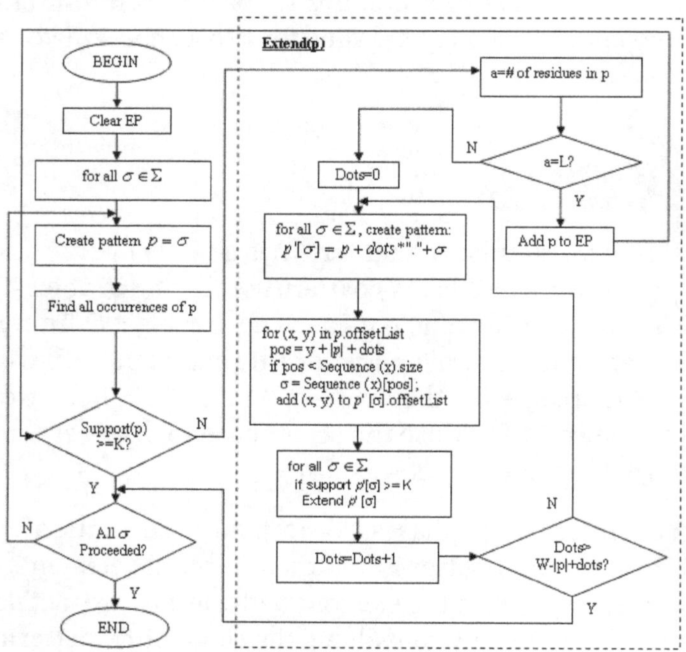

Figure 2: Flow Chart of Scan Phase

Convolution Phase

The term "convolution" is used here to represent the operation of the second phase of Teiresias algorithm. The principle here is quite clear: "Given any pattern with at least L residues, the prefix of p is the unique substring containing the first L – 1 residues of p. Similarly the suffix of p is the unique substring containing the last L –1 residues of p. Given two patterns p and q, p convolve q is the empty pattern if the suffix of p is not the prefix of q, otherwise it is the pattern p followed by the part of q which remains when its prefix is removed. The offset list of p convolve q is simply computed from the offset lists of p and q separately. Note that the prefix of $t = p$ convolve q is the prefix of p and the suffix of t is the suffix of q." The following figure shows an example of extending the elementary patterns.

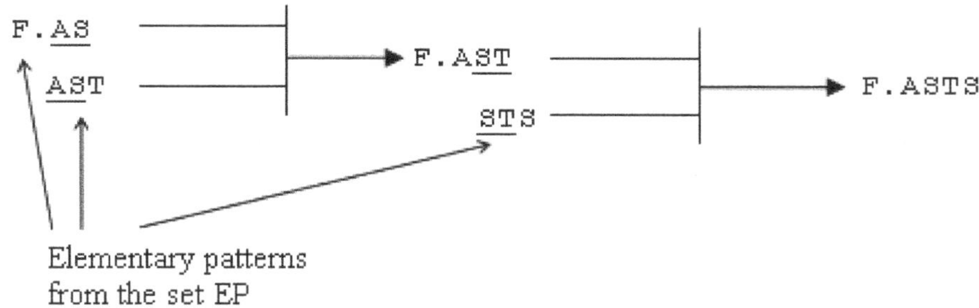

Figure: Extended the elementary patterns

Based on the algorithm, the convolution phase can also be divided into two sub-phases. Firstly, we need to sort all the elementary patterns by pair-wise < and then pick up their prefixes and suffixes. This can be called as "Pre-Convolution Phase".

Pre-Convolution Phase

The flow chart and a sample result of pre-convolution phase are shown in figures respectively. The main focus in this phase is to sort the elementary patterns. In our implementation, we used insertion sorting in generally. Moreover, we also designed a function big (string a, string b) to compare two elementary patterns.

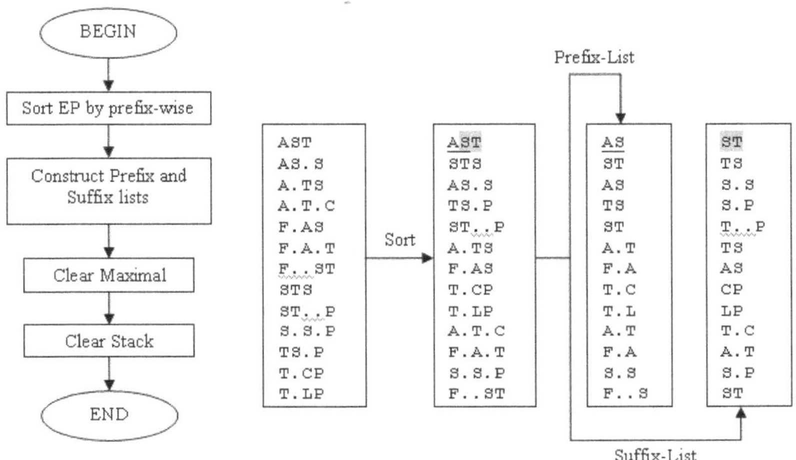

Figure: Flow chart of Pre- convolution phase Figure: Results of Pre- convolution phase

After sorting the elementary patterns, two structures are also produced: Left (prefixes) and Right (suffixes). Left [i] returns all the elementary patterns which can be convolved to the left of elementary pattern EP [i], and similarly Right [i] contains all the elementary patterns which could be convolved to the right of the elementary pattern EP [i]. "Each of the structures provide O(1) access to the needed patterns. However, Floratos implies that structures equivalent to Left and Right can be constructed in O(|EP|log|EP|) time, whereas the current implementation requires O(|EP|^2) time."

The main target of the operation of convolution is: For each elementary pattern P, try to extend the pattern with other elementary patterns by convolving them. The flow of the procedure can be summarized as:

- Find a short pattern that appears in K input sequences.
- Extend them until the support go below K.
- Once we find pattern that cannot be extended further, the patterns in maximal and can be written to output.

How to convolve and extend the patterns? Here are the steps to follow:

If there exists an elementary pattern Q can be glued to the left side of P.

{Take such Q which is largest in suffix ordering.

Let R be the pattern resulting from gluing Q to the left side of P

If ((R's occurrences >= K) && (R's occurrence is maximal with respect to the set of already reported patterns))

{Try to extend pattern R with other elementary patterns.}

If (R's occurrences == P's occurrences)

{P is not maximal;

Do not need to search for other extensions of P. }

Else

{P is not a significant pattern.}

}

Repeat the same process for the elementary patterns which can be glued to the right side of P (starting with the largest pattern in prefix ordering).

Report pattern P.

Figure shows the flow chart of the whole convolution phase.

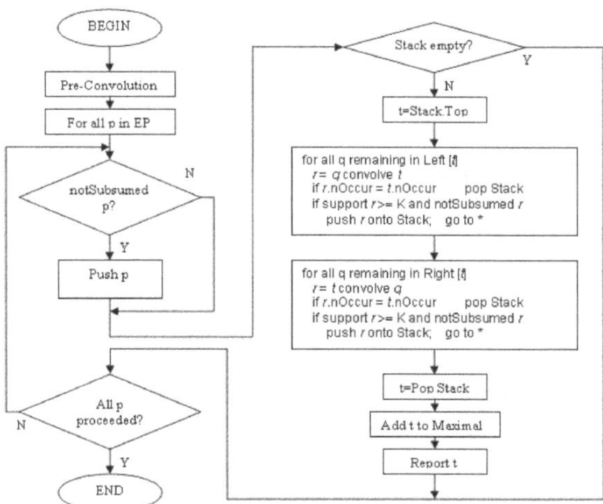

Figure: Flow chart of convolution phase

For the previous example, we get the final result which is shown in figure. Also we run our program on a complex data set, the original file is here, the result file is here.

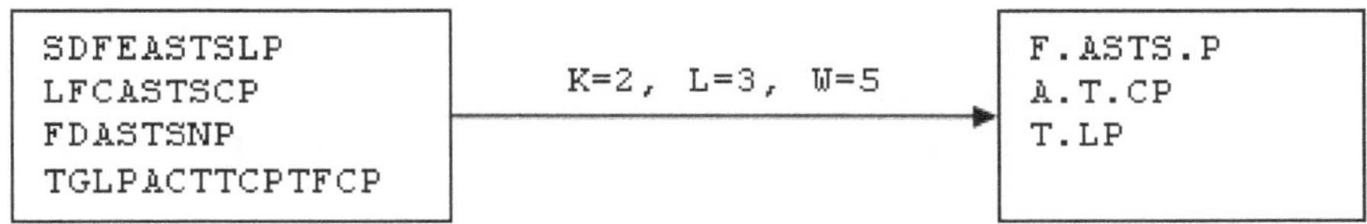

Figure: Final result of the example used in the report

Generally speaking, Teiresias do a good job when solving the pattern discovery problem of non-aligned sequences.

Teiresias and GYM are counterparts in motif detection area. The Teiresias algorithm is designed for non-aligned sequences. On the other hand, the GYM algorithm is efficient to process aligned motif sequences. The output pattern of GYM algorithm is like <amino acid, position>. Compared to GYM, Teiresias has a significant drawback: it can't find out the repeated pattern in one sequence. That is to say, different numbers of "ABC" mean different pattern. Also, in Teriesias, different number of "don't care" means different patterns.

WINEPI

WINEPI is a specialised algorithm for mining episode rules, based on a sliding window approach. WINEPI utilizes the concept of episodes which may be parallel, serial or composite. The idea is that to be considered interesting the events of an episode must occur close in time. The user defines how closely events must occur by specifying a time window and a step size defining the overlap of windows. The goal is the same as in regular association rule mining, to find all frequent episodes. This is done by counting in how many windows an episode occurs. If an episode a occurs in S, we write $S \models a$. The frequency of a in the set aw$(S,\ w)$ of all windows on S of size w is

$$fr(a, S, w) = \frac{|\{W \in aw(S, w) | W \models a\}|}{|aw(S, w)|}.$$

Given a threshold min $\_fr$ for the frequency, a given episode a is frequent if $fr(a, S, w) \geq min\_fr$. If an episode a is frequent in a sequence S, then all sub-episodes $\beta \prec a$ are frequent, as given by the A-priori property. The algorithm follows the same procedure as the A-priori algorithm iteratively alternating between building and recognition phases. First, in the building phase of an iteration i, a collection C_i of new candidate episodes of i elementary events is built, by joining the frequent episodes that share the $i - 1$ events. This can be done efficiently by representing an episode as a lexicographically sorted array of event types. Collections of episodes are also represented as lexicographically sorted arrays. Since the episodes and episode collections are sorted, all episodes that share the same first event types are consecutive in the episode collection. By storing the start point of blocks that share the $i - 1$ events the candidate generation can be done efficiently.

Then, these candidate episodes are recognized in the event sequence, and their frequencies are computed. When episodes are recognized in sequences it is done in an incremental fashion, and the sliding window is applied on the event sequence. The episodes that are totally covered by the window are counted for each step of the window. Two adjacent windows are typically very similar to each other. This is used as an advantage by after recognizing episodes in W_i, incremental updates are made in the data structures to achieve the shift of the window to obtain W_{i+1}. Parallel episodes are recognized by maintaining a counter and a window list for each candidate episode, and serial episodes are recognized by using a state automaton. In addition it is possible to recognize all forms of composite episodes when counting, not only serial or parallel episodes. This can be done by handling the candidate episodes as regular parallel episodes until all events of the candidate episode is inside the window, and then check for the correct partial ordering. This gives the ability to only consider rules on the form [parallel, serial], hence enforcing the rule syntax at runtime.

If $F(S, w, min\_fr)$ is the collection of frequent episodes in S with respect to w and min $\_fr$, it is possible to derive all frequent episode rules from this collection. Formally, a WINEPI episode rule is an expression $\beta \Rightarrow \gamma$, where β and γ are episodes such that β is a sub-episode of γ and both are frequent. This will give rules with multiple events on the antecedent and consequent side, but it is easy to restrict the rule generation to only consider rules where the last element of the episode, which should be the last occurring event time wise, is the consequent. In addition to enforcing the wanted rule syntax this greatly reduce the running time of the algorithm.

The fraction $\frac{fr(\gamma, S, w)}{fr(\beta, S, w)}$ is the confidence of the episode rule. The confidence can be interpreted as the conditional probability of the whole of γ occurring in a window, given that β occurs in it. As already noted WINEPI can produce the wanted rule structure and ordering. The semantics with respect to maximum time is also enforced naturally in the algorithm. However, WINEPI do not keep information about the occurrences of events, which makes it difficult to obtain the wanted time information in the rule syntax, and enforce the minimum time constraint.

Permissions

All chapters in this book are published with permission under the Creative Commons Attribution Share Alike License or equivalent. Every chapter published in this book has been scrutinized by our experts. Their significance has been extensively debated. The topics covered herein carry significant information for a comprehensive understanding. They may even be implemented as practical applications or may be referred to as a beginning point for further studies.

We would like to thank the editorial team for lending their expertise to make the book truly unique. They have played a crucial role in the development of this book. Without their invaluable contributions this book wouldn't have been possible. They have made vital efforts to compile up to date information on the varied aspects of this subject to make this book a valuable addition to the collection of many professionals and students.

This book was conceptualized with the vision of imparting up-to-date and integrated information in this field. To ensure the same, a matchless editorial board was set up. Every individual on the board went through rigorous rounds of assessment to prove their worth. After which they invested a large part of their time researching and compiling the most relevant data for our readers.

The editorial board has been involved in producing this book since its inception. They have spent rigorous hours researching and exploring the diverse topics which have resulted in the successful publishing of this book. They have passed on their knowledge of decades through this book. To expedite this challenging task, the publisher supported the team at every step. A small team of assistant editors was also appointed to further simplify the editing procedure and attain best results for the readers.

Apart from the editorial board, the designing team has also invested a significant amount of their time in understanding the subject and creating the most relevant covers. They scrutinized every image to scout for the most suitable representation of the subject and create an appropriate cover for the book.

The publishing team has been an ardent support to the editorial, designing and production team. Their endless efforts to recruit the best for this project, has resulted in the accomplishment of this book. They are a veteran in the field of academics and their pool of knowledge is as vast as their experience in printing. Their expertise and guidance has proved useful at every step. Their uncompromising quality standards have made this book an exceptional effort. Their encouragement from time to time has been an inspiration for everyone.

The publisher and the editorial board hope that this book will prove to be a valuable piece of knowledge for students, practitioners and scholars across the globe.

Index

CPSIA information can be obtained
at www.ICGtesting.com
Printed in the USA
BVHW051537060619
550362BV00002B/82/P